effusion of blood, which we have seen by the military in St George's fields
in the most frivolous pretext, and in the most inhuman way).

    I submit to you, Gentlemen, the propriety of a
publication of any letters which may pass between us. You are the
true judges for what may respect the new world. Perhaps while I
am doom'd to this prison, unfair advantages might be taken against
me which I should find it difficult to overcome. I leave however the
whole to your mature consideration, with the best assurance that in
whatever way I can serve the generous cause of liberty, I will
be active and zealous. You will always oblige me by pointing
out the particulars respecting yourselves.

        I am,
           Gentlemen, with truth & regard,
              your affectionate, and
                faithfull, humble,
                  Servant,

To the Gentlemen of the Committee
of the Sons of Liberty in the Town of Boston.
                    John Wilkes.

The Extraordinary
Mr. Wilkes

LOUIS KRONENBERGER

The Extraordinary
Mr. Wilkes

HIS LIFE AND TIMES

DOUBLEDAY & COMPANY, INC.
Garden City, New York
1974

PHOTOGRAPH CREDITS

Mary Evans Picture Library: photos 1, 14, 15, 16, 19.
The Granger Collection: photos 2–13, 17, 18, 21.
Radio Times Hulton Picture Library: photo 20.

The Massachusetts Historical Society and
the British Museum for endpaper photos.

Designed by Wilma Robin

To E. P. K.

CONTENTS

In writing this biography of John Wilkes —as it happens, the first biography of him by an American—I have been much indebted to many of the biographers and other writers listed under *Books Consulted*; and for the chapters on lower, middle, and upper-class life in eighteenth-century England, I have here and there drawn on my own *Kings and Desperate Men*.

L.K.

Preface

THE READER may find useful a short headlines history of John Wilkes's England. His life spanned three quarters of a predominantly sane and fruitful eighteenth century which, unlike the seventeenth, was not sanguinary, bigoted, and intense, running to Gunpowder Plots and Bloody Assizes. It was much more of an Age of Reason, of the Rights of Man, of Britons never will be slaves: the reign of divine right and superstition was ending and that of steam and smoke had barely begun.

Yet this century of consolidation was also one of conquest— England, in 1700 struggling for power and overshadowed by France, could long before 1800 boast great place and possessions. The century opened with a new sovereign, Queen Anne, and with an eleven-years-long War of the Spanish Succession, when England, Holland, and Austria opposed a Louis XIV whose dynastic ambitions threatened the balance of power in Europe. With the great Duke of Marlborough in superb command, the war could have ended much sooner; but while England's taxbled landowning Tories clamored for peace, its moneyed and profiteering Whigs prolonged the war from greed. England eventually came off with Newfoundland and Nova Scotia, Minorca and Gibraltar, rights to the African slave trade and immense commercial advantages: by dint of arms Marlborough had elevated England—which in 1707, by uniting with Scotland, had become Great Britain—to the most commanding position in Europe.

Anne's resplendent if fractious reign had seen not only the War of the Spanish Succession abroad, but what might be called the War of the Hanoverian Succession at home. For Anne would die without offspring, and since her successor must by law be a Protestant, her half-brother, the Tory-supported Catholic son of James II, was ruled out, with the throne to be inherited by a distant and Whig-supported German cousin. Anne's reign consequently swarmed with dark Jacobite conspiracies; but at her death in 1714 the crown passed peaceably to the Hanoverian George I.

Exultant from having brought France to her knees, a warwearied England had itself to be put on its feet. George I soon faced, among other things, a Jacobite rebellion; and a few years later, the collapse of the South Sea Company and many wildcat investments, in which vast numbers of people had dementedly speculated, became a national calamity. Fortunately, one man now managed to stabilize England. Sir Robert Walpole, at once a cynical manipulator and a supremely efficient statesman, set George I and then George II firmly on their thrones, while making sure that they were docile constitutional monarchs, not to say figureheads. Indeed, Walpole evolved what became for good and all Britain's form of parliamentary government, operating through the party system. But Walpole chiefly put England on its feet by enforcing upon it a long period of peace. Despite tempting opportunities on the Continent, despite much opposition from his own Cabinet, he clung to his peace policy, so that by the time public pressure drove him into war with Spain, he had made England not only secure, but prosperous. He had also, it is true, made it a nation of shopkeepers and a hive of corruption: in Parliament, he said, he was obliged "to bribe Members not to vote against, but *for* their conscience." Yet Walpole remains the greatest of English administrators; as someone said, the best eulogy of his regime was the "ten blundering years that came after it."

Soon after them, however, England's greatest *war* minister was in the saddle. Pitt the Elder, joining Frederick the Great against half of Europe in the Seven Years' War (1756–63), gained for England, among many other things, all of Canada, much of the great Louisiana territory, and a firmer hand on India. Indeed, by 1765 Britain had begun to govern India; and with this established, Britain could boast a mighty empire.

A little earlier there had come to the throne George III who was not, like his predecessors, docile: if, as he found, Parliament ruled the country, he would set out to rule Parliament, bullying it where he could, bribing it where he must. Using money, sinecures, pensions, promotions, promises, and threats, he was very often successful in his efforts: it took another war to foil him and simultaneously lose a large segment of the empire, which called itself the United States. This final lunge of George's for extensive power proved a decisive one: no subsequent British monarch would have any real power at all. When Pitt the Younger drew George's royal claws, monarchy in England for the most part became pageantry: before the eighteenth century ended, England would witness, in the French Revolution and the war it drew her into, the blood-red dawn of democracy; and in the emerging Industrial Revolution would sniff the eventual transfer of power to the middle class.

Part One

I

JOHN WILKES WAS born, according to his own statement, in St. John's Square, Clerkenwell, on the seventeenth of October, 1727, though there is considerable reason to believe it was two years earlier. In those days his birthplace was a prospering residential part of London and John's nonconformist father, Israel Wilkes, was a prosperous distiller whose "coach was regularly drawn by six horses," and who kept "an elegant and sumptuous table for all his friends." He was a pleasant man and parent—John was the third of six children—with a somewhat worldly outlook on life and a slightly malicious sense of fun. "Have you a purse?" he once asked a schoolboy John, who answered: "No, sir." "I'm sorry," said the father, "for if you had one, I would have given you money to put in it." When, some days later, he again asked John if he had a purse, John answered, "Yes, sir." "I'm glad of it," said the father. "If you hadn't, I should have given you one." John's mother, the daughter of a prosperous tanner, was a rigid Presbyterian lady who seems to have dominated, and drilled rectitudinous principles into, her husband. All her children survived, thanks not least to their mother's uncommon faith in fresh air and clean linen. She also collected china, ivories, and bronzes and was not so rigidly Presbyterian as only to collect pictures with religious themes: hers were for the most part pagan ones, along with six statuettes of Bacchus.

The children, who do not figure much in their famous brother's life, turned out rather one of a kind and not altogether a credit to the mother they had greatly respected. One son took over the distillery in a sound man-of-business fashion; another son was a drifter with little success; a daughter with a violent temper became the wife of three well-to-do businessmen; and a demure daughter, as she grew older, developed melancholia and skirted madness, living alone in a house where the blinds were always drawn and the windows were always shut; she is said to have suggested Miss Haversham in Dickens' *Great Expectations.*

Though little of his childhood has been charted—something balanced by his very animated and anecdotal later life—John seems to have been the favorite of his indulgent, Whiggish, businessman father. Pretty certainly he was singled out by both parents to be made the gentleman of the family—a decision which must have come of John's clever mind and pleasing personality, for there were certainly no social qualifications in his looks. He grew up extremely ugly: Sir Joshua Reynolds spoke of "his forehead low and short, his nose shorter and lower, his upper lip long and projecting, his eyes sunken and horribly squinting," and there was also a crooked jaw. In later years he was very conscious of his looks but so sure of his engaging qualities as in no wise to worry.

The gentleman's education he received was also something of a scholar's; as a boy he was taken in hand by two Presbyterians—nonconformists' sons were not welcomed at the great public schools or permitted at Oxford and Cambridge—and, at the various places where they successively taught him, he acquired a decent mastery of Latin and Greek. He grew up a toughened and thick-skinned youth, a hard fighter who never lost his temper but made other people lose theirs. One of his two clergymen teachers, the Reverend Mr. Leeson, caused his pupil "to associate earnestness with bigotry"—according to John, it was Leeson's habit to search through dull volumes for new heresies.

Yet, when John was nineteen, his parents were sufficiently pleased with Leeson to send him as their son's tutor and guardian to the University of Leyden, a traditional Whig choice. Master and pupil were unable, however, to get along there: the pupil shifted his allegiance to the religious Scots philosopher Andrew Baxter, who said of his charge, "If friendship could appear in human shape, it would assume John Wilkes's agreeable form." But Wilkes shifted again—to the circle of the agnostic, if not indeed atheistic, Baron d'Holbach. This took Wilkes into a more enlightened and exhilarating world, which may have had something to do with Wilkes's precocious and rakish progress—at any rate, he showed signs, according to one of his companions, of the "daring profligacy for which he was afterwards notorious." "My father," Wilkes wrote of his school and college days, "gave me as much money as I wanted"; and Wilkes divulges how it was spent: "Three or four whores—drunk every night —sore head next morning." Yet Wilkes made strides, while abroad, in what he was sent there for. He acquired the polished manners of a gentleman and the knowledge of a fledgling *homme du monde;* he became a brilliant talker and a welcome guest. When he left Leyden, d'Holbach said, "The enchantment ceases, the delightful image vanishes"—and having completed a chapter in his education, Wilkes in July 1746 came back to England, well equipped but with no chosen career.

His parents, impressed by the excellence if unaware of the excesses of his education, now felt very strongly that their well-turned-out young gentleman should be joined in marriage to a suitable lady. Mary Mead, the lady they chose, was an heiress to a sizable fortune and the daughter of an old family friend, Mary's mother being an even more Calvinist mother than John's. Mary herself was dull, fat, and thirty-two years old: John was not yet twenty-two. He dutifully, and she apathetically, acquiesced in so unpromising an alliance; disastrous in itself, it was made fiendishly worse by the unhappy pair's moving in with John's mother-in-law, who not just continually chattered, but chattered on theological subjects. Speaking of his marriage in middle age, Wilkes called it "a sacrifice to Plutus, not to Venus" and a matter of stumbling "at the very threshold of the temple of Hymen"; and he proceeded to ask: "Are schoolboys to be dragged to the altar?" The marriage had one substantial worldly merit. Mary Wilkes's large fortune, and her possession of a twenty-five-room country house at Aylesbury, in Buckinghamshire, enabled her husband to be—and not least in Aylesbury eyes—very much of a gentleman,[1] indeed a country gentleman, tending the estate, supporting the church, serving as a magistrate, as a trustee of the grammar school and the foundling hospital, and dispensing charity. He was also in a position to enjoy other ladies than his wife. But the marriage provided him with one tremendous satisfaction: in August 1750 was born a daughter Mary, always known as Polly, to whom—though Mrs. Wilkes cared very little about her —John would be greatly devoted for the rest of his life.

In the years following his marriage he assumed no greater role or responsibility than that of a proper Aylesbury squire who managed to vary his rustic pleasures with urban ones, indeed being often in London—a "charming, warm, wicked town"[2] that he loved—where he became a good deal of a joiner, whether as a Freemason, a Buck, a Fellow of the Royal Society, a member of the Loyal Association of 1745, or a member of the Sublime Society of Beefsteaks. The Sublime Society was made up of various sorts—actors and writers, men of business and men of fashion; the only food was beefsteaks straight off the grill; the chief attractions, wine, the thought of women, and song. Soon after his daughter was born, Wilkes is said to have taken a house in London, which "required an expensive establishment and

[1] Wilkes's father also settled on him properties in East Anglia worth around £350 a year, in today's money close to $15,000.
[2] When the mayor of Aylesbury said that London was full of rogues and prostitutes, Wilkes acknowledged that there were, no doubt, a few such characters to be found there.

introduced a style and manner of living very different to what Mrs. Wilkes had been accustomed to." And beyond the "splendid dinners almost every day," there was Wilkes's "introducing into his house a number of juvenile, gay bacchanalians of dissolute manners and vulgar language." Mrs. Wilkes first remonstrated, and then "abandoned his table, and left him to treat his guests as he pleased." Wilkes himself took a good deal of interest, more gastronomical than gluttonous, in food. "I can never have too much game," he wrote to the friend and gentleman-farmer who served as his gamekeeper and asked him on another occasion to procure for him a "fillet of veal, a sirloin of beef, four fowls, a couple of rabbits," and "all sorts of game." That he did not overdo is pretty well proved, C. P. Chenevix Trench remarks, by his never putting on weight or suffering from gout. But, assisted by the son of a deceased Archbishop of Canterbury, Wilkes became, in London and elsewhere, a great deal of a rounder: he stands out, indeed, as one of the great profligates of a profligate century.

Thomas Potter, the archbishop's son who led Wilkes about, was Member of Parliament for Aylesbury; and where he always led Wilkes was down a primrose path, whether in London, Bath, or Tunbridge Wells. Indeed, an early biographer of Wilkes said that Potter had "poisoned his morals." Potter definitely suggested to Wilkes that the two of them invade Bath "if you prefer young women and whores to old women and wives; if you prefer toying away hours with little Sattin Back to the evening conferences with your mother-in-law"—only for Potter, after a good many invasions, to declare that Wilkes himself has "done everything in his power to destroy his health by strong soups, filthy claret, rakish hours, and bad example." In venery they were doubtless a matched pair, Potter having said, "My dear Wilkes is one of those who never yet sent women empty away." Potter, however, had a visiting list of a different and su-

perior kind and indeed introduced Wilkes to Earl Temple of
Stowe, said to be the richest commoner in England and known
to be the owner of one of its grandest country houses. Temple
was also the brother of a well-known member of the political
world, George Grenville; and the brother-in-law of a very great
statesman, William Pitt. With its immense power and influence,
the Grenville connection was very much the sort that Wilkes,
who by now had eyed and grown ambitious about politics, was
extremely glad to meet. As something of a neighbor to Wilkes,
Lord Temple came to see a good deal of him, to enjoy his company, and to become in time his friend and patron. The Grenville triumvirate foresaw a decided check on the power they
wielded in the probably not-far-off accession of the future George
III, and they were anxious to recruit bright young men who
might help maintain their ascendancy. Hence in 1754 Wilkes
was named high sheriff of his county and not long after was
encouraged by Temple to stand for a place in Parliament—
Berwick-upon-Tweed, a rotten borough held by the influential
Delaval family in the north of England. Northward went Wilkes
to contest the borough and preserve its rottenness. (Potter had
found for Wilkes a vacancy at Bristol, much nearer home and
easier to win, but Temple was a man whose choice it would be
very impolitic to reject.) Wilkes bribed the captain of a ship—
laden with voters for his opponent—to land them in Norway. In
or near Berwick he bought more than three thousand pounds'
worth of votes, some of the money almost certainly his wife's and
his mother-in-law's. He electioneered in the most exalted terms:
"Gentlemen, I come here *uncorrupting* and I promise you I shall
ever be *uncorrupted.* As I will never take a bribe, so I will never
offer one." Thanks to such avowals he collected 192 votes, his
Delaval opponent collecting more than twice as many.[3] South-
ward he went, to be assailed by his wife and mother-in-law, who

[3] Wilkes petitioned Parliament on the result, charging Delaval with "flagrant,
notorious bribery." Parliament decided against him.

beyond deploring the lost campaign money[4] disapproved of his political aspirations.

The Berwick venture widened the gap between Wilkes and his wife, which was not helped by his mother-in-law's being constantly seated at her daughter's side. Their distaste for him was the merest fraction of his for them; and by the end of 1756 husband and wife had decided on a trial separation. Wilkes, many years afterward, spoke of his marriage—something he had done "to please an indulgent father"—as the great mistake of his life. Not long after the separation Wilkes's daughter, now six years old, contracted at school a serious case of smallpox. Wilkes hurried to her there and at once sent for his wife, who was living with her mother. For whatever reason, she refused to come, even when the crisis was over and the child was convalescent. Wilkes could only with great bitterness berate such a mother and legalize the separation for good and all: he granted his wife £200 a year, promised not to molest her, and permitted her to live with her family and to see Polly from time to time. The two never met again. While living with his wife Wilkes was said to have been "an extremely civil" if "rather cold" husband; but after the separation, being financially pinched, he maneuvered to get a legal release from paying the £200 a year, and to drag Mary Wilkes into court over the matter; but Lord Chief Justice Mansfield, whom Wilkes would meet again, ruled otherwise.

The year—1757—that brought an end to Wilkes's marriage also opened his political career. He stood again for Parliament, this time to represent the town he lived in, Aylesbury. Pitt having given up his pocket borough at Okehampton to stand instead for Bath, Potter, as M.P. for Aylesbury, agreed to take the vacated Okehampton seat and make Aylesbury possible for Wilkes. Potter wished him "a safe and cheap election," but Wilkes had

[4] Elections could prove too expensive for candidates; thus in Essex there was no contest from 1774 to 1810.

not only Aylesbury *douceurs* to pass out—he undertook the financing of Potter and Pitt. The bill came to £7,000, a sum that drove Wilkes, for the first of many times, to the moneylenders. Add to all this his taste for high living and it is no surprise that he had run into considerable debt. Yet he *was* now a Member of Parliament, someone to be counted in the ranks of the Great Commoner, Pitt, and of the great contriver, the Duke of Newcastle. At first, indeed for quite a while, the new honorable member for Aylesbury was not heard from in the House. He voted as the ministry of Pitt and Newcastle expected of him; and for political reasons he had to dispense in Aylesbury a rather disastrous amount of social hospitality, more than enough for him to declare that any M.P. who had to think of his purse and look to his cellar should never represent the town he lived in. He also took a commission in the Buckinghamshire militia, which Pitt had organized for home defense: this was needed with so many British troops fighting abroad and the French actually planning an invasion of England. First as captain and then as lieutenant colonel and second in command, Wilkes, it appears, performed very well, being praised for, among other things, his "humanity." In later years he sufficiently cherished, or romanticized, his military service as to wear his uniform long after he had no right to. (Britain during Wilkes's militia days was of course engaged with Prussia against France and Austria in the Seven Years' War, and in Hampshire a younger man of parts was also an encamped militiaman: Captain of Grenadiers Edward Gibbon. Some years later the two men would meet at dinner, with Gibbon morally shocked if excellently entertained. "I scarcely ever met a better companion," he wrote of Wilkes. "He has inexhaustible spirits, infinite wit and humor, and a great deal of knowledge. A thorough profligate in principle as in practice, his life stained with every vice and his conversation full of blasphemy and bawdry. These morals he glorifies in, for shame is a weakness he has long surmounted." Wilkes did not care for this portrait of himself and decided that Gibbon must have written it while drunk.)

But Wilkes, in his captain-of-militia days, did more than march and vote and regale his Aylesbury constituents. In public life he was also a turnpike trustee, a justice of the peace, and the governor of Aylesbury's foundling hospital—a suitable position, it was remarked, since he was accountable for so many foundlings. In private life, his fellow profligate and M.P. Thomas Potter had introduced him—he was by now in lusty bachelor pursuit of women—to a group of gentlemen who had included the Devil himself in their debauchery. Potter, who had in some degree played the amused tempter to Wilkes and who in both crude and decadent pleasures was Wilkes's evil spirit, seems to have outdone the reputed behavior of a minister's son; and seems, in his behavior, to have outdone any infant's father as well. For when his wife gave birth to a daughter, Potter—as he informed Wilkes—set forth from home to escape "the odious yell of a young female yahoo that thrust herself into the world yesterday." Potter, of course, had often set forth from home for various other reasons, one of them to meet the gentlemen whom he had Wilkes meet also.

These were the members of the extremely notorious Company of the Monks of St. Francis, known also as the Knights of St. Francis of Wycombe; sometimes referred to, because of the Gothic abbey where they met, as the Medmenham Monks— and on occasion "nuns"; and referred to, by the vulgar, as the Hell-Fire Club. Wilkes's entrance into this monastic society, which met on dubiously Christian soil or in weird subterranean caverns, had almost certainly come about from Potter's making him known to a libertine who outranked Wilkes and Potter both and who was the father superior and the canonized figure of the Monks of St. Francis. As Sir Francis Dashwood he also outranked Wilkes in better ways, being goodhearted rather than selfish; as devoted to his wife as he was dissolute; a patron of painters and sculptors; and one of the founders of the famous Dilettante Society, which would rank among the century's outstanding enterprises in art, architecture, and antiquities. Dashwood took a liking to Wilkes and made him one of the company.

The monks indeed lived up to their reputation for debauchery but were in other respects thoroughly disappointing. The roster of members perished when the order's minutes did: just before his death, a number of years later, the secretary burned all the records. But a fair percentage of the membership is known, and some of the full-fledged members—there are also "inferior" ones—are still notorious. Lord Orford was no worse than a halfwit and Bubb Dodington was very much a political turncoat. Lord Sandwich, who could be unscrupulous and unbearable, was without question one of the greatest of rakes, and so passionate a gambler that, rather than leave the card table for dinner, he had meat brought to him between pieces of bread and lent his name to the language. Lord March, best known and excoriated as "Old Q," was not far from villainous. Hogarth was perhaps one of the "inferior" members—he had attended at least once; and three of the monks were also poets, by far the best known of them being Charles Churchill, an Anglican curate who has been called "the most profligate rogue who ever wore the dress of a clergyman" and who was eventually Wilkes's closest friend. Once very famous for satires, many of them vituperative, Churchill at his best was far from lacking in merit. He could be very amusing, as in making sport of the historian William Guthrie, whose *Complete History of the English Period* was loaded with unbelievable inaccuracies:

> He, far beyond the springs of Nature led,
> Makes women bring forth after they are dead.
> He, on a curious, new and happy plan,
> In wedlock's sacred bands joins man to man.
> And to complete the whole—most strange but true—
> By some rare magic makes *them* fruitful too.

Despite the impressive roster of peers and poets, the order brought little that was ingenious or impressive to its rites, or for that matter to its orgies. The members wore Franciscan robes and had various names, Wilkes's being St. John of Aylesbury;[5] and all the members took an oath of secrecy, lest their ceremonies should "increase the number of divorces." The central ceremony was a Black Mass, which had an anti-Catholic coloration. Dashwood, when young, had run untrue to his goodhearted nature: noting, in the Sistine Chapel at Rome, that the sinners flagellated themselves "very lightly," he on Good Friday went to the chapel with a horsewhip hidden under his coat and when the lights were out brought down the whip on all sides, provoking agonized howls of pain and then—amid shrieks of "Il Diavolo!" —having to run for his life. From this performance there presumably emerged at Medmenham a parody of the Roman ritual and an elaborate ceremonial honoring the goddess of love. Wilkes, says Olga Venn, went at all this sacrilegious hocus-pocus with gusto, chiefly, perhaps, because many of his fellow celebrants had high-born names. As for anything further to the celebrants' credit, Wilkes himself confessed that Dashwood alone of them had any imagination.[6] As often happens, high birth had at Medmenham very low proclivities: the monks drank themselves under the table, took their "nuns" inordinately to

[5] In Charles Johnstone's once very popular *Chrysal, or The Adventures of a Guinea* (4 vols., 1760–65) there is material about Medmenham, its members, and its modus operandi. There were no servants, but the "inferior" probationers waited on the "regular" monks. Wilkes, as John of Aylesbury, is described in the book: "His wit gave charms to every subject he spoke upon . . . The vanity which first made him ambitious of entering this society only because it was composed of persons superior to his own rank in life, still kept him in it, though upon acquaintance he despised them . . . His humor was debased into buffoonery, and his wit was so prostituted to the lust of applause that he would sacrifice his best friend for a scurvy jest." *Chrysal* itself was spoken of as "the best scandalous chronicle of the day."

[6] Wilkes also said that Dashwood's "capacity did not extend to settling a tavern bill"; and amended this—when years later Dashwood was made Chancellor of the Exchequer—to "from puzzling all his life over tavern bills, he was called [upon] . . . to administer the finances of a kingdom over a hundred millions in debt." Dashwood called himself "the worst Chancellor of the Exchequer the country had ever known."

bed, and doubtless indulged their monastic tastes in farm-hand pranks and animal pleasures. Though theirs were near-orgies, Wilkes paid tribute to what he perhaps meant as their heterosexual tastes, by saying that "they seem to have sinned *naturally*." Whether the partners involved were ladies of the evening, or well-born ladies, or both, has not come to light.

The setting for all this was rather elaborate. The entrance to Dashwood's abbey bore the Rabelais-born and Rabelaisian-intended inscription, *Fay ce que voudras;* the vista included the Thames near Marlow where Dashwood had moored a gondola brought from Venice; the grounds were a jumble of phallic decorations and suggestive architecture—of symbolic vases, of priapic statues and pornographic obelisks, and of urns dedicated to Potiphar's wife and the Widow of Ephesus. Of the decor within the abbey, and the details of Medmenham ceremonials, not much seems to be known—though, in addition to frescoes parodying various Greek and Roman marriages, there was on the grand staircase a "very moral painting," which much impressed Wilkes, of "a maid stealing to her master's bed, laying at the same time her finger to her lips." The Black Mass was performed in a chapel, with its celebrants dressed in white suits and hats, while Sir Francis, as prior, wore a red bonnet trimmed with fur. On what might be called Medmenham's creative side there existed a sort of scrapbook named the *New Foundling Hospital of Wit,* to which the more inspired members contributed various sallies and salacities. The book also commemorated a kind of parlor game which consisted of reading a newspaper, not downward but crosswise from one column to another, and recording such resultant reading matter as

At a very full meeting of Common Council

the greatest show of horned cattle this season.

and

This day His Majesty will go in state

to fifteen notorious common prostitutes.

Wilkes seems, opinions to the contrary, to have enjoyed the amenities and opportunities of Medmenham—"amusement I must have," he wrote to a friend, "and it is the only one I take." But the elaborate ritualism and the obscene jocularities presumably became a bore, prompting Wilkes to pass judgment on such mumbo-jumbo with a prank of his own. He concealed in a box, inside the abbey, a large black baboon dressed as the Devil; and when Lord Orford was offering a prayer to Satan, Wilkes, by pulling a string, released the terrified baboon, which leaped onto an even more terrified Lord Orford's shoulders, only to dart outside the abbey, first to frighten and then to infuriate the townspeople. The prank succeeded, if in no wise else, in putting an end to the Company of the Monks of St. Francis: no further meetings were ever held and, very soon after, the members— many of them no longer diabolists—were apt to be politically at odds with one another. Furthermore, the perpetrator of the prank was by now becoming very much entangled, not to say imperiled, in weightier transactions.

2

WHEN IN 1757 Wilkes became a Member of Parliament and began as a very docile member in pursuit of a career, the framework of politics and, in consequence, the fortunes and future of England were by no means reassuring. England was involved in the Seven Years' War and failing to win it: Minorca was lost, thus making for Mediterranean troubles; across the ocean the French had beaten General Braddock in Pennsylvania and were inflicting fresh defeats in Canada; the long odds of the war would seem to be growing longer. Ever since the death of Queen Anne in 1714 the great Whig families had ruled the country, which is to say that whoever might be King reigned and in no respect governed. The immense patronage that the great Whigs commanded had come close to forging absolute rule. Although neither George I nor George II was a supine monarch, each had kept his throne through Whig support, which meant genuflecting to Whig supremacy. Both Georges, moreover, were stanch Hanoverians for whom England was much less a residence and a kingdom than a business address and a bank. In contrast, the Whig oligarchy equated governing England with gobbling up offices, with dipping into the privy purse, rifling the Treasury coffers, and, as good family men, with giving their sons and their sons-in-law, their infant grandsons and their aging uncles, and some of the ladies in the family, a variety of ill-defined jobs, undefined joblets, and lucrative sinecures. A baroness might be made Sweeper of the Mall, and so on; but if there was actual work to do, it was done by ill-paid subordinates. Such familial benefactions, however, were far exceeded by the gifts to political "friends" who, besides having their palms suavely greased, might with their well-trained fingers, pocket a borough or two. All this had gone on very smoothly, but soon after Wilkes became an M.P., England had been forced to part with here an island and there a colony, and the nation had begun to seethe with dissatisfaction and unrest.

At this point Pitt, at most a Whig by coalition, and certainly not by creed—he had been an Opposition figure during most of his previous career—took over. "I am sure," he said, "that I can save this country, and that nobody else can." And now, *encountering* opposition, he fell to: scornful of caution and shrugging at the economy, he assembled and sent forth fleets and armies. The war, he believed, was a struggle for empire between England and France, and though the grand issue was America, the conflict was global, waged on many coastlines and on several continents. Within two years he brought a host of great enterprises to the boil; and by Christmas of 1759 England could celebrate a host of great victories. Minden, Quiberon Bay, Madras, Guadeloupe, Lagos, and Quebec—such were the trophies, unequaled since the Middle Ages, that England's imperious war minister set before his aging King. Thanks to Pitt's tremendous success, the Whig oligarchy, though debilitated and divided, seemed secure.

But 1759 was the gorgeous sunset of George II's reign; in the following year he died. His successor was his grandson, twenty-two-year-old George III, who might seem, and who to the populace did seem, a very welcome monarch. He was young and good looking in a pop-eyed and Germanic way; moral in his thinking and outlook; and quite unroyally well behaved. To be sure—and partly *because* he was so well behaved—not a great deal was known about him. His father Frederick Prince of Wales having died when George was thirteen, the boy was brought up in seclusion by his German mother, whom George II called "cette diablesse, Madame la Princesse." In any case, she sought the counsel, and very possibly shared the bed, of a not very popular Scottish counselor, Lord Bute. This, together with other factors, had meant bringing George up at an Opposition court which abounded in out-of-favor and out-of-office Tories and Scotsmen; and what must well have been drummed into the future King's ears was quite out of line with the scrupulously constitutional policies and practices of the two kings who preceded him. Madame la Princesse's educative preachments were aimed at scaling and then demolishing the great wall of Whiggery and, as a matter of fact, at dispensing with constitutional rule. Her chronic and heraldic injunction was "George, be King!"—an injunction that, however peculiarly George might interpret it, was to a considerable extent inherent in him. He had a fistful of moral tenets: he would never be cynical, he would never be irresponsible, he would never be dissolute. He had also a head full of monarchical tenets and would make every effort to be a totally participating, a firm and unbudging monarch. He had grown up quite backward and dull; was still not able, when eleven years old, to read; and intellectually improved very little thereafter. He had also grown up to hate the Whigs and was thus resolved in every conceivable way to harry them. His most valuable tenet, acquired from Bolingbroke's *The Idea of a Patriot King,* was that a monarch should be altogether above faction and party, while empowered to control faction and party in Parliament. To be sure, a king at that period in English history, had much power of patronage, which could be crucial in elections[1] and had also the right to choose his own ministers.

[1] Chenevix Trench tells, apropos of this, of a candidate who, to gain his constituents' votes, forged a letter from George III, wishing the candidate success, assuring him that the Treasury was at his disposal, and concluding with "Charlotte [the Queen] and the children desire their compliments."

As what might be called a private person, George would be a very approachable, indeed "democratic" monarch who, with rustic tastes, rode around superintending his acres like any country squire and who, far from minding the nickname of "Farmer George," rejoiced in it. When at home, he both preached and practised thrift, personally inspecting the kitchen so that nothing should go to waste and incidentally forbidding servants to take tips. When he traveled he would stop at inns and chat with strangers; and, as domestic in his way of life as he was rustic, he quite merited—after a dozen of his wife's childbeds—the title of "Father George." He mingled freely with shopkeepers and tradesmen, and when he found he had no money on him to pay for what he bought, he left his watch with the shopkeeper as surety. Part of his being a good royal mixer was his being a notable gossip; part of it also, no doubt, was due to his undistinguished royal mind. And along with discussing crops and other country matters he took pleasure in doing his duty by the arts: he offered Rousseau a pension; he not only pensioned Dr. Johnson but gave him an audience which is one of the most famous pages in Boswell; and he gave Gibbon a near-sinecure on the Board of Trade bringing almost £800 a year (this maliciously ascribed to his keeping Gibbon from writing *The Decline and Fall of the British Empire*). Like all the Georges, he liked music; and he liked art, not least having his own portrait painted. On succeeding as King he became a patron of the Royal Academy but was a careful purchaser, finding sixty guineas rather too high for a painting of Richard Wilson's. If, said Wilson, the lump sum was more than His Majesty could manage, he was willing to be paid in installments.

As a great deal more than a private person, George III was also a great deal different. His chief virtue, a strong sense of duty, was true of the man and the monarch alike, but with unlike results. George saw himself as God's vicar as well as England's King[2] and as someone who should boast a virtuous as well as a victorious reign; who should do away with "those proud [Whig] dukes" and fearlessly wipe out corruption. And indeed the more he saw of corruption and felt surrounded by it, the more deserted and solitary he felt in his lofty rectitudinous aims, and the more self-righteously unyielding he grew. In short, his greatest virtue was married to his most costly fault, an unshakable stubbornness. Some part of this, to be sure, resulted from the evils he faced rather than the principles he formulated. He was indeed surrounded by careerism and corruption and was constantly vis-à-vis with intrigue; only two men, says R. J. White, possessed anything in the way of ideas and principles: Pitt, who would soon be ousted from power, and Edmund Burke, who would never be granted any. Men in politics were glaringly limelighted actors: as Mr. White puts it, "the public life . . . was a performance to be watched and enjoyed, hissed or applauded. Everything from an election to a hanging took place on an open stage, for all to see."

The central, most brilliantly lighted drama, which performed for six months every year, was Parliament. The real conflict had long been not between Whigs and Tories—the Tories were tagged as Jacobites and were quite without power—but between Whigs in office and Whigs out of it, or one species of Whigs and another. Party principles accordingly had little to do with political performances: in the general election the year after George III became King, not a single seat was won or lost on party grounds. Moreover, about a third of the House of Commons was made up of "the King's men"—placemen and courtiers often on the King's payroll—who supported the King's ministers simply because of their being the King's minions. Such men might be said to have permanent jobs. As opposed to this, per-

[2] He rebuked the Court chaplain, who had too profusely sung his praises, with: "I come to church to hear God praised, not myself." The chaplain in due course became a strong supporter of Wilkes.

haps a fifth of the House was a group made up of largely Tory-minded country gentlemen. They were not courtiers or careerists or "permanent" M.P.s, but men who supported the sovereign so long as they could without shaming their consciences or losing their constituents. They prided themselves, in fact, on being independents who might vote for either side, and thus they had always to be reckoned with. Walter Bagehot, in a later age, called them "the finest brute votes in Europe"; they had little interest in "Fine men in place / In cockade and lace" and, all in all, the squire would

> Vote as his father did when there's a call
> But had much rather never vote at all.

They were men George approved of and who, like George, disapproved of the arrogant Whigs and their high-handed presumptions; and more times than not they would give George an extra push toward fulfilling his God-ordained duty.

But the worst possible voice for George to respond to was Duty whispering low "Thou must." For in large degree it prevented his realizing that as an ignorant new broom, faced with so much to sweep away, he couldn't possibly sweep clean but could decidedly raise dust. "Any suggestion of reform," says J. H. Plumb, ". . . he regarded as a personal affront." What George needed in the service of virtue was a talent for judging people, joined to an ability to conciliate them: a stupid man, he was often no better a diplomat than he was a statesman. Thus, for one great example, George should have seen, not least from his *own* point of view, the political virtue as well as value in retaining Pitt; what he did, as we shall see, proved the worst sort of political folly.

On becoming King, George chose as the man to get rid of the Whigs his mother's counselor, Lord Bute. "My Lord Bute," George said to the Duke of Newcastle, "is my good friend. He will tell you my thoughts at large." Though George's father had

characterized Bute as a man who might make a splendid ambassador at a very minor court where there was nothing to do,
George—though at the age of seventeen he had been informed
of the gossip about his mother and his tutor[3]—greatly admired
Bute and, as a first step toward endowing him with power, gave
him a place in the Cabinet. Pitt was still needed to prosecute
the war, but it was Bute's great ambition to negotiate the peace.
Whatever his social background, Bute's political one was unpromising. He is said to have "edged into Court favor" by "making a fourth at cards when rain halted a cricket match in which
the Prince of Wales [George's father] was engaged." He did
have his points: on the death of his kinsman and fellow Scot
the Duke of Argyll, Bute would be left to oversee forty-five
Scottish M.P.s; he had, in Edward Wortley Montagu, the famous Lady Mary's husband, a very rich and stingy father-in-law
whose fortune, estimated at £1,300,000—close to $50,000,000
in today's money—descended to Bute's wife; and he had in Sir
James Lowther an even richer son-in-law and a Member of
Parliament. But as a politician Bute had very little else. Pitt
at this point found himself, in attempting to get on with the
war, prevented from doing so, wherever possible, by a stubborn
and strong Opposition. Both Newcastle and Bute,[4] among
others, wanted an end to the war, because so long as there *was*
one, Pitt was indispensable. Though himself no party man and
as hostile to faction as was the King—whom he very much respected as his sovereign—Pitt lacked the King's support. He
was, to go no farther, too great a leader for George to like or
approve of. Indeed, George saw him as having "the blackest of

[3] George's reaction was: "I do here in the presence of Our Almighty Lord
promise that I will ever remember the insults done to my mother, and will
never forgive any one who shall speak disrespectfully of her . . . I do in the
same solemn manner declare that I will defend my Friend and never use evasive
answers."

[4] Bute had been promoted to one of the Secretaries of State by means of
George III's retiring the incumbent, Lord Holderness, with an annual £4,000
pension ($150,000 today).

hearts" and as "an overmighty subject"; hated him as a "deserter" from his father the Prince of Wales's Opposition ranks and would hate him even more in the years—years that led to the American Revolution—to come. (Both men, it is perhaps worth mentioning, went periodically mad.) And in prosecuting the Seven Years' War Pitt, who among other things wanted to declare war on Spain and seize her trade,[5] found that he had more than the King's hostility to contend with: he had the Whigs as well and the opposition of his co-administrator Newcastle. Pitt thereupon imperiously resigned. Next it was Newcastle whom the King wanted out of office—Newcastle who, as First Lord of the Treasury, was not only Prime Minister but quite in command of the Treasury and a fountainhead of corruption. Newcastle, like Pitt, faced more opposition than just the King's; he faced it among his own colleagues, indeed among his Treasury board members; and he too presently resigned, conceivably in the belief that his resignation would not be accepted.

But it *was* accepted; and exactly three days later, on May 29, 1762, Bute was appointed First Lord of the Treasury—and the King's peacemaker. Bute's aim was one thing; his attaining it, not just despite his opponents but despite his colleagues as well, was another. As for the King's *place*maker, who should manage the House of Commons and continue Newcastle's corrupt Treasury performances,[6] the role passed not to Bute but to the paymaster of the forces, Henry Fox—Charles James's father—who was promised a peerage and became in 1763 Lord Holland. In the way of greasing palms while buttering his own parsnips—of buying votes, distributing places, and collecting commissions for himself—Fox had perhaps no equal; and the King, who realized his need to possess a majority in the House of Com-

[5] Pitt believed, says J. H. Plumb, that England's moral duty was to capture the trade of the world, if need be, by war.

[6] *The Concise Dictionary of National Biography* says of Newcastle, however, that "though a master of political corruption he was not himself corrupt and died £300,000 poorer [for being in politics]."

mons, bowed to the necessity of having to install "bad men to govern bad men." But in having chosen Fox the King might be comforted by two things in Fox's favor: first, that he apparently bribed nobody to *support* the peace; and second, that he never appropriated a shilling of the capital that was to be spent for public use—all he took for himself was the interest on it. As for Fox's attitude toward the "bad men" he had to bribe, Horace Walpole says he showed so little concern that at the Pay Office a shop was opened where M.P.s who were on Fox's books went regularly for their "wages." And Walpole's nephew, Lord Orford, took a bribe—a £2,200 rangership of St. James's and Hyde parks—and, by no means uniquely, never once voted with the ministry.

In such a setting, and with the support of the very rich and very pro-peace Whig Duke of Bedford, Bute opened peace negotiations. By late October of 1762 the preliminaries of a peace with France were drawn up. Whoever, among the Duke of Newcastle's men in office, opposed those terms was, at the King's command, to be instantly turned out or, with royal politesse, asked by Newcastle to resign. But there were enough men who favored the King to insure success when, in December, the preliminaries came before Parliament. Britain's victory over France was indeed a notable one and, from what Britain acquired through it, might seem notably rewarded. France gave Britain all of Canada; Cape Breton and the islands of the St. Lawrence; all of Louisiana east of the Mississippi; a number of West Indies islands; Senegal; and a much firmer hold on Minorca and India. Spain, which had joined France late in the war, gave Britain Florida. (As against this, Britain restored to France and Spain a number of conquests such as Havana and the Philippines, Guadeloupe and Martinique.) Yet for political reasons, and also for some that were practical, the terms in England were met with vehement attack. The most ironic reason was the strong disapproval of England's swapping Guadeloupe for Canada—Canada being in those days, as compared to the West Indies, a much less valuable purchaser of English goods or supplier of needed English imports. The really incisive reason, however, for disapproving the swap was the Duke of Bedford's argument that *fear of the French* in Canada was the chief cause of the New England colonists' adherence to Britain: relieved now, Bedford argued, of so menacing an enemy nearby, the colonies would look on a mercantile Britain as very little their friend.[7] There were other valid objections to the peace terms, such as that Britain, by its treatment of its enemies and allies—it welshed on its financial promises to Prussia—was isolating itself and destined to have no allies. On the other hand, and a most powerful argument, there was not just a strong popular desire for peace; there was a great financial need. On February 10, 1763, the Peace of Paris, with England, France, and Spain as signatories, ended the Seven Years'—as also the French and Indian—War. (George's mother is said to have congratulated him with "Now, George, you *are* King!") The House of Lords did not even take a vote, and the House of Commons voted 319 for the peace and 65 against it. The chief protest against it was Pitt's, who, agonized with gout, was carried—a mournful sight dressed in somber black—into the Commons to deliver an ineffectual and scarcely audible three-and-a-half-hour speech. Elsewhere there was also a considerable outcry, with Bedford stoned in the streets of London. This was perhaps less because of the terms of peace than because of the "peacemaker"; because of Bute for *being* Bute, a disliked and unattractive Scotchman[8] and the King's favorite; and because of Bute, and not Pitt, being in the saddle. (Bute's ministry would fall in less than two months.) Of all the

---

[7] "The Revolutionary War calamities of 1778–83," says R. J. White apropos Britain's taking Canada, "were to be blamed on the peacemakers of 1763."

[8] Bute found places, out of all proportion, for Scotchmen: "Of sixteen names on one list of gazette promotions, there were eleven Stuarts [Bute was himself named Stuart] and four McKenzies." Indeed, anti-Scots called the newly completed Buckingham Palace "Holyrood."

comments about the Peace of Paris the wittiest and best remembered is that "it is like the peace of God, for it passeth all understanding." The author of the remark, who had become very much of an author and would soon be the most talked about author of his time, was of course John Wilkes.

3

The accession of George III was to endow Wilkes with a new and by no means passive role. When Wilkes's patron, Pitt, resigned, Wilkes, who had scarcely made himself heard, rose in the House of Commons in Pitt's defense; but never was a great orator championed by a more ineffective one. Presumably aware that as a Member of Parliament he was an unskillful haranguer, Wilkes turned elsewhere and proved immediately gifted —indeed found his political métier—as a writer for the press. He was by now prepared to attack the Government in the service of the Opposition and, more particularly, in the service of Lord Temple and of Temple's bulging purse. Earlier, whatever his affiliations with Temple and the Pitt-Newcastle alliance, Wilkes, as an M.P. of no standing, had made strenuous efforts to be given an Administration post. He applied to Bute for the embassy at Constantinople, and being turned down he sought the governorship of a recently acquired Canada—there, he said, he would "reconcile" the French and the English and show the French "the advantages of the mild rule of laws over that of lawless power and despotism." There also, Wilkes added, he would himself be "conveniently remote." Turned down once again, he turned acrimoniously against the Administration.[1] Serving his

[1] Edmund Malone, writing contemporaneously, said that when Wilkes, with some backing, wanted to be made governor of Canada and the Duke of Bedford

friend and chief patron, Temple, with his pen was assuming no uncommon role: almost all political parties and factions needed propagandists and pamphleteers. The Bute administration had Bute's fellow Scot, Tobias Smollett, on hire; as it had also the support of a scoffer at everything Scottish whom Bute in the name of the King had recently pensioned: Dr. Johnson. Indeed in 1761 and 1762 Bute, at a cost of some £30,000, hired or pensioned a number of writers with an eye to their serving the Administration. Smollett edited the Administration's paper, *The Briton*, which denigrated Pitt; and Dr. Johnson's friend Arthur Murphy directed the Administration's *Auditor*.[2] And in June 1762 Wilkes, with the assistance of the Medmenham poets Charles Churchill and Robert Lloyd launched the anti-Administration *North Briton*. The title was chosen in part to make both fun and fools of *The Briton*[3] and its staff; and in part to pretend that, like Bute, it was Scottish-born—this expressly to defame Bute or to insult him. The anonymous "Scotch editor" of *The North Briton* announced that he was "unplaced and unpensioned," but that he hoped that this would soon be rectified. Bute was an early and easy butt, whether as a dispenser of places—as with the Stuarts and McKenzies—or as tied to the Tories and thus linked with the Jacobites, who had rebelled first against George I and then against George II. Some-

applied to Bute, Bute "would not listen to it, and even treated the affair with contempt." This intensified, and personalized, Wilkes's dislike of Bute and led him to say that he would never cease attacking him "till he had made him the most unpopular man in England." And Malone adds: "He kept his word."

[2] *The Auditor* ran a story that Wilkes met Bute's twelve-year-old son in a Winchester bookshop and drove him to tears by bullying him and saying that within six months his father would "be either beheaded or torn to pieces by the mob." Wilkes denied this indignantly in a letter which Churchill printed in *The North Briton*. There were further skirmishes, involving several people, but the truth seems to lie much more in *The Auditor*'s trying to discredit Wilkes than in Wilkes's trying to frighten Bute's son.

[3] Wilkes had gibed at *The Briton* by saying he had heard of *The Free Briton* and wondered why the "free" had been removed. He also, in his anti-Scottish way, translated *The North Briton*'s Vergilian motto *Nos patriam fugimus* as "We all get out of our country as fast as we can."

times *The North Briton* merely joshed the Scots by faking
letters from them, as in its praise of Scottish liberality:

> When Lord Darnley was married to Mary Queen of Scots he
> applied to the City of Edinburgh for a loan and . . . however
> incredible it may seem to our English readers, the City of Edin-
> burgh alone agreed to advance . . . the entire sum of *twenty
> pounds.*

The pretense of its Scottishness was dropped after twelve
issues; by then *The North Briton* had become required reading
in every coffeehouse, and Dr. Johnson had become a target,
his having recently accepted a pension being linked to his famous
description of one: "In England it is generally understood to
mean pay given to a state hireling for treason to his country."
(Wilkes himself referred to Johnson as "Pensioner Johnson.")
Earlier, in *The Public Advertiser*, Wilkes had caught him out
for saying "H seldom, perhaps never, begins any but the first
syllable." "The author of this remark," wrote Wilkes, "must be
a man of quick appre-hension and compre-hensive genius, but
I can never forgive his un-handsome be-havior to the poor
knight-hood, priest-hood, and widow-hood, nor his in-humanity
to all man-hood." More serious was Wilkes's clash with William
Hogarth. The two men had always been on friendly terms, and
Wilkes, hearing that Hogarth was doing a political cartoon,
"The Times," in which he, Churchill, Temple, and Pitt would
appear, wrote to Hogarth "that such a proceeding would not
only be unfriendly . . . but extremely injudicious" and asked
him not to publish it. Hogarth answered that he and Churchill
were not in the cartoon, though Pitt and Temple were. Wilkes
said in reply that reflections on himself were of no matter, but
that attacks on his friends would rouse him to reprisals. The
result was *The North Briton No. 17* in which Wilkes assailed
Hogarth's character—"the rancor and malevolence of his mind"
made it impossible to "treat of pleasant things." He then stressed

Hogarth's decline as a painter and denounced Hogarth's becoming an Administration man on grounds of "gain and vanity." Hogarth had, indeed, for not very admirable reasons become a King's man and was named "serjeant-painter" to the King. "I think," *The North Briton* article remarked, "the term means what is vulgarly called house-painter." Wilkes somehow thought that this and other unkind remarks would not offend Hogarth; indeed, when two months later he thought that Hogarth was dying, he told Temple that "Mr. Hogarth . . . believes I wrote that paper, but he forgives me, for he must own that I am a thorough good-humored fellow, only Pitt-bitten." But Hogarth spoke from no deathbed; he would live for two years more and was biding his time.

Wilkes also went frivolously after some of his old Medmenham cronies, among them Lord Sandwich. Sandwich had been appointed ambassador to Spain and Wilkes lampooned him in a childish salacious "instruction." He was to "preserve his energy" and not fight duels: "We must expressly restrain you to make all your thrusts at the women . . . I hope you will first carry the breastwork, then take the demi lune and at last plant your victorious standard in the citadel of every fair Donna." Though Sandwich would rather soon become hostile toward Wilkes, this sort of thing could scarcely have aroused the hostility of a notoriously lecherous peer; and a possible slur in the squib at Sandwich's courage, if a little more likely, still does not seem likely enough. Nor does Wilkes's famous retort on Sandwich's saying to him that he would either "die of a pox or on the gallows": "That depends, my lord, on whether I embrace your mistress or your principles." The real cause must lie elsewhere in their relationship and will be suggested in due course.

One more personal incident that arose out of Wilkes's rather facetious and technically anonymous *North Briton* joshings concerns George III's Lord Steward of the Household, the vain and arrogant Lord Talbot, who had gone to considerable trouble to train his horse to back away rump first in the presence of royalty. At George III's coronation, however, the horse backed rump first *into* the King's presence and never ceased—"throughout all subsequent maneuvres" and amid loud laughter and applause—to show the King such inelegant disrespect. Wilkes, in *The North Briton,* made fun of the incident at wearisome length: "A politeness," he wrote, "equal to that of lord TALBOT's . . . horse ought not to pass unnoticed . . . I appeal to the applauding multitudes—who were so charmed as to . . . clap even in the *Royal presence.*" This was at most what might amuse *North Briton* readers; there was a good deal more to tire them.

And there was a good deal more to infuriate Lord Talbot, who wrote to Wilkes asking if he was the author. Wilkes, who had nowhere admitted any connection with *The North Briton,* in turn asked what right Talbot had to "catechise me about an anonymous paper." Talbot persisted while Wilkes parried until, after seven letters had been huffily exchanged, Wilkes casually consented to a duel: "On Wednesday," he wrote to Talbot's second, "I will play this duet with his lordship." Refusing to take the challenge seriously, Wilkes arrived on the scene fresh from an orgy with Medmenham associates, proposing that he and Talbot, with their seconds, should dine together before they dueled and that the duel be put over till the next morning. But Lord Talbot—all this is taken from a letter Wilkes wrote to Lord Temple—was "in an agony of passion. He said that I had injured, that I had insulted him, that he was not used to be injured or insulted." Thereupon Talbot said that he insisted upon a direct answer, and that here, sir, were his pistols. Wilkes answered that Talbot would very soon use them, but once again refused to answer Talbot's question. "I observed," said Wilkes, "that I was a private English gentleman, perfectly free and independent"; and he made plain that he would not "submit" to the dictates of someone who, however superior in "rank, fortune and abilities," was no more than Wilkes's equal in "honour, courage and liberty." Talbot, insistent that they duel that evening, first railed at Wilkes and then bemoaned the situation. One minute he told Wilkes that he admired him exceedingly, only to assail him a minute later: "You are a murderer," Talbot cried out, "you want to kill me! But I am sure that I shall kill you . . . If you kill me I hope you will be hanged." "I asked," continued Wilkes in his letter, "if I was first to be killed and afterwards hanged; that I knew his lordship fought me with the King's pardon in his pocket and I fought him with a halter about my neck . . . He told me that I was an unbeliever, and wished to be killed. I . . . observed that we did not meet . . . to settle articles of faith, but points of honour." Then, except for the time he needed to write down his plans for his daughter, who was to be left, should he be killed, in Lady Temple's care, Wilkes put himself at Lord Talbot's service. This included letting Talbot have choice of weapons.

The duelists, around seven o'clock of a bright moonlit night, stood facing each other and, on signal, they both fired—using Talbot's large horse pistols—with neither man hit. Wilkes immediately walked up to Talbot to avow that he *was* the author; Talbot heaped "the highest encomiums" on Wilkes's courage, "and he said would declare everywhere that I was the noblest fellow God had ever made." Wilkes saw to it that his letter to Temple about the duel got published, which enhanced his popularity, not least among the ladies;[4] but it far from pleased either Lord Temple or Lord Talbot. Talbot, indeed, charged Temple with publishing it and now called *him* out; but he refused to come. Temple thought that Wilkes had behaved well about the duel, but objected to his publishing the letter and objected even more to the sort of frivolous communications he was getting from Wilkes by mail. He pretty snappishly exhorted

[4] "A sweet girl, whom I have sighed for unsuccessfully these three months," Wilkes wrote to Churchill shortly after the duel, "now tells me she will trust her *honour* to a man who takes so much care of his own. Is not that prettily said?"

Wilkes to concentrate on his labors in Parliament, and he twice
told him to stop sending him scandalous verse.[5] But Wilkes
was chiefly given to scandalous, and anonymous, prose: in *The
North Briton* he had accused Bute and his fellow Scots of seeking to govern England and had used harsh and unscrupulous
methods to denounce them or whoever else became a target.
Wilkes made a success of *The North Briton* as partly a scandal
sheet and partly a flagellant, having in the first number acclaimed "the liberty of the press" as "the birthright of every
Briton." As for Wilkes's ethics generally as a pamphleteer and
his frankness about them: "Wilkes said to me," Adam Smith
reported, " 'Give me a grain of truth and I will mix it up with a
great mass of falsehood so that no chemist will ever be able to
separate them.' "

As time went on Wilkes attacked the Administration more
directly and more crucially. With Henry Fox by now in the
Cabinet as, so to speak, Minister of Corruption, as well as behind the counter as paymaster of the King's mercenaries, bribes
were as common as breakfasts, and *The North Briton* took note
of them. For one example, it called Samuel Martin—a master
briber, a fellow M.P. of Wilkes's, and a former secretary to the
Treasury—"the most treacherous, base, selfish, mean, abject,
low-lived, and dirty fellow that ever wriggled himself into a
secretaryship." Wilkes went most, however, after Bute himself.
On March 15, 1763, he published in pamphlet form, dedicated
to Bute, a Wilkish introduction to an old play, *The Fall of
Mortimer*. Treating of Roger Mortimer, who was eventually
executed as not only the murderer of Edward II but more per-
tinently, the lover of Edward's Queen and for several years the
ruler of England under the youthful Edward III, Wilkes wrote:
"I purposely dedicate this play to your lordship because history
does not furnish a more striking contrast than there is between

[5] As the verses dealt with Bute and the Princess and the like, Temple—whose
mail was subject to examination—was perhaps more worried than disgusted.

73723

the two ministers in the reigns of Edward the Third and George the Third." Edward, Wilkes declared, "was held in the most absolute slavery by his mother and his minister, the first notables of England were excluded from the councils, and the minion disposed of all places of profit and trust." What, it would seem, most aroused George III, and later antagonized him, was not the charge of corruption or the making him a cipher, but the blatant insinuation about his mother and Bute. About Bute Wilkes grew bolder still, drawing on his love of amateur theatricals and his "achievements" as Lothario and Hamlet: "It is the warmest wish of my heart that the Earl of Bute may speedily complete the story of Roger Mortimer . . . Such a work will immortalize your name in the literary, as the peace of [Paris] will in the political, world." For a final gibe at Bute Wilkes said to Jeremiah Dyson, a venal Government hack: "It is usual to give dedicators something. I wish you would put his lordship in mind of it."

Though it is reported that in response to all this Bute was "crimson" and the King "livid," no action was taken against it; and Wilkes remarked that he had tested the temper of the Court by writing the piece and had found that they dared not touch him. When he was in Paris soon after, he was asked—some versions say by Madame de Pompadour—how far the liberty of the press extended in England. "That is what I am trying," answered Wilkes, "to find out." (Actually, in November 1762, a warrant was drawn up to arrest the editor and publisher of the first twenty-six *North Britons,* but it was later withdrawn.) Feeling rather triumphant Wilkes had ended the April 2, 1763, issue by saying: "We may safely conclude that a change is at hand." He had prophesied well: a few days later Bute, saying, "I am firmly of the opinion that my retirement will remove the only unpopular part of the Government," thereupon resigned. He resigned for a number of reasons, among them ill health (he suffered from worms) and lack of support from his own Cabinet; but he had been notably unpopular—as a Scot, a Mortimer, a peacemaker, and a sweeper of the Opposition out of office; and Wilkes could scarcely not exult from having in some degree intensified the unpopularity. Out of office, however, the King's "Dearest Friend" was by no means out of favor: within a few weeks of his resigning, he received some eighteen letters from the King seeking his advice about various political matters, as well as appointments and promotions. Soon after, while working to form a ministry, Bute told a friend: "Whatever the Ministers may think, they will find that I am a Minister still."[6]

On the heels of Bute's resignation Wilkes found there was new *North Briton* work to be done. Lord Temple's brother, George Grenville,[7] had succeeded Bute as First Lord of the Treasury, and an immediate policy of Grenville's was to silence Bute's opponents and assailants and to release the King from dependence on the Whig oligarchy. Two of Bute's most formidable assailants were Grenville's brother and brother-in-law, Temple and Pitt. Yet, out of some need or perhaps out of courtesy, Grenville sent his brother an advance copy of the King's forthcoming speech from the throne; and on their reading it over, Temple and Pitt found it as bad as they had feared. Wilkes, who was often in their confidence, happened just then to call on Temple on his return from a trip to Paris and was made privy to the speech and to their criticisms of it; and possibly on his own initiative, but rather more likely through their proposal, and even with their co-operation, he wrote an attack on the speech, which he published in the April 23 issue or, as it is far better known, *The North Briton No. 45*.[8] With this issue, Wilkes hurled himself into history.

[6] Oddly enough, George III long afterward declared that he had always been opposed to giving his Dearest Friend political power. Or giving it to anyone else, he might have added.

[7] George III invariably wrote to him as "Mr. Greenville."

[8] Some doubt has been cast on the origin of *No. 45* as coming from a single and not too reliable source, John Almon.

4

In ASSAILING the King's speech Wilkes had taken the precaution to say that it was *not* the King's: "It had always," the attack remarked, "been considered by the legislature, and by the public at large, as the *speech of the minister*." Wilkes indeed showed nothing but respect and praise for the King, at the expense of the minister: "Every friend of his country must lament that a prince of so many great and amiable qualities . . . can . . . give the sanction of his sacred name to the most odious measures"; indeed, "This week has given to the public the most abandoned instance of ministerial effrontery ever attempted." And again: "I wish as much as any man in England to see the honour of the crown maintained in a manner truly becoming Royalty"—which was immediately followed by: "I lament to see it sunk even to prostitution." Bute, though no longer Prime Minister, was battered in the *No. 45* for his peace treaty and not least for England's gaining it by not meeting its obligations to Prussia. Bute was further assailed as really running the Grenville administration, and "with a rod of iron": Grenville in fact, soon after and very peremptorily, had to call a halt on the King's constantly writing to Bute for advice.

The ministers were for retaliating on the *No. 45*; and the King, however respectful the references to him, was now fully aware that Bute's resignation in no wise ended Wilkes's assaults. The ministers themselves were not quite sure or stouthearted enough about how to proceed; but on approaching the Attorney General and the Solicitor General they were advised that *No. 45* could be adjudged "an infamous and seditious libel, tending to inflame the minds, and alienate the affections, of the people from his Majesty, and excite them to traitorous insurrections against his government." So advised—Wilkes originally was to be charged with "treasonable libel"—the Secretary of State, Lord Halifax, with behind him the Attorney General's and the Lord Chancellor's assurances that such a procedure was legal, issued a general warrant for the arrest of the writers, printers, and publishers of *The North Briton No. 45* and for the seizure of their papers. In the warrant no one but the printer was actually named. (Halifax, as he later admitted in court, drew up the general warrant, not only a day before he had a written statement from the Attorney General and the Lord Chancellor, but with no evidence of the authorship of *No. 45*.)

The four messengers and a constable who were empowered to make arrests went forth and in three days had seized forty-eight persons—a number of them having nothing to do with *The North Briton* and a number of them dragged from their beds—including the publisher of *No. 45* and the printer. (Also arrested was a printer of other issues of *The North Briton* but not of *No. 45*, and who some three years later was granted £400 in damages by the court.) Wilkes, however, was still at large and still trying to find out how far the freedom of the press extended in England. Dr. Johnson favored dispensing with any legal punishment for Wilkes; his own prescription was, "I would send half a dozen footmen and have him well ducked." Obviously the drama that was opening, and whose first act was chiefly a farce, appealed to Wilkes—appealed to the agitator in him that craved excitement, to the actor that craved the limelight, and to the man of parts that could trick out an insolent role with ready wit. The slow-footed constable and messengers would seem to have surmised that they were no match for him (the most trustworthy of them pleaded illness in a handwriting that was just a little too wobbly to be convincing). On April 29, however, two of the King's messengers did station themselves outside Wilkes's house in Great George Street, Westminster—where, just four houses away, Lord Halifax lived also. But when Wilkes came home that night the messengers—it is just possible that their palms had been greased—kept their hands off him; they afterward explained that he had been "in liquor." Such sensibility, however, does not apply to Wilkes's reappearance at six o'clock the next morning when, steady and resolute, he left the house, vouchsafing that he would be back for breakfast: again the messengers neither questioned nor laid hands on him. His walk before breakfast, which conceivably quickened to a canter, took him to a printing shop. There being refused admittance at the door by the printer's wife, but winked at should he break in, he climbed on a borrowed ladder to the loft. On entering it, he first took an impression of *The North Briton No. 46*, which had already been set up and contained a number of fresh gibes; he then pied the type, and possibly destroyed the original version of *No. 45* as well, along with whatever else might prove compromising. Then, at his ease, he strolled home. There the braver of the two messengers made a mild show of arresting him. Well aware and in perfect command of the situation, Wilkes insisted on seeing the warrant, which he dismissed as not a warrant: he asked why *he*—rather than the Lord Chancellor, or a Secretary of State, or Lord Bute, or indeed the man next door—should be served it. He informed the bearer of the warrant that it was of no concern to John Wilkes; he advised the man "to be very civil"; he warned him that if he attempted force he would put him to death with the sword he was wearing; and at length invited him to come into the house to hear in accurate detail why the document he carried was totally illegal. The warrant bearer acquiesced, came in, and—while various other messengers and their assistants arrived—was interminably harangued by Wilkes with arguments and rejoinders concerning how outrageously he had been treated. In the midst of all this, Wilkes's great friend Charles Churchill, who was also, as a *North Briton* writer, being sought out, pushed his way into the presence of the messengers, only to be saved by his host's presence of mind. Loudly greeted by Wilkes with a "Good morrow, Mr. Thomson," Churchill was next very loudly interrogated whether Mrs. Thomson wasn't planning to dine *in the country*. An alert teammate, Churchill answered that Mrs. Thomson had so definitely arranged to dine there that he could just pay Wilkes his respects before joining his wife. And indeed he darted home, grabbed his papers, and then fled, no doubt to the country. His escape—for he wasn't tracked down—was a good deal less remarkable than the reason for it: how anyone so well known and, with his burly bruiser appearance, so easy to describe, was not recognized by *any* of the King's deputies is only explicable on the weak grounds that tackling one Wilkes was enough.

Wilkes, after Churchill's exit, continued to hold forth—while, a few doors away Lord Halifax and his fellow Secretary of State, Lord Egremont, were waiting impatiently, and more and more irritably, for Wilkes to accept an invitation to join them. Wilkes answered that this was not possible, as unfortunately he had never been introduced to them. Exasperated beyond endurance by so immovable an object, the messengers threatened to rout Wilkes by sending for an irresistible force—a platoon of Foot Guards. Wilkes thereupon consented to call on Lord Halifax regardless of protocol, but insisted that a sedan chair be brought to convey him to his lordship's. The chair having been brought, Wilkes's love of the limelight was carried out with the utmost ceremony from one neighboring doorstep to the other. On entering Lord Halifax's house Wilkes was led "into an apartment fronting [St. James's] Park" where his host and Lord Egremont were seated at a table stocked with papers, pens, and ink and flanked by various lesser officials and functionaries. Pos-

sibly so formidable a guest list and so formal an atmosphere were
meant to disconcert, and perhaps frighten, their tardy guest;
and very possibly Lord Halifax, who was civil, and Lord Egremont, who was brutal, were determined, if not in one way then
in another, to bring him to heel. But far from this happening,
Wilkes when plied by Halifax with questions—and virtually
charged with being the author of *No. 45*—refused to answer the
questions; parried the accusation; himself made accusations for
being illegally arrested; and when the examination was over,
remarked that "all the quires of paper" on Halifax's table would
be "as milk-white" as at the beginning. He then treated their
lordships to a denunciation of the cabal of ignorant, autocratic
ministers who were ill ruling the country and whom (their lordships included) he would in due course impeach in the House
of Commons. Halifax's response was to give Wilkes his choice
of being imprisoned in Newgate, the Tower, or his own house,
to which Wilkes replied that he never accepted favors except
from a friend. He now advanced from insolence to insult, saying
to Egremont, apropos his having given verbal orders that Wilkes
be dragged out of bed at midnight, that "your lordship is very
ready to issue orders which you had neither the courage to sign
for nor, I believe, to justify." He was soon after informed of the
decision of the secretaries: he would be sent to the Tower. While
waiting to be taken to the Tower, Wilkes—left in Egremont's
charge when Halifax absented himself—strolled so nonchalantly
about the room and so debonairly offered his opinion of the pictures on the walls that a fuming Egremont absented himself
also. Thereafter, it appears, two men (one of them an M.P.)
who had that morning been in the Court of Common Pleas
when on Wilkes's behalf a writ of habeas corpus was applied
for and granted, went at once to Lord Halifax's asking to see
Wilkes. "After some hesitation" this was acceded to, but only
in the presence of Philip Carteret Webb, solicitor to the Treasury, and Lovell Stanhope; and when the two men told Wilkes

of the habeas corpus writ permitting him to be brought to court rather than to the Tower, the information was received by Webb and Stanhope with contempt. Moreover, Halifax and Egremont, in order to evade the writ, drew up a new warrant and took Wilkes out of the custody of one set of messengers and put him into that of another; and in this fashion Wilkes's custodians changed "four times in half a day"—the last being the deputy-lieutenant of the Tower.

On arriving at the Tower Wilkes asked to be put in a room—"if it is possible to find one"—where no Scotchman had been imprisoned, this on the ground that he was afraid of catching the itch. Wilkes also asked, according to Horace Walpole, to be put in the same room where Egremont's father had been confined, charged with being a Jacobite. Wilkes was held in the Tower for three days, with his friends permitted neither to see him nor to stand bail for his release. Temple's reaction was that what he thought to be the Tower he found to be the Bastille: Temple and the Duke of Bolton had offered to stand bail, in some accounts for as much as £100,000 each. (Another account reports that Wilkes had previously, with martyrdomic acuteness, turned down any thought of being let out on bail. A letter exists, however, wherein Wilkes wrote asking the Duke of Grafton to go bail for him, as he had also asked Temple; and a letter exists from Grafton to Temple saying that he would refuse Wilkes's request.)

It furthermore transpired that no sooner had Wilkes left his house for Halifax's than Government agents, still using a general warrant, ransacked the place, smashed open "every closet, bureau and drawer in the house," and piled up all Wilkes's papers which, in the presence of an Under Secretary of State, were stuffed into a sack. Closing "the mouth of the sack" were Wilkes's will and his private pocketbook; also among the contents, Wilkes afterward maintained, were a silver candlestick, an indiscreet letter from an M.P.'s wife, and two "cundums." The stuffed

sack was taken to Lord Halifax. Soon after, Temple, as lord
lieutenant of the county, was ordered to strip Wilkes of his
colonelcy in the Buckinghamshire militia; and, for showing concern about Wilkes, Temple soon after was himself dismissed,
Halifax writing to him curtly that "His Majesty has no further
occasion for your service as Lord Lieutenant." Temple's successor as lord lieutenant was Lord le Despencer, formerly Sir
Francis Dashwood.

Meanwhile Wilkes, in the Tower, had finally been allowed
visitors; the governor of the Tower, however, had orders to take
down the name of everyone who came visiting. When one of
Wilkes's custodians had asked him if he had any requests to
make, he replied grandly: "All I can say to you, sir, is that if my
valet de chambre is allowed to attend me in the Tower, I shall be
shaved and have a clean shirt; if not, I shall have a long beard
and dirty linen." The valet was allowed him. The writ of habeas
corpus—something that Wilkes, should he be arrested, had
planned with Temple to apply for—had not, as would have been
the usual procedure, been sought of the Court of King's Bench,
which was presided over by a foe of libelers and a friend of the
Government, the famous Lord Chief Justice Mansfield; a writ
had been, for the first time since the reign of Charles II, sought
of the Court of Common Pleas. There sat a notably open-minded
Lord Chief Justice Pratt (the future Lord Camden)[1] and on
May 3 Wilkes appeared before the court. He spoke to it, or
might better be said to have spouted to it, first summarizing all
the wrongs he had been victim of and then trusting that his
Administration wrongdoers would be taught that "the liberty of
an English subject is not to be sported away with impunity in
this cruel and despotic manner." Those who heard him—obviously his admirers—enthusiastically huzzaed him; but the Lord

[1] So great did Pratt's reputation become—he was known as "the incorruptible
judge"—that, we are told, "distinguished foreigners who had listened to Pitt
at Westminister, and Garrick at Drury-lane, were taken to hear Camden as the
third wonder of London."

Chief Justice held over giving an opinion until May 6 and sent Wilkes back to the Tower where, Pratt remarked, he was sure the time would not be misspent.

On May 6, the case having become a great public event, the court was packed with adherents on both sides. Wilkes—the time had not been misspent nor the cheers of the crowd underestimated—spoke again, on this occasion sounding a new note: "The liberty of all peers and gentlemen," he said, "and (what touched me more sensibly) that of all the middling and inferior people who stand most in need of protection, is in my case this day to be finally decided upon; a question of such importance as to determine at once whether English liberty shall be a reality or a shadow." Not by accident the "middle and inferior people" he spoke of were in large part the people he was speaking to. The politician, not to say the demagogue in him, and his showman's sense of timing were not lost: Wilkes clearly foresaw a great gain in followers from a segment of the population that, as Steven Watson puts it, "would enjoy a little rioting to the accompaniment of rhetoric."

In delivering his opinion Pratt began on the cold side. He allotted the Secretaries of State, and indeed any magistrate, the right—which Wilkes had protested—to issue a warrant sending Wilkes to the Tower; and he denied that, in sending him there, it was necessary to cite "particular libelous" passages from *No. 45* (adding, to quote from Wilkes's own notes on Pratt's judgment, that the issue before the court "was not the nature of the offence but the legality of the commitment"). However, continued the judge, there was something else to consider: Wilkes's privilege, which Wilkes had pleaded, as a Member of Parliament. The only charges, said Pratt, for which privilege could be suspended were treason, felony, and a breach of the peace; and the only one of these which might even be considered—a breach of the peace—was insufficient. Wilkes thereupon stepped down a free man.

He thanked the court; and in the courtroom rose a roar of satisfaction and delight, caught up and kept going by the crowd outside where, possibly for the first time, there sounded the cry that would resemble a firm name, with both members very prominent: "Wilkes and Liberty!" Two further particulars are to be mentioned, and one postscript. Lurking behind a pillar during the proceedings and sketching away with a pencil was a man as little Wilkes's friend that morning as was George III, and for the same reason of having been attacked in Wilkes's paper: William Hogarth. The caricature of Wilkes that he produced is certainly unflattering enough, but not nearly so vicious as it has sometimes been judged: the squint, the leer, the grin, the self-confident posture are more theatrical than menacing and come closer to the diabolical décor of Medmenham Abbey than to any portrait of satanic evil.[2] The second particular is the arrival, after the proceedings before Justice Pratt, of a procrastinating Attorney General and Solicitor General, who wanted to debate the matter of privilege and who were informed that the case was closed. As for Wilkes himself, he immediately sent from Great George Street a postscript of sorts to Halifax and Egremont:

> My Lords:
>   On my return from Westminister Hall, where I have been discharged from my commitment to the Tower under your Lordships' warrant, I find that my house has been robbed and am informed that the stolen goods are in the possession of one or both of your Lordships. I therefore insist that you do forthwith return them to
>   Your humble servant
>   John   Wilkes.

[2] The famous German physicist and aphorist G. C. Lichtenberg, who knew England and knew Wilkes and who wrote a brilliant book on Hogarth's engravings, thought the portrait a caricature, insisting that it overdid the squint and lacked the "noble look" of Wilkes's profile.

Wilkes thereafter went to the police office in Bow Street, seeking a search warrant to enter the secretaries' houses so that he might regain his papers; but this was refused him. However, Halifax and Egremont were sufficiently enraged by his letter to produce a reply, in which they accused him of *"indecent* and *scurrilous* expressions" and of publishing "infamous and seditious libels." They also informed him that he was to be prosecuted by the Attorney General and that his papers would be retained until those proving his guilt could be come upon and removed. With his love of provocations Wilkes happily answered them at considerable length, saying that only his respect for the King kept him from answering in the "billingsgate" they had employed; and that if they acted about Wilkes's papers on the basis they had mentioned, they would all "be returned to me. I fear neither your prosecution nor your persecution, and I will assert the security of my own house, the liberty of my person, and every right of the people." He then printed his exchange of letters with Halifax and Egremont and circulated them all over London. The "middling and inferior people"—a phrase he used again—rallied round him: when the ministry subpoenaed Wilkes to attend the Court of King's Bench that they might prosecute him for seditious libel and he failed to appear and nothing came of it, the public exulted. A club which met at a pub in Wapping swore, while celebrating Wilkes's release, to get drunk annually on his birthday, but wrote to ask when that was, since otherwise —to be sure of keeping their vow—they would have to get drunk every day in the year. The merchant class sympathized with Wilkes and, as they dominated most juries, were able to impose substantial fines on officials, while having substantial damages awarded to the printers and compositors who had been dragged out of their beds and arrested on the general warrant. The matter of the warrant's legality had still to be passed upon and when Wilkes, bringing a damage suit against Under Secretary Wood for the seizure of his papers, was awarded a much welcomed

£1,000, Chief Justice Pratt, in his direction to the Court of Common Pleas, ruled that general warrants were illegal.[3] The crowds, we are told, cheered Pratt even louder than they did Wilkes.

But cleared though he was in court, and cheered in the market place, Wilkes was elsewhere not on very favorable ground; and the hero he had become only lent encouragement to the *enfant terrible* and the spendthrift he long had been. Financially he was far from well off and had grown so dependent on Lord Temple to lend him money as well as influence that in something like six weeks he was given more than £1,000 by his patron. In return he paid Temple only perfunctory deference. Having, for the only time known, denounced George III by name—"Hypocrisy, meanness, ignorance and insolence characterize the King I obey," Wilkes wrote to Temple—Wilkes also wrote to him "I am my own man, and Lord Temple's." But seeking help from Temple was one thing and not heeding his advice and disapproval quite another. When he asked leave of his patron to visit Polly in Paris for a month, his patron disapproved; and when he then asked Temple's consent to reprint all the issues of *The North Briton* (which had ceased publication after *No. 45*) Temple disapproved even more. Despite Temple's reactions, Wilkes went ahead with both projects. He informed Temple that he was "the entire and absolute master of my conduct and engagements"—but he informed him from Paris. Before he went there, not finding a printer "brave enough" to reprint the whole of *The North Briton,* Wilkes had installed a printing press in his

[3] As a result of Pratt's *personal* ruling, Wilkes would later boast that "general warrants are absolutely illegal" and that "the seizure of papers, *except in cases of high treason,* has been declared illegal." Prior to Wilkes's day, it had—legally or not—long been common practice for Secretaries of State to issue general warrants on grounds of seditious libel; in pronouncing them illegal Pratt confessed that he stood alone. Two years later, however, the whole bench of judges concurred; later Pratt, as Lord Camden, pronounced general warrants null and void, and in 1766 the House of Commons condemned them as "illegal and obnoxious."

own house and had hired journeymen printers who, along with their wages, were given board and lodging. On finding that *The North Briton* was not yet ready to put in type, Wilkes had run off, for private circulation and for no one to be allowed to read, twelve copies of an *Essay on Woman*—a very salacious parody of Pope's *Essay on Man*—which Wilkes no doubt thought his Medmenhamite brethren might savor. Though Wilkes very likely wrote the notes and two short poems appended to the *Essay,* the best opinion is that he did not write the *Essay* itself. In any case, the extreme pornography of the poem and its many personal gibes could, if printed in *The North Briton,* make it a target for Wilkes's detractors to shoot at; and the already vulnerable contents of *No. 45* could, if reprinted, provide his enemies with something to shoot at once more.

Wilkes thought that the reprinted *North Briton* would have an immense sale and bring in a great deal of money. He ran off two thousand sets of two volumes each, priced at half a guinea; but he soon enough wrote to Temple that there "are not 120 subscribers" and that he was "not a little out of pocket." He added, however, that *"North Briton* and Wilkes will be talked of together by posterity." He had, of course, not dared to advertise, which should have restrained any thoughts of reprinting. Temple, despite his strong disapproval of the *North Briton* project (he knew nothing of the *Essay on Woman*), paid the printing bills, at least in the form of loans which Wilkes with insolent grandeur kept asking for. Seeking of Temple a "last sum of £400 or £500" Wilkes said: "I make no apology to Lord Temple. I am proud to have an obligation to Lord Temple." Lord Temple, aware that the reprint of *The North Briton* might provide proof of Wilkes's authorship of *No. 45,* along with other damaging evidence, had offered Wilkes any sum of money he might name if he would get rid of the printing press, but Wilkes obstinately refused to do so. Before he left for France, however,

the type of the *Essay on Woman,* which was left quite unfin-
ished, was broken up.

In France, Wilkes stayed not for the month he had stipulated
to Temple, but twice as long. Comparing the poverty-stricken
French provinces with a luxury-bloated Paris, he predicted revolution; and for himself was assaulted by a Scot named Captain
Forbes, who charged him with insulting the Scottish nation and
demanded a fight "without seconds." This Wilkes refused on
the ground that he had first to call out Lord Egremont and
could accept no other challenge until that was settled. When
Forbes—who was apparently one of a number of violent and
unscrupulous Jacobites—persisted, friends of Wilkes in France
got a police warrant for Forbes's arrest. Forbes thereupon fled
to England where, almost simultaneously, Lord Egremont died.
On hearing of Egremont's death—"What a scoundrell trick has
Lord Egremont played me!" wrote Wilkes—he informed Forbes
that he would meet him on September 21 at Menin in Austrian
Flanders. On the day set Wilkes arrived at Menin to find no
Forbes, and no letter from him, waited for him throughout the
next day in vain, and never again heard from him at all.[4]

In England, meanwhile, difficulties were awaiting Wilkes;
various forces, while he was abroad, had set to work. He had
enlarged the number of his political enemies in England and
had acquired opponents among the Opposition as well. And
his refusal, when subpoenaed, to appear at the Court of King's
Bench had roused the ministry to take action elsewhere. It was
to be double-barreled and punitive action, first planned schem-
ingly behind the scenes and then played out on two of England's
most celebrated stages.

[4] When Forbes said at the outset, "Your name is Wilkes; do you not write?"
Wilkes responded characteristically that he now and then wrote receipts for his
tenants. After fleeing to England, Forbes sailed (with help from Lord Sandwich) for Portugal, "where he was taken into the Portuguese service." Mr.
Chenevix Trench adds, on the word of a "Portuguese correspondent," that
Forbes became a general and that when Napoleon drove the royal family out
of Portugal, he escorted them to Brazil.

On the fifteenth of November, 1763, seven weeks after Wilkes's return from France, Parliament reopened.[5] There were great crowds outside, and inside the corridors were packed with members of both Houses. The benches in the Commons were soon packed as well, with many members standing, and with everywhere an atmosphere of excited expectation. Wilkes arrived, ready to start matters by raising the question of parliamentary privilege. As soon as new members had been sworn in and the clerk was about to open the session by reading a bill, Wilkes jumped up asking to be heard on a matter of privilege. Equally agile was the Prime Minister, George Grenville, who proclaimed that he was carrying a message from the King. Although, with parliamentary precedent, the claim of privilege had a prior right to be heard before any other business, the Government had carefully planned, not least through gaining the co-operation of the Speaker, to reverse matters. A stormy five-hour debate now ensued as to whether privilege took precedence of everything else—a message from the King might be an exception—with Pitt and the Opposition Whigs contending that it did, but with all the King's hirelings and many other members insisting that it didn't. Finally put to a vote, the reversal was overwhelmingly approved, and the message from the King was then read. It asked the House to look into the matter of *No. 45* and of Wilkes's avoiding trial by pleading parliamentary privi-

[5] From October 31 through November 13, the Secretaries of State had Wilkes's every movement watched, with daily reports such as the following: "*Thursday Nov. 3.* Mr. Wilkes went out this morning at half an hour after eight o'clock to Mr. Woodfall's, printer, Charing Cross; stayed ten minutes; from thence he went to Mr. Onslow's in Curzon Street, May Fair, and stayed an hour and a half. Mr. Wilkes brought Mr. Onslow in a hackney-coach to Spring Gardens, where Mr. Onslow got out . . . but would call on Mr. Wilkes presently . . . from thence [Wilkes] went home; soon after Mr. Cotes came . . . At half after two o'clock Mr. Wilkes, Mr. Onslow and Mr. Cotes came out together and parted at the top of George Street. Mr. Wilkes then went to Mr. Thornton's in Chapel Street, but did not stay; from thence he went home. A little before seven o'clock he went out in his chair to my Lord Temple's and left him there at nine o'clock."

lege. Once the King's message was read and the King was thanked for it, the Administration machinery worked smoothly. Lord North rose and moved that *No. 45* be voted a "false, scandalous and seditious libel containing expressions of the most unexampled insolence and contumely toward His Majesty, the grossest aspersions upon both Houses of Parliament, and the most audacious defiance of the authority of the whole legislature"—a libel, North continued, which would also disaffect the people toward the King, instill disobedience to the law, and incite insurrection against the Government. There followed something like seven hours of wrangling—could "false" be applied to *No. 45*? could "traitorous"?—and of debate, led masterfully by Pitt who, though denouncing *The North Briton,* understood that "the supremacy of the Commons over the King" was at issue and argued that the Administration had violated the liberty of the subject. During the debate Wilkes was permitted to speak his piece, stressing the breach of privilege he had suffered from; but a House that had resisted Pitt's eloquence in Wilkes's behalf reacted either phlegmatically or, because of Wilkes's behavior toward the King, indignantly toward Wilkes himself. Having protested his treatment by the Government, Wilkes wound up, to the surprise of the House, by promising that if it declared him entitled to privilege, he would waive his rights and accept a trial by jury. It was almost 2 A.M. when the House voted, 273 to 111, for North's motion, after adding to it that *No. 45* be publicly burned. Horace Walpole, attending as a Member of Parliament, wrote of the occasion:

> The campaign is open, hostilities begun, and blood shed . . . The Parliament met on Tuesday. We sat . . . till two in the morning . . . The business was a complaint made by one King George of a certain paper called "The North Briton, No. 45," which the said King asserted was written by a much more famous man called Mr. Wilkes . . . Mr. Wilkes with all the impartiality in the world . . . sat and heard the whole matter

discussed, as if the affair did not concern *him*. The House of
Commons . . . did divide twice on this affair. The first time,
one hundred and eleven, of which I had the misfortune to be
one, had more curiosity to hear Mr. Wilkes's story than King
George's; but the three hundred being of the contrary opinion,
it was plain they were in the right, especially as they had no
private motives to guide them. Again, the individual one hundred and eleven could not see that "The North Briton" tended
to foment treasonable insurrections, though we had it argu-
mentatively demonstrated to us for seven hours . . . but the
moment we heard two hundred and seventy-five gentlemen
counted, it grew as plain to us as pike-staff.

Meanwhile, on the second stage—the House of Lords—a gross
and nasty farce was being enacted. The *Essay on Woman* was
wheeled before the footlights, and since the name of one of the
House's lords spiritual, William Warburton, Bishop of Gloucester, had been bracketed with some of the notes to the *Essay,*
Wilkes was to be decried for libeling a member of the Lords.
Wilkes's Medmenham companion Lord Sandwich, who, at Lord
Egremont's death, had replaced him as Secretary of State, had by
now turned against Wilkes (as had Sir Francis Dashwood, who
it was that got Wilkes thrown out of the militia). By this time
Sandwich had become a great deal more alienated from Wilkes
than he might have seemed associated with the *Essay;* and he
stood up to lead the attack by reading aloud to his fellow peers
both the *Essay* and the notes upon it. He did this in the most
oily and pharisaical manner possible, relishing what he pre-
tended to reprobate and stopping every so often to express how
shocked and horrified he was by such scandalous and salacious
writing—so much so, indeed, that his fellow peers were both
amazed and amused at his newborn piety. He was ticketed not
only as an old crony of Wilkes's and as himself a master of
obscene language, but as one of the most dissolute rakes alive
and as having been expelled from the Beefsteak Club for blas-

phemy. Dashwood, now Lord le Despencer, remarked of Sandwich's performance that it was the first time he had ever heard the Devil fulminate against sin; and Lord Lyttleton was so revolted by the contents of the *Essay,* and even more by Sandwich's unctuous pleasure in reading it, that he insisted the recital be stopped. But the assembled lords insisted it not be—crying out, "Read on! Read on!" On Sandwich's retiring, the libeled Bishop of Gloucester rose, choking with rage, to call Wilkes "a buffoon without wit," "a debauchee without delicacy," "a fine gentleman . . . without letters." He also denounced the *Essay's* blasphemies as more than "the hardiest inhabitants of hell" could listen to "and in due course begged the Devil's pardon for comparing him to Wilkes." He also called on God as his witness that he had written none of the notes. Though truly libeled, Warburton was also so unpopular that to argue with him, it was said, was as degrading as wrestling with a chimney sweep; and Churchill described him as

> . . . so proud, that should he meet
> The Twelve Apostles in the street
> He'd turn his nose up at them all
> And shove the Saviour from the wall.

And Churchill said of Sandwich that he

> Wrought sin with greediness and courted shame
> With greater zeal than good men seek for fame.

Lord Temple's efforts to defend Wilkes went for nothing, and the lords who would not take no for an answer in having the *Essay* read to the end, now pronounced it—indeed joined in the House's unanimously voting it—a "most scandalous, obscene and impious libel."[6] Sandwich further moved to name

---

[6] The *Essay* was not an offense for the House of Lords to deal with, if there *was* an offense; it only squeaked through because Warburton, as a bishop, was a peer, and to mock him would be a "breach of privilege and an outrage on the Chamber." Furthermore, says A. S. Turberville, "in a case of criminal libel,

Wilkes the author, but even an unsympathetic Lord Mansfield
contended that before condemning a man, he should be heard
in his own defense; and further action was put off till the next
week. Sandwich's spurious piety met its match when, a few
days later, at a performance of *The Beggar's Opera*, Macheath's
remarking "That Jemmy Twitcher should peach on me, I own
surprises me" produced throughout the audience a deafening ex-
plosion of laughter. For the rest of his life Sandwich was everywhere known as Jemmy Twitcher. When he tried to be elected
lord steward of the University of Cambridge and as a candidate
dined at Trinity, the scholars, to show their disapproval of him,
walked out in a body. Unattractive looking, he also walked with
a roll and someone seeing him said, "I'm sure it's Lord Sandwich, for look, he's walking down both sides of the street at
once"; and Lord Chesterfield said what a mercy it was "that
God should have raised up the Earl of Sandwich to vindicate
our religion and morality." Yet he was not without ability and
held Cabinet posts with success. As for his turning against
Wilkes, it probably derived from an offer to help him. In a letter
of March 1763, presumed to be written to Wilkes, Sandwich
offered to support him for election to the East India Company's
court of directors—a juicy sinecure. It is also presumed that the
offer was withdrawn when, in April, *No. 45* appeared; but
when, in September, Sandwich sought Wilkes's very likely prop-
agandist services, Wilkes "desired it to be understood" that he
was "entirely devoted" to the Opposition. Thereafter Sandwich
would have none of him.

The events of one day in both Houses of Parliament ended
with the salacious libel that Wilkes was accused of, stealing the
show from the seditious one. The next day more trouble would

the prosecution would have had to prove publication. Here the only publication
was by those who themselves brought forward the case." The lords presumed on
parliamentary privilege to apply the law of libel so that the Government could
be rid of a hated adversary.

arise for Wilkes, who was by now being hounded—while being elsewhere huzzaed—from many sides; and with, now, the *Essay* the talk of the town, we can find no better moment to talk of it too. A parody of Pope's *Essay on Man*, the *Essay* itself is, in content, of the most minimal value; and the immense disproportion it displays between the crudest kind of bawdry and barely passable wit is perhaps the best argument that Wilkes was not to any great extent the author. The far more likely fact is that Wilkes's old crony Thomas Potter wrote most of it—it was composed in the early 1750s—and that Wilkes touched it up, along with supplying many or all of the notes. Moreover, a great deal of the *Essay* is very close to Pope's original—a number of lines, indeed, are the same as Pope's—so that most of what is new is merely dirty words and innuendos. Itself a mere fragment of the poem—Wilkes said that "not quite a *fourth* part" was put in type—the whole thing runs to only ninety-four lines. The first twelve lines are, as parody and as pornography, in no way inferior to any other passage in the poem ("Fanny" is Fanny Murray, a well-known prostitute of the 1750s; though the first three words, it appears, were originally: "Awake, my Sandwich"):

> Awake, my Fanny, leave all meaner things;
> This morn shall prove what rapture swiving brings!
> Let us (since life can little more supply
> Than just a few good fucks, and then we die)
> Expatiate free o'er that loved scene of man,
> A mighty maze for mighty pricks to scan;
> A Wild, where Paphian thorns promiscuous shoot,
> Where flowers the monthly Rose, but yields no fruit:
> Together let us beat this ample field,
> Try what the open, what the covert yield,

> The latent tracts, the pleasing depths explore,
> And my prick clapped where thousand were before.[7]

The notes, with their horseplay from the classics, perhaps have an iota more of merit, and hence of Wilkes; for example, "Priapus was worshipped at Lampascus—but indeed *is* everywhere"; or, the "doubting Frenchman who asked the fair, 'Madame, est-ce que j'ai l'honneur d'y être?'" But the notes can hardly be less condemned than the verses, and the notes that are fathered on Warburton are in every sense wretched. What is clear, however, is that a piece of work so glaringly libelous and so merely lewd —printed with a large phallus on the title page—was never meant to be circulated beyond the Medmenham brethren, let alone offered to the public. Nor are the additional verses printed with the *Essay* any more inspired or any less indecent. One of them, a thirteen-stanza travesty of *The Universal Prayer* concludes:

> To thee, whose fucks throughout all space
> This dying world supplies,
> One chorus let all being raise,
> All pricks in reverence rise.

Almost certainly, except for a small mischance, such verses would never have been relayed into hostile hands, nor, but for a quite unrelated reason, have been voted libelous by a hostile Lords.

As for the small mischance Wilkes, in setting up his own

[7] Herewith the first twelve lines of Pope's *Essay on Man*:
> Awake, my St. John! leave all meaner things
> To low ambition, and the pride of Kings.
> Let us (since Life can little more supply
> Than just to look about us and to die)
> Expatiate free o'er all this scene of Man;
> A mighty maze! but not without a plan;
> A Wild, where weeds and flow'rs promiscuous shoot;
> Or Garden, tempting with forbidden fruit.
> Together let us beat this ample field,
> Try what the open, what the covert yield;
> The latent tracts, the giddy heights, explore
> Of all who blindly creep, or sightless soar.

printing press in Great George Street, hired as foreman a printer named Michael Curry who, in printing for Wilkes the twelve specified copies of the *Essay*, struck off an extra proof copy for himself. In an affidavit made five years later, Curry acknowledged that he had been under orders from Wilkes to let no one see the copies he had printed; but Curry said that a journeyman printer named Jennings got hold of several pages of his copy and that as a result of this Curry was bribed into putting a complete copy of the *Essay* into Administration hands. In any case, Philip Carteret Webb, who had played an Administration role in the *No. 45* proceedings, got a copy from Curry, who had been assured of being "taken care of" for handing it over, but who, should he not, could be prosecuted for having printed it. By way of Webb, it reached Sandwich, who agreed to read it in the House of Lords. "I wish," he told Webb, "to play a forward part in this business"; and, as we know, he played it with relish. A different version, which is the Administration one, has Jennings pick up some proof and wrap some of his lunch in it, whence follows a confused account of its passing upward from one hand to another until it reaches the Reverend John Kidgell, the chaplain of the infamous Earl of March, to whom he showed it and who saw that it could do Wilkes harm. This led to much maneuvering until Curry eventually handed over a set of proofs, which Sandwich read to the lords. As for Jennings, his wrapping his lunch in such very confidential proof sheets seems all too facile and opportune; as for Curry, who hoped by complying to be given a Government appointment, he was anything but well taken care of; and as for Wilkes's having private copies of the *Essay* run off, it would never have got into the story had it not been a fine additional weapon in the Administration's attack on *No. 45*.[8]

[8] Neither the original manuscript nor any of the original printed copies of the *Essay* have survived, though one copy was said to exist until late in the nineteenth century. The excerpts from the *Essay* that are quoted in this book come from the edition printed in 1871 by John Camden Hotten which answers

ARCUI MEO NON CONFIDO

IOHN WILKES Esqr:
Member of Parliament for Aylesbury Bucks.
Great without Title, beyond Fortune bleſs'd;
Rich, ev'n when plunder'd, honour'd, while oppreſs'd;
Lov'd without Youth, & follow'd without Power;
At Home, tho' exil'd; free, tho in the Tower. Pope

Groß, ohne Staat; im Elend auch beglückt;
Reich und beraubt; geehrt, und unterdrückt;
Geliebt, nicht jung; nicht stark, bedient mit Treu;
Verjagt im Land; und im Gefängniß frey.

John Wilkes when M.P. for Aylesbury.

Charles James Fox.

James Boswell.

Charles Churchill.

Edmund Burke.

George Grenville.

The Earl of Sandwich.

John Stuart, third Earl of Bute.

During the eight-hour session in the Commons which voted *No. 45* a seditious libel, Administration M.P.s, according to Horace Walpole, talked now of expelling Wilkes, now of putting him in the pillory, and even of cutting off his ears. And during those eight hours a member of the House of Commons —the Samuel Martin whom *The North Briton* had violently attacked, describing him as a "mean, abject, low-lived, and dirty fellow"—rose to attack in turn "the author of the article." In the course of his denunciation he twice called "the author," who, he said, had stabbed him in the dark, a "cowardly, malignant, and scandalous scoundrel," all the time "looking at Wilkes . . . with such rage and violence that he owned his passion obliged him to sit down." Under Martin's assault Wilkes showed no slightest sign of having anything to do with Martin's scoundrel; but the next morning he sent Martin a note reading:

> Sir,
> You complained yesterday, before five hundred gentlemen, that you had been *stabbed in the dark;* but I have reason to believe that you was not so *in the dark* as you affected to be. To cut off every pretence of ignorance as to the author, I whisper in your ear, that every passage of 'The North Briton' in which you have been named or even alluded to was written by
> > Your humble servant,
> > John Wilkes.

Martin, who was probably very little surprised by Wilkes's letter, was not long in answering it:

> Sir,
> As I said in the House of Commons yesterday that the writer of the North Briton, who had stabbed me in the dark, was a cowardly as well as a malignant and infamous scoundrel . . . I must take the liberty to repeat that you are a malignant

---

to all the bibliographical specifications, set forth by the Reverend John Kidgell, deemed necessary for any genuine and complete copy of the original "edition."

and infamous scoundrel, and that I desire to give you an opportunity of shewing me whether this epithet of *cowardly* was
rightly applied or not.

I desire that you meet me in Hyde-Park immediately with
a brace of pistols each, to determine our difference.

I shall go to the ring in Hyde-Park, with my pistols so concealed that nobody may see them, and I will wait in expectation of you one hour. As I shall call in my way to your house to
deliver this letter, I propose to go from thence directly to the
ring in Hyde-Park, from whence we may proceed if it be necessary to any more private place, and I mention that I shall
wait an hour, in order to give you the full time to meet me.

I am, Sir, your humble servant,

Sam Martin.

Wilkes responded at once. The two principals met, walked
toward a more private part of the park, stood themselves fourteen
yards apart, fired, and missed. Firing again, Wilkes missed again,
but this time Martin seriously wounded Wilkes in the groin.
When Martin rushed up to him, he—believing the wound to
be fatal—urged him to hurry away. After starting off, Martin
came back to ask if he could be of help, but was once more
urged to hurry. Wilkes, carried home with a high fever and in
great pain, ordered that Martin's letter be given back to him so
that no incriminating evidence could be found; nor would he
speak to the surgeon of more than "an affair of honour." Wilkes
somehow emerged from the duel full of approbation of how
well Martin—a thoroughly corrupt politician, a lackey to Lord
Bute, and a man whom Wilkes himself had excoriated—had behaved. Wilkes subsequently treated him with every courtesy;
two days after the duel, when he was out of danger, Wilkes
wrote of the whole affair to Polly in Paris:

At the second fire I was wounded by a ball which entered the
lower part of my belly on the right side. I was carried home in
a chair, and a surgeon has extracted the ball. The pains I have

suffered are beyond what I can describe, but both physician and surgeon declare me out of all danger . . . You may depend upon seeing me at Paris before Christmas . . . It was an affair of honour, and my antagonist behaved very well.

But a great many people, Wilkes's detractors among them, thought differently, believing that this had been a deliberate, cold-blooded, indeed trickster attempt to kill him. It became known that Martin had, every day for months, been taking practice shots at a target; that, as the challenger, Martin had very unfairly usurped Wilkes's right to choose the weapons; that he had not given Wilkes time to acquire a second[9] or a doctor; while many years later Wilkes discovered that in the very year he had denounced Martin and dueled with him, Martin "under the head of secret and special service" had "received from the Government £41,000," which might have been payment toward getting rid of Wilkes. There was considerable feeling, intensified by the challenges of Talbot and Forbes, of an Administration plot to this effect.

While Wilkes was lying in bed and slowly convalescing, his champions multiplied. "Wilkes has been shot by Martin," wrote Walpole, who was no champion but also thought the duel was a plot, "and instead of being burnt at an *auto da fé*, as the Bishop of Gloucester intended, is reverenced as a saint by the mob." But Wilkes received, and on the same day, two more serious wounds. The first was a House of Commons resolution, passed on November 23, that "the privileges of Parliament do not extend to the case of writing and publishing seditious libels." The second was Pitt's brutally deserting Wilkes while nominally defending him. The House's greatest member, and by all odds its greatest speaker, Pitt, emerging from retirement, arrived dur-

---

[9] This is a moot matter. Wilkes appears to have had with him, whether or not as a second, his friend and admirer, a wine merchant named Humphrey Cotes. Walpole says that Cotes waited "in a post-chaise to convey Wilkes away if triumphant"; and Cotes may have—and someone must have—been present to get Wilkes carried home "in a chair."

ing the debate on the resolution. Though suffering from gout and hobbling on crutches he rose, a majestic figure and a histrionic one, to denounce the entire roster of *North Britons* as "illiberal, unmanly and detestable . . . His Majesty's complaint was well founded." He went on to thunder that Wilkes "did not deserve to be ranked among the human species—he was the blasphemer of his God and the libeler of his King." Furthermore, Pitt said twice that he had "no connection with any such writer" —he who had dined with Wilkes, laughed with him, counseled him, and waved him on into politics. No doubt politics, now that Wilkes was in bad political and parliamentary odor, had something to do with Pitt's desertion of him; but denouncing Wilkes so harshly seems, to say no more, excessive. To Wilkes, Pitt's speech came as a knockout blow, all the more as he now felt deserted by virtually every friend except Temple and Charles Churchill.

Still bedridden, Wilkes still had much to harass him. A Scottish officer named Dun twice tried to break into his house with intent to murder; to the disappointment of the Wilkites he was proved insane and put in a madhouse.[10] Wilkes's house, as Wilkes well knew, was being watched and his mail intercepted. His other House—on the parliamentary pretense that he was exaggerating, if not indeed feigning, his illness—was sending doctors to Great George Street to look him over. The House, he fired back, "had desired [the doctors] to visit him, but had forgotten to desire him to receive them," which he decidedly would not do. To the doctors themselves he wrote that he was sorry not to receive them just then, but would ask them to dinner when he got well. He then proceeded to send for two other doctors, remarking that as they were both Scotch and both connected with the royal household, they must certainly give satisfaction as spies.

[10] Nine years later Dun wrote in a friendly way to Wilkes, soliciting a subscription to his latest literary work.

But however many his jests, his future remained in jeopardy; and though he had a multitude of "friends" among the "middling and inferior people," he could not but feel bereft of his old ones. The multitude, however, must have raised his spirits when on December 3 it rose, as "the greatest mob" that Sheriff Blunt had known in forty years, to stop the hangman from burning *No. 45*. The burning produced verse against Bute:

Because *The North Briton* inflamed the whole nation
To flames they commit it, to show detestation.
But throughout old England how joy would have spread
Had the real North Briton been burnt in its stead.

At length, at a serious risk to his health, for his wound had not yet healed, he managed just before Christmas to escape detection from the spies outside his house, to go by post chaise to Dover, and to cross the next day to France. From Dover he wrote how badly jolted and harmed his wound had been while going through "the rascally towns of Stroud, Rochester and Chatham" and that the two previous days were "the most unhappy days I have known." His chief reason for going would seem to have been a reunion in Paris with Polly, for whom he needed, among other things, to find a chaperone, and with whom, now that he was faced with prison, he would certainly wish to be while he could. It was pretty surely not his intention to remain abroad in order to avoid punishment; indeed, he wrote to Temple from Calais that he would be back by mid-January. Just before then, however, he wrote to the Speaker of the House of Commons asking, on a plea of illness, for leave to stay in France, and enclosing a certificate signed by two surgeons. To be sure, he had to face indictments for libel in both Houses and had every reason to think that the cases would be tried—indeed, that the cards would be stacked—with the full ruthless force of the Government. Nor, to act, did the Government wait on his return. On the twentieth of January 1764 it went beyond having indicted him; it had the Commons expel him. In doing this the Commons was not only acting in his absence, it was prejudging him—for, as the basis of expulsion, it used the publication of *No. 45* before the case had come to trial.[11] A month later, on February 20, in the Court of King's Bench presided over by Lord Mansfield, Wilkes, apropos the *No. 45* and the *Essay*, was found on both counts guilty of libel. Setting up a press and reprinting *No. 45* in his own house, which Temple had so much opposed, contributed greatly to Wilkes's conviction, for he was never convicted of the original publication in *The North Briton*. Lord Mansfield did no sentencing after the verdict, but issued a writ for Wilkes's arrest.

Looking at it afterward Wilkes's supporters had reason to think that the trial had been a good deal that it should not have been: the Government had sought and gained a small alteration, though actually to Wilkes's benefit, in the phrasing of the indictments; again, certain jurymen had been informed not to show up in court because—which was quite untrue—it had adjourned; and Wilkes's solicitor, Alexander Philipps, would seem to have been bribed or to have behaved discreditably. But it is possible that by not returning to England Wilkes did himself more harm than an unscrupulous lawyer may have done, or a slanted jury. By appearing and attacking in his best style or defending himself in the form of attack, he might have infused drama into his expulsion and have much enlarged the multitude of his sympathizers all over London; and he might have injected a winning defense into key moments of his trial. Indeed his very presence might have rallied forces that his absence quashed. To be sure, he might have done none of these things. But now, however he acted, his position was very much weakened: to

---

[11] When the Speaker read Wilkes's medical certificate to the House, he commented that it bore no notary's name nor other certification. Wilkes, on hearing of this, sent certification by two notaries, as well as by the English ambassador; but by then, of course, he had been expelled.

return, now, after all advantages had been forfeited, was to lay himself open to arrest and to whatever sentencing and imprisoning a vindictive Government could contrive, while to stay on in France put a slur on his courage.

He had, it is true, debated the matter of going back to England, both with himself and with people he wrote to. He gave his reasons for deciding not to go: he was prepared, or alleged himself prepared, to come to an accommodation with the Government, but he was quick to add that the King would never hear of such a thing. As for the "public cause" or the chief cause, liberty, he felt that the matter had been resolved: "The two important decisions in the Court of Common Pleas and at the Guildhall have secured forever an Englishman's liberty and property. They have grown out of my firmness and the affair of *The North Briton;* but neither, in this case, are we or our posterity concerned whether John Wilkes or John a Nokes wrote or published *The North Briton* or the 'Essay on Woman'." Thus the public, he felt, had no call on him and had nothing to lose by his absence.[12] But Wilkes saw himself in decided jeopardy. No man with the condemnation of both Houses behind him could, he declared, face Mansfield's sentencing. He seriously believed that Mansfield would sentence him to life imprison-

---

[12] Indeed, they had something, rather ungratefully, to gain. Wilkes, more than anyone else in the Opposition, had roused enthusiasm and protest and had done most to embarrass and weaken the Government. With Wilkes out of the way, the Whigs could now take up his cause without the drawbacks of his character, could, without making him the protagonist, return to Revolution principles. As Horace Bleackley said, "The man who kindled the fire was cast out into the cold." And indeed in February 1764 the Opposition introduced a motion that "a general warrant . . . is not warranted by law"—though in this they obviously could not, with any hope of succeeding, bring Wilkes's name into their arguments. The debate on their motion, with all the great guns of eloquence firing away, kept the House from adjourning on one night until half past five in the morning and on a second night until half past seven. The twice-voted motion was lost on both occasions by a very narrow margin. In order to succeed, the Government had in wintry weather to call forth all its invalids; and to carry them forth, "muffled in shawls" and "wrapped in blankets." "The floor of the House," said Walpole, "looked like the pool of Bethesda."

ment, with the pillory to boot, and as a result he passed sentence of another kind on himself: "I think myself an exile for life."

Some six months later, however, Wilkes veered around to a different way of thinking: the one card he still held was his charges against Halifax for breaking into his house under a general warrant and stealing his papers. But the card would not win the trick if, as seemed probable, Lord Mansfield should declare Wilkes, for failing to appear at his trial, an outlaw. He decided accordingly to return to England and, with his advisers' approval, to "go North" to keep his "great cause"—that is, his suit against Halifax—from being smashed. He arranged to meet his friends Humphrey Cotes and Charles Churchill in Boulogne to talk over the matter; but, for whatever reason, the meeting came off five weeks later than the time set—two days *after* a very cogent "Letter to the Electors of Aylesbury," which Wilkes had written, was published. On meeting, moreover, the three men took to drink rather than discussion, and five days after they met, Churchill, who had been drinking excessively, became ill—not, it turned out, from drink but from typhus. Physically exhausted by too dissolute a life, he grew steadily worse and in less than a week was dead, his last words an appeal to his "dear friend, John Wilkes"—in whose arms he died—to serve as his literary executor.

The death of his best and loyalest friend drove out of Wilkes's mind all thought of England where, on November 1, for not appearing to hear judgment passed, he was declared an outlaw. Prostrated and unable to adjust to Churchill's death, he went back to Paris where he wrote of himself that he "was long in the deepest melancholy" and passed day and night in tearful agonies of despair. Emotionally his sense of desolation and of his own dark future was interwoven with the death of Churchill, though "at last the three great remedies mentioned by Cicero came to his aid, *necessitas ipsa, dies longa, et satietas doloris.*" Wilkes had long been urging Churchill to join him in Paris and

share its pleasures, and this time he had planned to bring Churchill from Boulogne to Paris and help him paint the town red,
"unless," Wilkes added, "constancy has changed her name to
Churchill." When it turned out that Churchill was just then
very constant to someone named Elizabeth Carr, it was planned
that after Boulogne, Wilkes, Churchill, and, for part of the way,
Elizabeth Carr should set off on a trip to the South of France and
Italy. The two men had always got along extremely well, though
where Churchill showed small interest in anything except poetry,
the bottle, and the bed, Wilkes had, besides politics, many interests. He greatly admired Churchill's talent as a poet—he was
said to have written "the best political satire since *Absalom and
Achitophel*"—and he could indeed be savagely witty. He had half-
revenged Hogarth's engraving of Wilkes with verses on a self-
centered, emulous Hogarth; and he hit straight and hard at Lord
Sandwich:

> Nature designed him, in a rage
> To be the Wharton of his age;
> But having given all the sin,
> Forgot to put the virtues in.
>
> . . .
>
> To knock a tottering watchman down,
> To sweat a woman of the town,
> By fits to keep the peace, or break it,
> In turn to give a pox, or take it,
> He is, in faith, most excellent.
>
> . . .
>
> Hear him but talk and you would swear
> Obscenity herself was there.

As Churchill's admirer and literary executor, Wilkes "in the
first flush of enthusiasm" said he would spend the rest of his life
arranging a completely annotated edition of Churchill's poetry.
And at the end of a year Wilkes could exult in "how pleased is

the dear shadow of our friend with all I have done!" But this was virtually all he would ever do, which constituted, at Wilkes's death thirty-odd years later, a small fraction of the undertaking —a matter not of lessened affection but of temperamental incapacity: Wilkes was no sedentary, years-long worker in a library, constantly checking, collating, correcting in someone else's behalf, though he would have done far more than he did just by identifying the pseudonymous targets of Churchill's satire. Even more, though Wilkes had a scholarly side which in his later years bore fruit, he lived, and wanted to live, out in the world: it was not people in a friend's folios that he could really care about; it was people in the flesh. Late in life, however, Wilkes did erect in his garden a nine-foot-tall pedestal, supporting an urn with a Latin inscription that celebrated Churchill as a divine poet, a charming companion, and a citizen worthy of his country's high esteem. And, however inspirited he might be by temperament or consoled by time, he had lost—and pretty surely knew that he had lost—his most devoted friend.

5
_____

CHURCHILL'S ILLNESS and death and, much more, Lord Mansfield's pronouncement of outlawry, which the *Annual Register*
described as completing Wilkes's ruin, fully decided him against
returning to England. His position in exile, though far better
than one in prison which Mansfield might decree, was scarcely
encouraging: to begin with, there were his scant and uncertain
finances.[1] His father, who died in 1761, had (in view of what
he had already settled on him and given him as gifts) left him
no legacy. His friend Cotes and his brother Heaton set to work
selling his Buckinghamshire properties which, though there were
no bids for them when put up for sale, were bought by friends
of Wilkes at generous prices. The lease on 13 Great George
Street was taken over; Prebendal House and the manor of Aylesbury were sold for £4,100; and Wilkes continued to own some
small estates in East Anglia. His patron, Temple, wiped out
Wilkes's debts to him, and there was the £1,000 from Under
Secretary Wood which he had been awarded but which had not

[1] He did move to less expensive lodgings, but kept a coach and retained all
his servants; and every time that he wrote to the faithful Cotes about his econ-
omies, he borrowed £150 or £200. It was said that should he return to England
and be expelled by the House, the "creditors might prove more dangerous
enemies than the ministers." But Wilkes on his uppers could be extremely
grand, for which Mme. Geoffrin once scolded him: "When one hasn't a shirt,
one mustn't have pride." "On the contrary," Wilkes answered, "one *must* have
it, so as to have something."

yet been paid. His income could be fixed at no more than £500 a year—by no means bad for those days, but brutal for the likes of Wilkes. He resolved, however, to live sensibly, to economize by going to Italy, and to get seriously to work writing a book for which he received an advance. The book was to be a history of England—"this is the work for my fame and my purse"—obviously just the sort of knickknack he could toss off in no time at all without the slightest trouble. Indeed, he did write the introduction, described as "an unsatisfactory performance," and thereafter let history sit waiting. And he did, with much sense and doubtless at a sacrifice to himself, send Polly to England, to be cared for by his brother, which ultimately but not at first seems to have worked out. For Wilkes's wife had obtained a legal ruling that gave her a half share in looking after her daughter and tried to get Polly to live with her, the last thing Polly wanted. But the next time Polly visited her, Mrs. Wilkes would not let her go, and there was a scene, with Polly crying that her father would never forgive her. With the help of lawyers, a compromise was finally reached, Polly dividing her time between her uncle and her mother. Heaton Wilkes, a very decent but very practical and conventional man, regarded his fourteen-year-old niece as an overindulged, wasteful, all-too-French young thing. She had arrived with her own French maid, without whose assistance, she maintained, she could not possibly dress herself. Her uncle, however, promptly sent the maid back to France and spoke anything but well of her father. Her father, on hearing all this, spoke anything but well of her uncle. "By God," he exclaimed, "Heaton is a barbarian!" But Heaton, it seems, brought Polly around.

Deprived, but also made free, of the daughter he loved—"How do you like England? . . . Is it not a little *triste*? The Sundays especially . . . are very dull," he wrote to her—and having put an end to his history of England without adding a word to it, Wilkes had every encouragement to become a rake-about-town.

The most extensive of his amours was with an extraordinarily beautiful Italian girl, twenty years younger than he was, named Gertrude Maria Corradini. Brought up in Bologna, she had acquired in Venice, as Wilkes put it, "the only education fit for a courtesan"—"the art of adorning gracefully her person, and a flexibility of the limbs worthy the wanton nymphs so celebrated of Ionia." In Venice she had performed as a dancer and been the mistress of the British consul. When her bedroom charms had rendered him bankrupt, she was forced to look elsewhere and went to Paris. There, very early in his exile, Wilkes met her and, after something of a struggle, won her favors, very probably by the well-timed gift of a crucifix to replace one that had been stolen from her. "She was so struck," Wilkes wrote in his diary, "with the mark of attention, that the same afternoon she ceased to be cruel." He set her up in fine style in lodgings that over-looked the gardens of the Palais-Royal. She was something of a type, given to stormy emotions which Wilkes had constantly to contend with and soothe; and she had a mother who in genteel fashion saw to it, despite her daughter's air of not being inter-ested in money, that there was always a quite suitable amount of it. At the outset, however, Wilkes was passionately drawn to the Corradini and was enchanted by her resourcefulness in giv-ing sexual pleasure, by what he was pleased to call her "divine gift of lewdness, offset as it was by her innocent look and vir-ginal manner." Physically "she was a perfect Grecian figure, cast in the mold of the Florentine Venus, except that she was rather fuller, and had flatter breasts." Her stormy nature, however, was not her only imperfection. She was "born," Wilkes wrote, "with little or no wit," which is to say quite stupid and, in con-versation, very dull; she had precarious health and gave way to nervous outbursts that proved exhausting; she cared tremen-dously about money; and she could be fantastically jealous and embroil Wilkes in painful scenes.

After a while—for, no matter how much was lacking, her

love-making triumphed—Wilkes let his Paris lodgings to David Garrick, and he and Gertrude traveled to Italy together. Wilkes never forgot the bedroom she had in Bologna: on the bare walls were two miserable images of the Virgin, while above the bed was a picture of the Virgin and Child, and whenever Gertrude made ready for carnal ecstasy, she would draw a green silk curtain over the picture. This show of modesty and piety, said Wilkes, was only "the more amusing because there were no curtains either to the bed or to the windows," so that what went on was for anyone to see. Their union continued, with Wilkes happily enchained: "So sweet a situation," he wrote of it, "and so beautiful a woman." Their agreeable travels proved also expensive ones: from Bologna they went to Florence, and from Florence—with a stop at Sienna to see the cathedral—to Rome. There, we are told, Wilkes met the archaeologist and secretary to the Vatican, the famous Abbé Winckelmann, who in addition to taking Wilkes on archaeological expeditions, would call on him in his lodgings and stay on, talking with the Corradini's mother when her daughter and Wilkes had made themselves scarce. From Rome, where Wilkes also met Dr. Johnson's great friend and host Henry Thrale, the lovers went to Naples where, in February, the air was "silky soft" and the gardens and groves and flowers and fruit were enchanting. While in Naples Wilkes learned that a printer named Williams had been put in the pillory for printing *The North Briton*. Williams' real punishment depended on how the public reacted—two years earlier a man in the pillory had been stoned to death. But Williams' ride in a coach marked "No. 45" was a triumph; while he was standing in the pillory for an hour, the crowd roared "Wilkes and Liberty!" and raised more than two hundred guineas for him in a purse.

After six weeks in Naples Wilkes rented a country house just outside of it. Its immediate surroundings and splendid view delighted him, and he was particularly taken with the mosquito nets he saw, which suggested Mars and Venus caught in Vulcan's web. But much at odds with the loveliness of the setting was the behavior of Wilkes's companion, who had become more and more difficult and trying. She kept losing her temper and lengthening her demands; she constantly quarreled with Wilkes's faithful valet, Matthew Brown; and after a while, having announced that she was with child, and Wilkes having gone to Ischia to see a friend, she took off for Bologna whence she sprang. She also took with her, besides her mother and her "uncle," as much silverware as all three of them could grapple with. Wilkes was hard hit by the performance but—though the Corradini had counted on his doing it—he refused to follow her. He sent her a friendly letter and £100 but, leaving Naples, he would not even risk passing through Bologna "lest the dear enchantress should again draw him within her powerful circle, and melt down all his manhood to the god of love." Thus ended a relationship that, for a seasoned libertine, seemed a good deal more romantic than merely rakish. Or was it distance that lent enchantment?—for much about the liaison that I have been quoting was written by Wilkes some thirty years after the liaison broke up.

In any case, there was much else during Wilkes's exile to brighten rather than embitter his life—much else, though of shorter duration, with women who attracted him; and a good deal also in Paris, among people of distinction. There he was received in a number of salons and saw informally David Hume, then secretary to the British embassy; his old friend Baron d'Holbach;[2] a French friend, the rich, rakish scientist and dramatist

[2] D'Holbach was perhaps the most unwholesome, though pragmatic, of moralists: "So long," he said, "as vice renders [a man] happy, he should love vice." In personality he had something of Wilkes's appeal, in that his good points, we are told, won him "the friendship of many to whom his philosophy was repugnant," and the two men's personalities certainly won them the friendship of each other. Dr. Johnson's famous Club was perhaps outranked in celebrities by d'Holbach's dinner table: he kept "open house for Helvétius, D'Alembert, Diderot, Condillac, Turgot, Buffon, Grimm, Hume, Garrick, Wilkes, Sterne,

the Comte de Lauraguais;[3] and others. The doors of all official government places were of course closed to Wilkes, and he seems to have avoided places and people that might get him in hot water, for should this happen, it was as much as any envoy's post was worth to lift a finger to protect him. While traveling he met one man who was on the way to fame and another in vast possession of it. Twice during the Corradini's reign Wilkes encountered the young author of *An Account of Corsica*, whom he had known slightly in London: James Boswell. When Boswell heard that Wilkes was in Turin he "was very curious to see him in his misfortunes" and sent him the following note:

> Sir: I am told that Mr. Wilkes is now in Turin. As a politician, my monarchical soul abhors him. As a Scotsman I smile at him. As a friend I know him now. As a companion I love him. I believe it is not decent for me to wait upon him. Yet I much wish to see him. I shall be alone and have a tolerable dinner upon my table at one o'clock. If Mr. Wilkes chooses to be my guest, I shall by no means oppose it. I may venture to say he shall be very welcome, and do promise him a feast of most singular and choice conversation.

The note reached Wilkes when he wasn't at home, but he left a card on Boswell. However, going to the theater in Turin, Boswell caught sight of Wilkes at a distance and was so full of "romantic agitation" that he thought not only Churchill but Wilkes had died and that he was now viewing him "in the Ely-

---

and, for a time, J. J. Rousseau." Among others, the first three of these men, besides responding to Wilkes's wit, strongly sympathized with his protests and his plight.

[3] Lauraguais pushed through an important theater reform—forbidding spectators to sit on the stage. Wilkes must have met his mistress, the famous opera singer Sophie Arnould, known, like Wilkes, for her wit. When a rival singer got from her lover a great *rivière* of diamonds whose length, someone remarked, fell too low on the singer's person, Sophie answered: "C'est qu'elle retourne vers sa source." And when the Opera House burned down and a Court lady asked for particulars of "cette terrible incendie," Sophie said: "All I can tell you, Madame, is that *incendie* is a masculine noun."

sian Fields." But, being Boswell, he abandoned fantasy for fact and wrote a second time to Wilkes at his Turin lodgings:

> I am sorry you could not dine with me . . . I would wait upon you, were I not an old laird and a steady royalist. Since Churchill's death, I have had a serious sympathy with you . . . Might we not have an interview? . . . To men of philosophical minds there are surely moments when they set aside . . . all that they have suffered in this jumbling world . . . John Wilkes, the fiery Whig, would despise this sentiment. John Wilkes, the gay profligate, would laugh at it. But John Wilkes, the philosopher, will feel it, and will love it. You have no objection to sitting up a little late. Perhaps you may come to me tonight.

Wilkes, it would seem, complied. They met briefly in Rome, then met again in Naples—Boswell going there partly in pursuit of Wilkes—where they climbed Vesuvius and struck up an agreeable friendship despite all the factors that might militate against one. Indeed, Wilkes praised Boswell for being notably liberal-minded, "a citizen of the world, free from the prejudices of any country." (They were very similar in being incorrigible rakes, in being full of faults and yet very well liked by most people they met.) When, however, they had parted and some time had elapsed, Boswell, being more Boswell than ever, wrote to his new friend a kind of lament for all his weaknesses and a recital of his good qualities: "O John Wilkes, thou gay, learned, and ingenious private gentleman, thou passionate politician, thou thoughtless infidel, good without principle and wicked without malevolence, let Johnson teach thee the road to rational virtue and noble felicity." (Johnson will presently appear in a famous and felicitous, but far from didactic, scene.) Wilkes, on his part, thought another declaration of Boswell's wildly unreasonable, in particular coming from the mouth of a rake: "Better occasional murders than frequent adulteries."

The Wilkes-Boswell talks at Naples, as recorded by Boswell, were very much in character. Wilkes told Boswell that he loved the Corradini but could not bear her relatives; that his "eyes were open to them and his pockets shut"; and that he had never for a moment been low-spirited. When Boswell asked why Wilkes spent time with him, Wilkes answered that he was an "original genius" who would be spoiled in Paris. When Boswell, on the supposition that both he and Wilkes should die in Naples, said, "How they would write about us!" Wilkes said that if *he* died and Boswell lived, a Middlesex jury would find him guilty of Wilkes's murder. (The point, no doubt, was their tremendous political differences.) When Wilkes dined at Boswell's and talked of his wife, and a fellow guest said with surprise: "Have you a wife?" Wilkes answered: "Yes, Sir; very much at your service." Boswell's account of his and Wilkes's last get-together in Naples ends: "Up all night, &c."[4]

The man at the height of his fame whom Wilkes met—as the doorbell-ringing Boswell had done a little earlier—was Voltaire. This was after the break with the Corradini, when Wilkes made many stops on his way to Paris. He found Geneva, where the very grave of Calvin was thick with nettles and thistles, extremely unattractive; but at Ferney the greatest intellectual voice and figure of the century was throwing forth vibrations felt all over Europe. Logically enough, the two men—what with their kindred wit, audacity, and cynicism—got along extremely well. Voltaire, indeed, spoke later very highly of Wilkes as a social figure, while Wilkes during a longish visit said that "the laugh of Voltaire banished all the serious ideas the Englishman

[4] Boswell later boasted: "When Wilkes and I sat together, each glass of wine produced a flash of wit, like gunpowder thrown into the fire." D. B. Wyndham Lewis, in *The Hooded Hawk*, sees in the Wilkes-Boswell relationship a "tempting parallel of Mephistopheles and Faust." He finds something very Wilkish in "some of the polite raillery Goethe puts into the tempter's mouth" and cites the following examples: "My friend, the time has come to indulge ourselves in a little discreet debauchery." . . . "One dare hardly name to chaste ears what chaste hearts can never tire of." . . . "I can think of nothing more ridiculous than a devil who despairs." . . . "I wish thee much pleasure in lying to thyself from time to time."

nourish'd of love and the fair Italian." And to Polly, Wilkes wrote: "He put me to the blush by the many compliments he paid me. . . . I do not know when I have been so highly entertained." Voltaire also, it appears, suggested that Wilkes make use of his printers; but Wilkes refused to become involved in business arrangements with so supreme a master of both malice and money.

At last back in Paris late in September 1765, Wilkes moved about in a society full of Englishmen, which included a gout-ridden Horace Walpole, who wrote: "Wilkes is here and has been twice to see me in my illness. He was very civil but I cannot say entertained me much. I saw no wit: his conversation shows how little he has lived in good company, and the chief turn of it is the grossest bawdry. He has certainly one merit, notwithstanding the bitterness of his pen—that is, he has no rancour, not even against Sandwich." Wilkes also met Colonel Isaac Barré, an Irishman of French descent, a fine soldier, a fine orator, and a radical M.P. who had constantly voted against the Government in all matters concerning Wilkes and as a result had been tossed out of the British Army by George III. In America the two men would live permanently side by side in the city named after them. (A town and a county in North Carolina are named after Wilkes alone, as was John Wilkes Booth, whose grandfather was distantly related to Wilkes.) Wilkes also saw Boswell again in Paris. In Italy Boswell had met Lord Bute's twenty-one-year-old eldest son and had come to think that Bute was a fine man and a statesman with splendid intentions; but what Wilkes and Boswell argued about was not politics—it was writing and religion. Wilkes found nothing new in Christianity but the resurrection of the body and said: "I care no more to be raised in the same body than in the same coat, waistcoat and breeches." Before Boswell hurried off to Scotland—for Wilkes had been with him when Boswell discovered, while reading a newspaper, that his mother had died—he told Wilkes: "You'll think as I do one day," to which Wilkes replied: "You'll probably think as I in State [i.e., politics], and I as you in Church."

The return to Paris brought Wilkes into much closer contact with what was happening in England. He wrote in December of 1765 to an unnamed Englishman: "I love and honour many of the present Ministers . . . I am at their service . . . and I wish they would never bring things to the alternative either of their finding employment for me or of my finding enough for them." The English news sounded good: during the summer of 1765 the Grenville administration had fallen; and, though he was Temple's brother, Grenville had had no more regard for Wilkes than Temple's brother-in-law Pitt had come to have. Grenville showed the greatest respect and concern for the dignity of the House of Commons and, fussy about his own dignity, was fussy and pedantic—was much less parliamentarian than man of business—about much else. (It was said of him that he preferred "a national saving of two inches of candle" to all the victories of Pitt.) George III himself had said of Grenville: "That gentleman's opinions are seldom formed from any other motive than . . . may be expected to originate in the mind of a clerk in a counting house"; and said on another occasion: "When he has wearied me for two hours, he looks at his watch to see if he may not tire me for an hour more." Despite all this, Grenville's ministry had its merits, including a certain unitedness, but history can hardly do worse by him than his own Parliament did. The Grenville administration got Wilkes expelled from the House of Commons and got the Stamp Act imposed on the American colonists.

Grenville's fall naturally caused Wilkes's hopes to rise. Under Lord Rockingham's new Whig administration, he thought it very possible to be in some sense reinstated, and conceivably rewarded; and he thought it pretty certain that he would be granted a royal pardon. But Wilkes was more aware of his past services (as he regarded them) than of the present situation in

England. It is true that he was still a symbol and a slogan: at the end of this very year, 1765, on Edmund Burke's election to Parliament, the toasts had been "Wilkes and Liberty!" "Burke and Wilkes!" But it was less true that the new Administration had in it, as Wilkes thought, men who were his allies. For obviously Wilkes could embarrass the new Administration; it would have not only an outlaw's politics to account for, but his obscenities as well, not to mention unpredictable performances of his in the future. Burke, then Rockingham's private secretary, wrote to his brother: "[Wilkes] ought to be sensible that though the true *motives* for his prosecution were political, the prosecution he actually labors most under is not at all political"; it was, rather, for an offense against the ordinary laws. "Between ourselves," Burke added, "lord Rockingham is extremely averse from asking anything for [Wilkes] from the K[ing], at the same time that he is willing to do almost anything for him from his private pocket." Clearly it was as difficult to rehabilitate Wilkes as it would be easy to treat him as a kind of remittance man. Matters were made worse by the much more promising, the even enthusiastic, letters that came to Wilkes from lesser but respectable members of the Administration and of Parliament. Indeed, he was encouraged, though not without some doubts, to suggest posts he would like to be given; and he wrote, much as he did earlier, that an ambassadorship in Constantinople "is by far the most preferable." But as time passed—with Wilkes, in addition to being anxious, well-nigh penniless—and nothing happened, he wrote, perplexed and somewhat indignant, to one of his avowed supporters, George Onslow: "I ought to have had [from the new Administration] a pardon under the Great Seal without my asking it," and he added that he would be prepared to take "the Governorship of Jamaica, or perhaps the Leeward Islands." What he ultimately received was an offer "in the name of some of the ministry" of £1,000 a year—this clearly not even a gov-

ernment pension, but something taken out of the ministers' salaries, terminable whenever they gave up office. Furthermore,
not a word was said about a pardon. (It was feared that if Wilkes
got back into England pardoned or released from outlawry, he
would try to get back into Parliament.) He wrote in answer to
the £1,000 offer that it was "equally precarious, eleemosynary
and clandestine; I claim from the present Ministers a full pardon . . . for having served my country . . . If this is denied
me, I shall not look upon these ministers as my friends and
provoco ad populam like an old Roman." To Cotes he wrote of
the ministry that "if we are not friends, I am their implacable
enemy, ready to give the stab where it will wound the most."
Stony broke and having got no part of the £1,000 the Court
of Common Pleas had awarded him, he was forced to draw
upon the £1,000 that "some of the ministry" had deposited in
Paris. Chenevix Trench says that £500 on deposit for Wilkes
in Paris was "the first (and only) instalment" of Rockingham's
humiliating annuity; and Wilkes now felt forced to go, for a
short time, secretly to England.

He went in May 1766, so secretly that at Dover the bells
pealed for him and admirers swarmed around him. In London he
was given a Holles Street "hiding place" by a friend, and he
was invited to confer with Edmund Burke as representing the
Government. The two men met five times: their conversations
were not recorded, but in exchange for his grandiose demands of
the ministry—he is said to have asked for "a free pardon, a grant
of £5,000 and a pension of £1,500 a year on the Irish establishment"—he was offered nothing but the £1,000 a year allow-
ance, which was to be paid to him outside England; and he was
given not even the hope of a pardon. (He had earlier been told
that the difficulty lay in his needing two "pardons"—from the
sentence imposed by the court and from the hostile sentiments
held by the King.) While Wilkes persisted and had Burke con-

vey his protests to a Prime Minister who refused to see him,[5] he was reminded of the danger of being an outlaw; and when pointedly warned of an arrest that could only tie the Government's hands, he went back to France. With the least possible politeness, he had been shown the door.

Further attempts which Wilkes made from France, by way of Burke, got him nowhere; and Temple, who only by resuming office could be of real use to him, was unresponsive even to the letters Wilkes wrote about politics. Indeed, Temple lent a hand to a pro-Opposition piece of writing in which Wilkes came off very badly. Wilkes himself was low-spirited from his poor prospects; but the fall of the Rockingham ministry in July 1766, which resulted in Pitt's forming an Administration, gave Wilkes, because of Temple, fresh hopes. Temple, however, was given no place in the Administration—indeed, he quarreled with his brother-in-law; and his brother-in-law's moving, as Lord Chatham, from the House of Commons to the House of Lords and taking a sinecure office in the ministry, left the Duke of Grafton its nominal head.[6] Again Wilkes took hope, particularly from a letter, which he treated as an invitation, that the Duke of Grafton's brother had written to him. Moreover, George Rudé says it was Pitt who rejected Wilkes. Accordingly, in October 1766, four months after he left England, Wilkes went back again, feeling sure of a pardon and sending off at once a friendly application to Grafton, which concluded with a plea to remain in England: "I now hope . . . that I may be allowed to con-

[5] Burke, before Wilkes came from France, made plain that the Rockinghams "had not the least intention of taking up that gentleman's cause: he is not ours, and if he were, is little to be trusted: he is a lively, agreeable man, but of no prudence and no principles." And after Wilkes went back to France, a friend wrote: "Your so-called well-wishers stand in need of having their memories jogged so [that] it is a rather unfavorable symptom."

[6] Burke described the Pitt-Grafton coalition as "a piece of joinery so crossly indented and whimsically dovetailed; a Cabinet so variously inlaid, such a tesselated pavement without cement . . . that it was utterly unsafe to touch, and unsure to stand upon."

tinue in the land, and among friends of Liberty. I wish, my lord, to owe this to the mercy of my Prince. I entreat Your Grace to lay me with all humility at the King's feet, with the truest assurances that I have never . . . swerved from the duty and allegiance I owe to my sovereign." Grafton showed the letter to the King, who would have none of it. Chatham is said to have been shown it and to have thought it best "at present" to take no notice of it. Thereupon Grafton coldly, and in the presumed circumstances craftily, sent a message to Wilkes that "Mr. Wilkes must apply to lord Chatham." Even allowing that Chatham was not shown Wilkes's letter, to be made to seek help of a man who had deserted and denounced him and had lately quarreled with his patron (for Temple would have resented Wilkes's appealing to Chatham) seemed to Wilkes outrageous. On the same day that he heard from Grafton, he left England and set out for Paris, for during this visit he had been given no hideaway. Back in Paris, he wrote and published one of the most effective of his political pamphlets, "A Letter to the Duke of Grafton," which was in great part a diatribe against his "marble-hearted friend" Chatham.[7] After reproaching, not to say accusing, Grafton for such an about-face (in view of the assurances Wilkes had had from Grafton's brother), Wilkes proceeded to assault Chatham in a fashion that, beyond its own interest, displays Wilkes's denunciatory approach:

> Every tongue was wanton in his praise . . . With what anguish were we at last undeceived! . . . how he is changed! how fallen . . . his glorious sun is set . . . We long hoped, my lord, that public virtue was the guide of his actions . . . but private ambition was all the while skulking behind the shield of the patriot . . . As I had made no discovery of a new wonderful pill or drop, nor pretended to the secret of curing the gout or toothache, I never thought of soliciting lord Chatham . . . His

[7] The version quoted here, which is that given in *The Correspondence of John Wilkes* by John Almon, is a "corrected" one printed in Berlin.

lordship's office was neither important, nor responsible . . . I
believe that the flinty heart of lord Chatham . . . and the fine
feelings of humanity . . . are both formed to be admired, not
beloved. A proud, insolent, overbearing, ambitious man is always
full of the ideas of his own importance . . . Friendship is too
pure a pleasure for a mind cankered with ambition or the lust
of power . . . He has received obligations of the first magnitude
from [Lord Temple]: yet what trace of gratitude or of friendship was ever found in any part of his conduct? and has he
not now declared the most open hostility? . . . He may remember the compliments he paid me on two certain poems in
the year 1754. If I were to take the declarations made by himself and the late Mr. Potter *à la lettre,* they were more charmed
with those verses after the ninety-ninth reading than after the
first . . . [I] will now submit to your grace whether there was
not something peculiarly base and perfidious in Mr. Pitt's calling me "a blasphemer of my God" for these very verses . . .
The reason of this perfidy was plain. He was then beginning to
pay homage to the Scottish idol, and I was the most acceptable
sacrifice he could offer at the shrine of Bute . . . He was a few
years ago the mad, seditious tribune of the people . . . now he
is the abject, crouching deputy of the proud Scot whom he declared in Parliament to want wisdom . . . Was it possible for
me after this to write a suppliant letter to lord Chatham? I am
the first to pronounce myself most unworthy of a pardon, if I
could have obtained it on those terms . . . Conscious pride of
virtue makes me look down with contempt on a man who . . .
could in the lobby declare that I must be supported, and in the
House on the same day desert and revile me . . . But I have
done with lord Chatham.

On finishing with Chatham, Wilkes gave a lengthy account
of the 1763 scene with the constables at his house and, thereafter, of his session at Lord Halifax's, which culminated in his
being sent to the Tower (this account actually being the major
source of what happened that day). The "Letter" is not lacking
in animation and impudence and would seem to have had an

effect, in terms of both its substance and its manner. According to Wilkes's brother Heaton, it strengthened Wilkes's support and "has done you infinite service in the City and the exchange." This put Wilkes in better spirits, but hardly in a better position, all the more as his finances were in ruin. Cotes had gone bankrupt; Temple was irritated by Wilkes on several counts; and Heaton wrote that a letter Wilkes had published about his duel with Lord Talbot "has done you a great deal of harm." Nor was Wilkes able to raise the large advance he asked for on the history of England, despite his claim that the first volume was almost finished and that there could not be "a single libelous word" in it (which it is quite easy to believe). Hence it was "the persistence of his Paris creditors" rather than his political hopes that, late in 1767, led him to make a very brief visit to London for conference and advice with his friends. Some weeks before, he had publicly indicated in a London newspaper that he would come to England and stand as a candidate for Parliament in the general election of 1768.[8] Afraid, in London, that his creditors would have him arrested, Wilkes hurried away from it, shifting his continental base from Paris to Leyden, where he enrolled at the university as a student, since students there could not be arrested for debt. His alma mater, he later wrote to Polly from The Hague, "received me with raptures and congratulated herself on having produced so illustrious a son." He added to Polly: "You have been at the play and the opera; pray tell me how you find Corradini's 'dancing'"; also, "The Dutch . . . are round me to see if I am like my print [the Hogarth]." Soon after he crossed the Channel again, from Ostend, and on February 6, 1768 he arrived, where he would permanently remain, in London.

[8] Mr. Chenevix Trench says that the newspaper announcement was made *after* Wilkes came to London.

Part Two

I

ON ARRIVING in London[1] Wilkes decided with his usual sense of drama to stand for a very newsworthy seat in Parliament—one of two seats representing the City of London. The City itself represented a fairly "democratic" mixture of constituents, for one reason because many conservative well-to-do merchants and the like had moved beyond City limits nearer to the fashionable West End or had become the followers, and in some sense the acquaintances, of influential lords. This left smaller tradesmen and skilled and unskilled workers with a majority of City votes. Seeing the possibilities here—all the more because of declining wages and the specter of unemployment—and well aware of the publicity, Wilkes rejected the advice that he stand for a pocket borough of Lord Temple's, which he could be sure of winning and which the House of Commons could scarcely dispute. (It would infringe Temple's right of ownership and his prerogative to tell his electors how to vote.[2]) In choosing to stand for a City seat, however good in itself, Wilkes suffered from the circumstance that with the election only a month away he was left with very little time to organize, carry out, or finance

[1] Wilkes at first stayed with his "brimstone" sister Mary—a pugnacious Wilkite who, when someone ran Wilkes down and said, "I wish the King had his head," retorted: "I wish the King had half his head."

[2] Sir William Rough, the very intelligent husband of Wilkes's illegitimate daughter, Harriet Arnold, argued that had Wilkes stood for Temple's pocket borough and, thanks to Temple's position, been seated, the *Sturm und Drang* of the next few years would never have come about.

a campaign. The six rival candidates were already chosen, and Wilkes himself, a blatant outsider, lacked even the required qualifications for standing. When someone, saying "Good God, Mr. Wilkes," asked what his qualifications were, he answered: "General Warrants and the good nature of my fellow citizens." With, however, all sorts of people supporting him, it was not difficult to acquire qualifications: he was made a free man of the Joiners Company and thereafter presented himself as "John Wilkes, joiner." Yet it was much easier to qualify than to outvote candidates who, on the one hand, had powerful Court or party backing and, on the other, represented a liberal point of view. On this latter head, Wilkes was likelier to split the liberal vote than to get himself elected. To be sure, he had an army of supporters in England, even in greater London, but the crucial question was how many of them were City men with the right to cast a ballot. As for Wilkes's opponents, the Grafton ministry—since it thought Wilkes had no chance of being elected—decided to ignore him and not enhance his "martyrdom" through molestation. Hence he appeared everywhere and advertised himself with printed attacks on his enemies. He got good publicity; indeed a caricature of him as Hercules cleaning the Augean stables had a great sale.

Twelve days before the polls opened, Wilkes sent a letter to the King in which he respectfully sought "that mercy and clemency which shine with such lustre among your many princely virtues"—in other words, a pardon. That the letter was belated and, instead of being presented at Court, was handed in by a footman did not improve its all but impossible chances; and no letter was received in reply. The King and his party certainly felt rancorous toward Wilkes as an insolent hothead; but in matters like Wilkes's letter, he might very easily also be a hot potato. Grenville, Halifax, and others had come up against Wilkes's pranks and pleas, his tricks and jests, and very likely King and Court thought it best to let a barking dog lie. Wilkes, however, rose up on his haunches to bark as a candidate, stressing "the two important questions of public liberty, respecting *General Warrants* and the *Seizure of Papers.*" Bets abounded on whether he would be elected; other popular bets dealt with whether he would be put "in durance vile." Before the election he appeared, with the six other candidates, at the Guildhall where the crowd gave him a tremendous reception: "The acclamations of joy," said the *Annual Register*, "were inconceivable." "I stand here, gentlemen," he told the crowd, "a private man, unconnected with the great, and unsupported by any party. I have no support but you, I wish no other support. I can have none more certain, none more honorable." On the first day of voting there was a prodigious roar from the mob and a great rush of voters for Wilkes. His friends were indefatigable, one even going to the trouble of voting a second time, wearing his coat inside out; Wilkes said this was impossible, since none of his supporters had a coat. On the third day Wilkes was cheered and chaired to a cry of "By God, Mr. Wilkes, we'll *carry* you whether you carry your election or not." But the poll was open for a full week and with every day Wilkes lost ground. The two liberalistic "patriot" candidates had been promised most of the "radical" votes; and there were a great many voters—workingmen afraid of losing their jobs, shopkeepers afraid of losing their customers—who dared not vote for Wilkes. This was appraised by a commentator as the deciding factor in Wilkes's defeat; but as he came in last, with 1,247 votes as against the two leaders' 3,729 and 3,678, there were clearly other factors. Yet, since voters had to sign their names and the names of their choices, fear and caution could have made a considerable difference. As it was, Wilkes's chief support came from the loudest champions but the least "important" voters, which is to say the least well-off ones. When one of these men was accused during the election of being a turncoat, Wilkes punned again on the same word, saying that none of them had a coat to turn.

Wilkes himself, however, at once found a candidacy to turn to. Blaming his City defeat on his lateness in entering the field —which Benjamin Franklin, despite thinking Wilkes "of bad character" and "not worth a farthing," agreed with—Wilkes spoke to a new electorate: "Gentlemen, permit me to address you as Friends of Liberty and Freeholders of the County of Middlesex, declaring my intention of appearing as a candidate to represent you in Parliament." At once his hearers seized his carriage, set free the horses, "and dragged the carriage themselves, with Mr. Wilkes and another gentleman in it, from the Mansion House to the George and Vulture tavern" in Cornhill. At once in Wilkes's favor was the fact that in Middlesex voters did not have to sign their names or indicate whom they were voting for; also in his favor were two enthusiastic supporters or campaign managers. One was an old associate, Serjeant Glynn, who had defended Wilkes at the time of the general warrant uproar and who— except as Wilkes might occasionally flout Glynn's advice—kept everything on the side of the law. The other man, John Horne, was a clergyman—"in so far as a bishop's hand had waved over him"—and of a sort congenial to Wilkes himself, being ribald, witty, and bold, with strong democratic sympathies and dissolute habits. (He is far better known today as Horne Tooke, who would become an ultimately dubious philologist, the author of *The Diversions of Purley*, and who would get into trouble for his radical views. He was sent to prison for trying, during the American Revolution, to raise money for the American colonists, and during the period of the French Revolution he was tried for high treason but acquitted.) It is said that under Horne's guidance, the Middlesex freeholders met and agreed to finance Wilkes's candidacy; and it is also said that Horne pledged his credit for Wilkes's expenses. Of decided help to Wilkes was Lord Temple's gift to him of a piece of land worth £600 a year, which would make him, as a Middlesex freeholder, an eligible candidate for Parliament. The land was not granted outright to Wilkes because an outlaw's property was forfeit to the Crown, a proceeding which Temple did not welcome. It was arranged that should Wilkes be asked while campaigning to indicate his £600 property, he would "decline the poll," but it never occurred to his opponents to ask him.

Wilkes's campaign, though lacking the support of influential personages (Temple assigned land but provided no other support) was well handled by himself and his two aides. They had only twelve days to work in, but Horne in particular electioneered tirelessly for Wilkes; their close-to-modern type of slogan, "Register, register, register!" proved effective; and Wilkes, in an age of personal canvassing, at which he was quick-witted and friendly, rather than an age of formal speeches, at which he could easily fall short, found something to say to everyone. To a man who informed him that he would rather vote for the Devil than for John Wilkes, he tossed back politely: "But . . . if your friend should not stand?" The campaign extended as far as the churches, several of which carried the notice: "The prayers of this congregation are earnestly desired for the restoration of liberty, depending on the election of Mr. Wilkes." Wilkes had two opponents in the election. One was George Cooke, an aging and ailing joint paymaster of the forces and an adherent of Pitt's, who thought that if he took no part in the election he might (should Wilkes run) gain the other of the two seats, since the third contestant, Sir William Beauchamp Procter, was an affluent but ill-tempered barrister. Having to make a speech while standing for Parliament, Sir William said: "Gentlemen —er—I thank you—gentlemen . . . Oh, what must I say next? What *must* I say next?"

In the midst of the campaigning Wilkes wrote to the Solicitor of the Treasury—perhaps in good faith, perhaps from defiance —that as the election would by then be over, he would present himself at the Court of King's Bench on the day the court opened. The Wilkites, during the campaign, were electioneering with tremendous ardor. They chalked "45" wherever possible, but particularly on coaches, and went so far as to drag the Austrian ambassador out of his coach and chalk "45" on the soles of his shoes. The half-crazy Alexander Cruden (famous for his Bible *Concordance*) trudged after the Wilkites with a sponge, muttering to himself while he rubbed out their "45"s.[3] Wilkes's supporters put his picture in every pub they could or had it hang outside as an inn sign. Wilkes himself told of walking behind an old lady who, looking at one of the signs, said, "Aye, he swings everywhere but where he ought!" Horace Walpole tells of one of Wilkes's feminine admirers who, when someone said, "He squints," answered, "If he does, he squints no more than a gentleman ought to squint." Walpole also said that "the only good thing" he had heard apropos the election was of someone who began a letter with "I take the Wilkes-and-liberty to assure you . . ."

The Middlesex election on March 28, 1768, opened on a fine morning with, it was reported, nearly 250 coaches filled with Wilkites setting out to vote. Forty thousand handbills—should it not have been forty-five?—had been printed and passed along, urging Wilkes's supporters "to preserve peace and good order . . . to convince the world that Liberty is not joined with licentiousness." Wilkes himself went to the hustings in Brentford "attended by an amazing number of people" and riding in a "coach drawn by six long-tailed horses" with no disturbance on the way. "Weavers &c," wrote Walpole, "took possession of Piccadilly . . . and would suffer nobody to pass without blue cockades," and papers inscribed "No. 45, Wilkes and Liberty"; and

[3] The number "45" took on, as time passed, cabalistic significance: thus, a composition of Handel's was found to contain exactly forty-five bars; clergymen preached on the text of "If I find the forty and five"; and the forty-fifth article of Magna Charta had a sentiment apposite to Wilkes and liberty. Among colonial sympathizers in America, there was a "gathering of forty-five New Yorkers, on the forty-fifth day of the year 1770, to consume forty-five pounds of beefsteak cut from a bullock forty-five months old."

"tore to pieces the coaches" of both of Wilkes's rivals. (Coaches were not allowed to go through St. James's Street for fear of personal demonstrations against the King.) At the polls Wilkes himself "lest it should be declared a void election . . . had the sense to keep everything quiet." Cooke, who was ill, did not appear, and Wilkes and Procter sat next to each other on the hustings.[4] The whole thing proceeded in orderly fashion and many of those "who lately voted against Mr. Wilkes at Guildhall were the first to poll in his favor at Brentford." From the beginning Wilkes was ahead, and it was only the need to determine which of his two opponents had also been elected that slowed down posting the result, which was not announced officially until the next day. Wilkes got 1,292 votes and Cooke outran Procter 827 to 807. It was said of the whole occasion that "there has not been so great a defection of inhabitants from London and Westminster to ten miles distant, in one day, since the prophecy of the earthquake . . . in 1750." And in as many years, perhaps, there had not been so great a hubbub as what followed that day. Despite Wilkes's appeal for order, in returning to London Wilkes's "mob," as it was called, stopped every carriage without a "No. 45" and scratched one on it; forced everybody, including Walpole on his way to a party, to huzza their hero; threw dirt and stones; and smashed the windows of coaches. Other enthusiasts, while getting drunk, smashed windows in houses all over town and at 1 A.M. started rioting before Lord Bute's house. All houses in London were, under threats, to be illuminated; even the aunt and brother of George III had to light up their houses, and at two or three in the morning occupants were waked up to relight candles that had sputtered out.

[4] Wilkes, it is said, indicating his noisy supporters, remarked to Procter: "I wonder, sir, whether there are more knaves or more fools down there." Procter answered: "I'll tell them what you said and they'll put an end to you"; to which Wilkes is reported to have answered: "It's you they'd put an end to, for I would tell them yours was a falsehood and they'd finish you off in the twinkling of an eye."

In two nights, Benjamin Franklin calculated, London had used £50,000 worth of candles. Franklin wrote also of Wilkes: " 'Tis really an extraordinary event to see an outlaw and exile of bad personal character . . . come over from France [and] set himself up as a candidate for the capital of the Kingdom." But he added: "I went last week to Winchester and observed that for fifteen miles out of town there was not a door or window shutter next the road unmarked [with "No. 45"]; and this continued here and there quite to Winchester, which is sixty-four miles." (Boswell had noted the same thing while traveling to Oxford on a visit to Dr. Johnson.[5]) And Franklin, to quote him once more, had, amid the rejoicing and rioting for Wilkes, made his famous remark that if George III had had a bad character and Wilkes a good one, George might well have been toppled off his throne. And indeed, had Wilkes himself not called for order and patrolled the streets with his own committeemen, matters might have become far worse than they became. Actually, few people were hurt and the damage to property was chiefly a lot of broken windows and the need to repaint coaches and front doors. The principal loss evoked the jingle:

> Like many of the upper class
> They liked the sound of broken glass.

A Crown prosecution avowed that, notwithstanding the Lord Mayor's "vigilance to suppress the riots and disturbances" the goings-on extended, almost every night, from the twenty-eighth of March to the twelfth or thirteenth of May. When the City's trained bands—or militia—were called upon to serve, very few came forth, and those who did found that "six thousand weavers"

[5] Boswell turned up at Brentford on the first day, but kept out of Wilkes's sight. A bit earlier he had been approached by a man who inquired if his name wasn't Wilkes; and when Boswell said yes, the man said he had "today" got him twenty-five votes. Boswell bowed and talked of "liberty and general warrants and I don't know what all." He told Dr. Johnson—apparently this is what had surprised him most—that he didn't know he was so ugly.

had come forth also, supporting Wilkes and prepared to chase
the trained bands off the streets. The situation was not just a
spontaneous overflow of high-spirited misbehavior; it was be-
gotten of years of highborn misbehavior; of stupidly autocratic
actions by King and Court; of ineffective opposition by the
Whigs, hence of worsening hard times and resentful reactions
among the respectable poor and of much stronger emotions in a
street-roaming, half-homeless, fiercely dissatisfied rabble. We
shall in due course say more of this: the riots, partly from
Wilkes's refusal to encourage them, partly from the mob's mood
of being more often boisterous than vicious or rebellious, did
not cause anything like major damage or harm—no Wilkite
mob, it has been asserted, ever killed anyone and, unlike the
Gordon rioters, none ever resorted to arson.

As for Wilkes's election, there were a number of reactions
from men in politics and power. Lord Chancellor Camden
(formerly Mr. Justice Pratt) was thoroughly aroused that "a
criminal should in open daylight thrust himself upon the county
as a candidate, his crime unexpurgated"; but Temple emerged
enough to say that, despite enormous faults, Wilkes "had suffered abundantly" and must be saved from "Ministerial injustice"; and Edmund Burke, who had thought Wilkes would be
defeated, made the sagacious comment that "the crowd always
want to draw themselves from abstract principles to personal
attachments." Moreover, two great Whig dukes spoke in Wilkes's
favor. Whatever Wilkes's private character, said the Duke of
Richmond, he won his election by being supposed a friend to
liberty, which must show the Administration that however they
might "buy" or manage Parliament, they were not "so much
approved of by the Nation"; and the Duke of Newcastle spoke
to much the same effect. Wilkes himself, in his address of thanks
to his constituents, introduced something new: he asked them
to give him their *instructions*. Even if this was mere tactics,
it voiced a significant note.

Wilkes, after a postelection jaunt to Bath,[6] came back to London and on the first day of the Easter term, April 20, appeared, as promised, at the Court of King's Bench to surrender himself as an outlaw. Troops guarded the approach as a worried crowd escorted Wilkes almost to the very door. All over London precautions had been taken lest there be renewed agitations— troops were stationed in such places as the Tower, the Savoy, and the War Office, and magistrates were posted in public buildings, coffeehouses, and the vestry rooms of churches. Inside the Court of King's Bench Lord Mansfield was himself rather flustered and nervous, wanting, it would seem, to sentence Wilkes but worried about the consequences. He sat with his head back listening to Wilkes's defense and to the arguments between the Attorney General and Wilkes's stanch Serjeant Glynn, to announce at length, to everyone's amazement, that there was nothing to pass judgment on: Wilkes had not been arrested and until a writ of *capias utlagatum* arrested him, Wilkes must go free.[7]

Wilkes very much relished the technicality that gave him his freedom, and his followers went in for a certain amount of noisy celebrating, although one of them wrote to the Duke of Newcastle that "there has not been the least riot, tumult or Mob than is usual on the first day of the Term." As to the future, Wilkes was said to be "cleared till the Parliament sits, then he is to be tried by the House of Lords." Wilkes himself, however, chose to await no such doubtful event. Having, on being set free, enjoyed himself for a week, he is reported to have sent for a sheriff's officer with the request that he be "kind enough to

[6] Wilkes went to Bath, not as a politician or M.P., but as someone privately taking the waters. It was not an altogether successful junket: he became a kind of sight to behold at a distance, but elsewhere to shun or look away from; here Lord Chancellor Camden, in line with his comment on the election, cut Wilkes dead. On the other hand, a young lady at Bath had her hair curled to resemble "45" and was looking for a forty-five-year-old husband.

[7] One version has it that seven sheriff's officers stood outside the court "with the requisite *capias*," but no one dared to serve Wilkes with it.

arrest him"; this done, Wilkes had his lawyer inform the Attorney General that it was the prisoner who saw to the arrest. Taken before Lord Mansfield he was refused bail, entered an appeal against his outlawry, and was committed to the King's Bench prison in St. George's Fields on the Surrey side of the Thames. He then, accompanied by the tipstaff and John Horne, left the court in Westminster Hall at 6:30 P.M., only for crowds to form not just close by, but all along Westminster Bridge; and as both Wilkes and the mob got close to the Surrey side, a group of his followers took the horses off his coach, reversed the coach's direction, and on leaving the bridge drew it from the Strand into the City, pursued unsuccessfully by the famous blind judge and half brother of the author of *Tom Jones*, Sir John Fielding, accompanied by his clerk. Presently Wilkes was allowed to get out and rest, and he shortly after appeared in an upstairs tavern window from where he responded to the halloos of his adherents. Late at night he stole off, disguised, in a private carriage; knocked, on arrival, at the prison gates; and delivered himself to the jailers.[8]

Wilkes's refusal to exploit the situation and his "wise and humane discouragement of all tumult and disorder" pleased Temple, who at once wrote to him in very friendly terms and offered to pay him a visit. But Wilkes's supporters were very much inclined to exploit the situation, and the day after his entering the prison it was "surrounded by a prodigious number of persons"; after dark there was action and disturbance, with, shortly past midnight, a "Captain Guard" dispersing "the Mob." There were, however, arrests, and one rioter was sentenced to a year in prison. This did not prevent subsequent crowds from surrounding the King's Bench, or from manhandling an unsympathetic watchman, or from tossing a "well dressed" man who spoke ill of Wilkes into a pond and making him kneel while

[8] Many people, it was said, have stolen out of prison by disguising themselves, but this was the first time anyone had done so to steal in.

shouting "Wilkes and Liberty!" It was on May 10, however—the opening day of Parliament—that a serious clash arose, of sufficient intensity to become known as "the Massacre of St. George's Fields." Increasingly unsuccessful in handling matters, the Government became so much so that the crowd, which had done slight mischief, made monkeys of the officers of the Crown for their feeble and fatuous performances. The Government thereupon determined to stop the crowd's behavior by replacing feebleness with force. Fearing that there would be particularly large and unruly crowds on the opening day of Parliament, the authorities ordered "a troop of horse and a hundred men of the Third Regiment of Foot Guards" to the King's Bench prison, while the Lord Mayor gave orders to keep young journeymen and apprentices off the streets. But from mid-morning on, and from all over London, crowds quickly assembled. There were rumors that Wilkes would be carried to the Commons and seated as an M.P.; that he would be brought to trial; and that a movement was afoot to set not just him but all his King's Bench fellow prisoners free. Early in the day the crowd proved unmanageable enough for the prison marshal to ask for help. When help arrived and tore down a wretched poem that the Wilkites had pasted up and that began

> Venal judges and ministers combine
> Wilkes and English liberty to confine

the crowd grew more unmanageable, enough for a "stupid, over-zealous" justice to read the Riot Act, which was met—the crowd largely unaware of what had been read—with a "volley of stones." When the justice had been hit in the head by a "man in a red waistcoat," he ordered the guards to go after the man. An observer of all this—that even greater rake than Wilkes or Boswell, William Hickey—wrote in his enjoyable *Memoirs* that

> the pursued man ran round a windmill; when finding himself in danger of being overtaken he made for an inn . . . kept by a

Mr. Allen . . . darting through a barn used as a cow-house, having a door at each end . . . At the very instant he passed the second door, the son of Mr. Allen entered by the opposite one, and unluckily having a red waistcoat on, one of the soldiers . . . fired, killing him upon the spot. All this was the work of a minute, my companion and myself being witnesses of the whole bloody transaction. The mob, now justly irritated at the brutality of the soldiers, became outrageous, and volleys of stones flew in every direction. The soldiers loaded and fired again and again, by which many lives were wantonly sacrificed.

There had indeed been a second reading of the Riot Act and an order for foot soldiers and Horse Guards to fire into the crowd. More people were wounded and killed "returning to town": two men were stabbed with bayonets, a farrier was "shot through the breast as he was fitting a hay cart in the Haymarket," and a woman selling oranges there was killed. A constable testified later, at the Old Bailey trial, that the people merely "huzza'd and hissed" while "the soldiers fired at random. A great number of them loaded three times and seemed to enjoy their fire."[9]

At night hundreds of disorderly persons "left the mob to revenge the shootings" by pulling down the houses of two magistrates and later stealing a twenty-gallon cask of spirits worth several hundred pounds. Elsewhere, as rioting spread through London, "a brand-new saw mill" was pulled down, there was rioting outside the House of Lords, and considerable throwing of stones at people and windows. Horace Walpole, in his unsympathetic and not too accurate account of the proceedings, does make a very sound point in attributing the disordered attitude of the crowds to other causes than Wilkes: "We have independent mobs . . . who only take advantage of so favorable a season. The dearness of provisions incites, the hope of increase

[9] Almon reports that "Mr. Wilkes wrote a pamphlet on the transactions of the disgraceful day," which he entitled "The Inhuman Massacre in St. George's Fields on the 10th of May 1768" but "it was never published."

of wages allures, and drink puts them in motion." Indeed, some four thousand sailors had left their ships seeking higher pay;[10] so too there were "stoppages" among watermen, hatters, tailors, and coal heavers. "To all these men, needy and angry as a result of economic conditions," wrote Steven Watson, "Wilkes became a kind of symbol: he had no economic programme, but he was in revolt, and they were in revolt also."

Whatever the excesses of the crowds, very little credit redounded to the Crown. Its military tactics had been far less preventive than provocative, going so far as to shed blood. The Crown's behavior was condemned when the inquest into the death of the wrong red-waistcoated man found all three of his assailants "guilty of deliberate murder." Furthermore, all three were Scotsmen, that hated breed in England. A bill for willful murder was also found against the justice who gave the order to fire; he, however, was acquitted. The Government was indeed the Government and could, and did, defend the actions of its servants: "His Majesty," wrote "silken, fawning" Lord Barrington as Secretary at War, "highly approves of the conduct of both the officers and the men . . . In case any disagreeable circumstances should happen, they shall have every defense and protection that the law can authorise and this office can give." One of the assailants charged with deliberate murder was on that very day given, on behalf of the Government, a purse of thirty guineas. When the "massacre" was brought before a grand jury, the jury's membership was overloaded with Government

[10] The day before the "massacre" "a large body of sailors," William Hickey writes, "made their appearance, some of whom, like monkeys scrambling up the wall, were in a minute at the window of Mr. Wilkes's apartment; when they offered directly to liberate [him] . . . Mr. Wilkes very prudently begged them to desist, arguing that the law would doubtless do him justice and asking them to be patient, upon which they gave three cheers and dispersed, saying they would come again the next day, in case [Wilkes] should change his mind and wish to come out." Next day "at ten o'clock, full a thousand seamen made their promised visit . . . offering him liberty if he chose it, notwithstanding the presence of the 'lobsters' (as they called the soldiers), Wilkes renewing his entreaties that they would depart quietly. They, as before, cheered and did so."

people, landowners, and the like, and a true bill was refused. In Parliament the Opposition was somewhat of two minds about the "massacre," seeking to uphold law and order while striving to discredit Court and King. "We must either be governed," said Newcastle, "by a mad, lawless Mob, or the peace be preserved only by a military force, both of which are unknown to our Constitution." Wilkes, some weeks after the "massacre," was able to make public the instructions that authorized full military action should rioting occur. (George III, moreover, had written to Lord Weymouth, apropos the riots: "Bloodshed is not what I delight in, but it seems to me the only way of restoring a due obedience to the laws.") This made the "massacre" no ad-hoc performance but part of a deliberate policy so far-reaching as to have Englishmen killed by non-English muskets. Such proceedings could not but strengthen the Wilkite cause by winning over people who, whatever they felt about Wilkes, felt great concern for liberty.

Wilkes himself, however, had now his own freedom to fight for. On June 8 he appeared once again at the Court of King's Bench in the matter of his appeal against outlawry. Though he had presumably shown no fear—had, indeed, after the manner that befitted and often became him, been casual in company and ribald in conversation—what he faced could be decidedly severe. Legally, too much time had passed for his outlawry to be reversed; legally, if condemned as an outlaw, he would be quite without rights, in fact quite without identity. An outlaw's head was, from the Dark Ages, a "wolf's head," something to be killed at sight; and in contemporary practice he could be imprisoned for any length of time until the King should choose to pardon him. Furthermore, his fate lay ominously in the hands of his former antagonist, Lord Mansfield.

"The greatest lawyer of the century, but also a legal statesman," William Murray (1705–93), eventually the Earl of Mansfield, was the son of an impoverished Jacobite Scottish lord.

He early made a name for himself in the House of Commons, where in middle life he was judged the greatest orator after Pitt. But his ambitions resided in the law rather than politics, and he was Lord Chief Justice of the King's Bench from 1756 till he resigned in 1788. In his political thinking "the father of modern Toryism," he was also considered a notably impartial judge, his judgments on the liberal side running to the decision that a slave is free when standing on English soil; that a Quaker, rather than take an oath, could be permitted to "affirm"; and that the rights of conscience should be protected, so much so that his protection of Roman Catholics gave rise to rumors that he was a Jesuit and led to the burning of his house during the Gordon Riots. He could also be extremely cautious, as in some of his dealings with Wilkes. He insisted that libel was something for the judge rather than the jury to decide—a belief that was overturned by Charles James Fox. As a man he had elegant manners and social charm, but had one great fault, said Campbell in his *Lives of the Chief Justices*: a want of heart. And a great modern admirer of Mansfield's, John Sparrow, has said that he moved about "scarcely doing or saying a single thing that proves him a human being."

On June 8 at the Court of King's Bench, Mansfield, after both sides had put forth their arguments concerning Wilkes's outlawry, began to pass judgment. He spoke formally and lengthily, his theme being a judge's duty, in rendering justice, to abide by his conscience and his knowledge of the law. He went on to speak of his *personal* determination to be guided by this. Listened to in absolute and admiring silence, he continued to keep all those present in a kind of dazed suspense until, rather suddenly, he gave forth judgment that the outlawry was void and must needs be canceled. He then set forth the grounds for the cancellation: there was an error in the writ. The words for holding the trial had been "at the County Court for the County of Middlesex"; they should have been, ruled Mansfield, "at the County Court of Middlesex for the County of Middlesex."

It would be hard to say whether the Wilkites were more surprised by Mansfield's decision or more elated: for many of them, both surprise and elation might well have given way to bewilderment. But a plausible explanation of so surprising a verdict was not hard to come by. The verdict was not the result of a ridiculous pedantry, but of a need to be cautious in the light of Wilkes's mounting support and conceivably of a certain anxiety on Mansfield's part concerning himself.[11] (On that very day he had suffered from rough treatment on his way to court.) Had he found Wilkes guilty of so punishable a crime, a vast rabble and a vocal citizenry, already smoldering after the "massacre" and long inflamed by the Government's treatment of Wilkes and mistreatment of law and liberty, might have translated anger into action and rioting into revolt. One can only speculate on what *might* have happened, but in a cause that grew ever louder and stronger, and in a century given to both Jacobite uprisings and Jacobin uproar, almost anything could have. The verdict, in any case, was met with rejoicing by Wilkites all over England; but ten days after it was handed down Wilkes, with a cordon of Foot and Horse Guards guarding the court, was brought before Mr. Justice Yates for sentencing on the two indictments which, five years earlier, he had been found guilty of. For publishing the *Essay on Woman* Wilkes was fined £500 and sent to prison for twelve months; for republishing *No. 45* he was fined £500 and given ten months more. ("I will not believe," said Burke, "what no other man living be-

---

[11] It is interesting to compare Mansfield's verdict with what, only a short time before, he had told those present in the courtroom: "It has been said that consequences of a frightful nature will follow the . . . punishing Wilkes for outlawry . . . The people expect its reversal, the temper of the times demands it, the multitude will have it so. These are arguments which weigh not a feather with me . . . If insurrection and rebellion are to follow our determination, we have not to answer for the consequences. We can only say *fiat justitia, ruat caelum.*"

lieves, that Mr. Wilkes was punished for the indecency of his publications or the impiety of his ransacked closet.") The fines were paid by adherents of Wilkes, and he himself proceeded from the King's Bench court to the King's Bench prison.

THE RIOTOUS CLASS

MUCH OF LOWER-CLASS life in Wilkes's England is buried in anonymous and pestilent darkness, while much else stomps rowdily, and sprawls drunkenly, and turns riotous and lawless, in hideous squalid streets. What proportion there was of industrious, hard-working, and well-behaved "poor people" it would be very hard to say; perhaps their numbers are swelled by those who sufferingly endured their plights or died miserably in their verminous beds. Lower-class life was worst in the second quarter of the century, during the first twenty-five years of Wilkes's life and the period when crime most alarmingly increased. While England itself was otherwise prospering, was indeed moving toward the first place in Europe, its lower depths were menaced not only by brutality and violence, but by filth and starvation and by living quarters so ravaged and vile as to become street-long and acre-wide deathbeds. The period was little touched with public spirit or philanthropy and would have been little improved without a great deal of both. Besides being greedy men, George I and George II were Germans for whom London had little meaning and in whose inhabitants they took no interest at all. Though Sir Robert Walpole, as Prime Minister, struggled with great success to keep England at peace, he never once lifted a finger to mitigate poverty. Necessarily, England's poverty grew worse, its prisons became overpopulated, its slums became subhuman sties. Every lower-class evil increased, because what the poor snatched at for relief became their undoing.

What this meant was that within a few years a phenomenon swept over lower-class life and sentenced it to a far worse fate. Gin drinking became the mania, and one might almost say the menu, of the poor. Once beer and ale had sufficed for them; but when they became aware of the potency of gin, it became their mainstay and their obsession;[1] and once it became their obsession it spelled their ruin. It ruined their ability to work, it wrecked their health, it menaced their sanity, it destroyed their respect for the law, it incited or drove them to crime. Henry Fielding, a great novelist who was also a humane magistrate, said, "Gin is the principal sustenance of an hundred thousand people in this metropolis." Hogarth, the greatest painter of the day, with little exaggeration pictured, in *Gin Lane*, the hideous effects of gin. It was sold in every kind of shop—in chandlers' shops, in weavers' shops, in shops that were also brothels and receivers of stolen goods. There were streets where every fourth house was a dram shop (metropolitan Middlesex had 7,000 shops in all); and signs outside the shops would announce satirically that you could get "drunk for a penny, dead drunk for twopence, straw provided free." Gin sales, which had already climbed to three and a half million gallons in 1727, went to over eight million in 1743.

For a long time there was no attempt from above to cope with the situation, for distilling had become a highly prosperous and Government-favored trade (indeed employers, we are told, "sold gin to their work people.") Parliament took no action until gin drinking reached horrifying dimensions; it then imposed a very heavy tax on spirits in an attempt to materially reduce their consumption. But the tax could not be enforced and led to bootlegging, to considerable rioting, and to the murder of informants. Bootlegged gin became so profitable that the Gov-

---

[1] But hard-working laboring men, it appears, continued to drink strong beer.

George III.

"Beer Street," engraving after the original by William Hogarth.

"Gin Lane," engraving after the original by William Hogarth.

Lord North, subsequently
second Earl of Guilford.

William Pitt, Earl of Chatham.

ernment, having lost revenue from the high tax, substituted an extremely low one. Only tremendous middle-class protest and pressure on the Government—this in the teeth of vested interests—led to regulating the sale of gin and to forbidding it in many places. The drinking, as a result, was substantially reduced.

However much the craze for gin worsened the conditions of the poor, it arose out of extremely bad ones. The lower classes, haunted by poverty and all too often faced with hunger and homelessness, lived all too often at the mercy of their betters, not just landlords and employers, but parsons and the police. Great numbers of them lived in decayed, tumbledown dwellings that would literally cease to exist (Dr. Johnson described London as a place where "falling houses thunder on your head.") The houses lay in London's most unsavory and unsafe neighborhoods where, said Fielding in 1751, an "immense number of lanes, alleys, courts and bye-places" seemed designed for concealment and were a virtual forest for criminals to hide out in. The tottering houses were sometimes patched up into flophouses and brothels or were taken over by homeless beggars, or by people who took away timber they might sell. A night's lodging in the worst flophouses was often twopence for a single person, threepence for a couple. As late as the end of the century, very poor families slept three to eight people, of various ages, in a bed and did not "put clean sheets on their beds three times a year." There was fetid air and "putrid excremental effluvia"; there was tainted food; and whole large-sized families lived in one room. Fielding saw two filthy small houses emptied of seventy lodgers who collectively possessed a shilling (except for one girl who had "recently robbed her mistress").

The eighteenth century thought it had found a panacea for all these economic evils in the creation of the workhouse, which could salve the national conscience without draining the national purse. As a result, workhouses sprang up everywhere; but workhouse life was so harsh that many people would not submit to it, which caused them to forfeit their right to relief. Moreover, workhouse management was corrupt: the managers were paid lump sums per capita and best profited by underfeeding and overworking their charges, with vermin and jail fever quite as bad as in actual jails. Great numbers of children were placed in workhouses, "with," says Dorothy Marshall, "the most appalling results"—workhouses being nothing less than death traps. Of fifty-four children born or placed in one particular workhouse, not one remained alive for a year. At another time, thirty-nine workhouse children were put in three beds, to contract a variety of "disorders from each other." The workhouse movement failed, first from its not being able to make its inmates self-supporting, and again from jobbery and corruption that put into unscrupulous pockets what was designed for the poor man's plate.

In mid-century the deaths in London "greatly exceeded the births";[2] 80 to 90 per cent of children who were thrust upon the parish died, and of those received when less than a year old, 99 per cent. In 1757 it was reported that officers in Westminster were given money to rear over five hundred bastards "and reared but one." Late in the century "half-starved, miserable, scald-headed children" abounded. Nor was the plight of infants always due to natural causes: they might be deserted or murdered at birth—often left lying dead in the streets; and "wicked and barbarous nurses would, for small payments, ill feed children, make them beg and steal—and, so that they might gain extra pennies by arousing pity," have the children "blinded or maimed."

As for those who survived and became adults, the "workingman" was all too often not associated with work: thus in 1773

[2] When deaths far outranked births, the fact that a great number of jobs became available tended to reverse matters: jobholders proceeded to have children, and births for a period could outrank deaths.

a writer speaks of "workmen of every species in or near the capital" as "justly reputed idle, profligate and debauched." Less sweepingly another writer had in 1765 cited "porters, sailors, chair men, and day laborers who work in the streets as an insolent rabble, far worse than even the lowest class of shopkeepers." The age, as Dorothy George says, was one of "minute social distinctions, with not only a decided difference between skilled and unskilled labor, but even between slight variations involving merchandise": the daughter of the famous actor Colley Cibber, when in pinched straits, sold sausages in the streets, but indignantly denied a report that she sold flounders. Laborers' wages before 1765 ranged from nine to twelve shillings a week; the highest kind of skilled labor, such as the jewelry and optical instruments trades, ranged from one pound a week to three or four. What with so many widows, deserted wives, and unmarried mothers in need of work, women were worse off than men— their markets overstocked and their pay exceedingly low, sometimes a mere three shillings a week. Bread and cheese were the workingman's staple; how often his family had meat is hard to determine, but one such family of six had only half a pound of bacon a week and other meat "only at celebration meals." Ordinary seamen, it appears, were given "roots and greens," along with fresh meat, because of the Navy's fear of scurvy.

To be sure, not all working people were distressed: Voltaire mistook English servant girls and apprentices in their best clothes for "people of fashion"; but even people who worked in shops had a grueling day. In mid-century, shops opened at 7 A.M. and shut down at 8 P.M.; later, it might be 7 A.M. to 10 P.M.; and there were only three holidays a year—Easter, Whitsuntide, and Christmas. In many trades, however, there were additional holidays—the eight "hanging days" at Tyburn.[3] Lower-class

[3] The two-mile procession, from Newgate to Tyburn, of criminals condemned to hang, with the streets packed with cheering or taunting spectators, had become an unofficial holiday; but this grisly march was abolished in 1783. In London, between 1752 and 1772, more than half of those condemned to death went to

socializing was chiefly in taverns and alehouses or in young
workingmen's "clubs." Thus, a "punch club" with thirty members met on Mondays at 8:00 P.M. and "terminated when all
the members were drunk"; at "cock and hen clubs" young men
and prostitutes met "to drink and sing songs." The proprietor
of one club stated that his customers changed every six months
owing to "hangings, drownings and sudden deaths." The pleasures and pastimes of the lower classes were limited and not very
lustrous—occasional pageants or trips to the big London fairs;
watching cocks fight and bears baited; and gambling, which
might end in picked pockets and a broken head. Many workers
were paid on Saturday at midnight, with the wives present,
trying to get a small part of the wages before they were spent on
gambling or drink. There was also a public house in every prison,
and there were sometimes actual small prisons inside public
houses. At Wilkes's affluent King's Bench prison there were, at
one period, thirty gin shops.

But prison life for the poor, or for hopeless debtors, was quite
unlike what Wilkes encountered; was often, indeed, beyond description. Of a prison common room, a contemporary wrote:
"When first we entered, the mixture of scents that arose from
mundungus-tobacco, foul sweaty toes, dirty shirts, stinking
breaths and uncleanly carcases, poisoned our nostrils far worse
than a Southwark ditch." Men lived, underfed and overcrowded,
—fifteen might at night occupy a space barely six feet square—
in cold and darkness and the most outrageous filth and want.
The drainage made them sick, and water from the floor of their
cells rose up and slowly rotted away their beds. Prisoners might
be thrown into dungeons—far from dungeons being got rid of,
new ones were still built—lying over sewers full of corpses, a
state of things that produced epidemics of jail fever.[4] Moreover,

the gallows, whereas in Norfolk less than a third did and in the Midlands less
than a fourth.

[4] Jail fever (typhus) could be so bad that when, in 1750, a hundred prisoners
from Newgate were brought to trial, four of the six judges and over forty jurors
and minor officials died.

the treatment meted out by rapacious prison attendants vied with the horrors of the prison: debtors who could not tip adequately were thrown among prisoners with smallpox, or were denied food and a bed, or were put in irons, or were totally ignored when sick. Before 1774 prisoners discharged or acquitted might still have to languish in prison for not paying jailers' or sheriffs' fees. The public had glimpses of all this, seeing dirty specters standing behind windows, chanting "Pray remember the poor debtors"; but, though passersby might toss debtors a coin, they never protested their plight. Writers, to be sure, described prison conditions, hoping that legislators would act, but the evils were very little mended: in the earlier part of the century there was almost no public pressure for lack of public indignation: the identifiable philanthropists could not begin to alter a thoroughly unphilanthropic age. Despite the indefatigable, first-hand, physically horrendous investigations of the penologist and reformer John Howard, whose findings were a monumental exposé and indictment of prison life and prison administration, it was comparatively very little the eighteenth century, and very much the nineteenth, that benefited.

The prominence of prison life in eighteenth-century England obviously throws a spotlight on crime. The period was a lawless one, equally notorious for ruffians and robbery and for violence and murder. Those who carried out the law were themselves often lawless: constables, when drunk and even when sober, turned to theft and to arm-twisting blackmail. The more chicken-hearted constables hugged the warmth of beer houses or, when it seemed expedient to make arrests, arrested innocent people. So crowded, foul-smelling, and verminous was home life that the streets were the real home of the poor; and they took over the streets, jeering and menacing, and turning Sundays into "days of riot, excursion and dissipation." For ill-used people, or starving or desperate ones, dark streets were an open invitation to crime. If as the century advanced private philanthropy grew better, the already shocking penal code grew worse. Philanthropy saw a number of great hospitals founded,[5] and thereafter the dispensary movement, which gave poor people medicine and advice, began to make headway. Parliament passed a bill compelling London parishes to send infants into the country to be nursed; paving and drainage in London improved; and there were early attempts at slum clearance. But such humanitarian efforts paled beside the inhuman penal code. In a kind of brutal lethargy Parliament, as the century advanced, had piled new capital offenses on an already vast number of them, so that by 1786 there were 160 felonies "worthy of instant death." The penal code was not only harsh, it was also absurd. When the nineteenth century dawned, it was still a crime punishable by death to steal a horse, to take linen from a bleaching ground, to cut down trees in a garden, or to pick a pocket for more than a shilling. On the other hand, it was only a misdemeanor for a man to attempt his father's life. Again, if seen stealing from a shop, you could be transported, but if you stole without being seen, you could be hanged; stealing fruit already gathered was punishable by death, but to gather fruit and then steal it was only a trespass. England's penal code was so severe that juries, rather than send men to their deaths for trifling offenses, would often acquit them. For the most part, however, jurors were irresponsible: they ate and drank, they got drunk and fell asleep in the jury box and woke up to be talked by fellow jurors into any sort of verdict. Trials, moreover, were kept short to avoid being costly; one day at most was the general custom.

After the middle of the eighteenth century one big change for the better came into the life of the poor: London's gin drinking greatly declined. This was due partly to Government intervention; partly to a rise in the standard of living; and

[5] However, John Howard, who studied hospitals as he had jails, found them unsanitary—there was little ventilation, no end of vermin; washing was considered "weakening"; patients with different diseases would be put in one bed; and the nurses were frequently drunk.

partly, perhaps, to the terrible consequences of the habit, which even a lawless and desperate populace could not but notice.[6] The lawlessness itself, in any case, declined very little. And though R. J. White might speak truth in saying that "there was a peculiar savagery about the violence of the Londoners, as compared with provincial people," this was to some extent of a deceptive nature. For though the London mob was very easily aroused, by some instinctive code it seldom went too far. It might be a rabble, snapping its fingers at constables; it might respond to slogans without quite knowing what they stood for; but if violent, it was seldom stealthy or vicious. This was true of mob action in 1733 against Sir Robert Walpole's excise tax; in 1751, to get back the eleven days which the Government, by reforming the calendar, was cheating them of; in 1753, to refuse rights to the Jews; in 1763 and 1768, for "Wilkes and Liberty."[7] The great exception was the Gordon Riots, when "No Popery" could drive the mob hot and heedless through the City, burning, butchering, pillaging.

The actual criminals were numerous, and the age of crime was swelled by the awareness that if a man was to hang for theft, he had no incentive for foregoing murder. Yet, as Fielding put it, "The sufferings of the Poor are indeed less observed than their misdeeds"; and, as he went on to point out, though they "beg and steal and rob among their betters," they also "starve and freeze and rot among themselves." There would be reforms of sorts and philanthropists seeking to relieve a life that was indeed "mean, nasty, brutish and short"; but the reforms were not extensive, and though the philanthropies might be, they had

[6] The Gin Act in 1751, which both imposed a heavy duty on gin and required a license for selling it, considerably cramped the income of Wilkes's distiller father and largely explains Wilkes's not being helped by his father when he stood in need of money.

[7] There were also riots by arrogant and misbehaving footmen when they were shut out of the theaters, by soldiers who detested their "Hanover" shirts, by workmen against the threat of cheap Irish labor, in addition to High Church riots and other-than-Wilkes election ones.

oftenest the utilitarian motive of "teaching the duty of obedience to [one's] social superiors"—all this prompting Steven Watson to say that "at the end of George III's reign [1820] . . . the situation was not perceptibly better than in 1760."

2

___

THE KING'S BENCH PRISON belied its name and had for Wilkes most of the attributes of a gentleman's residence. Except that he was confined to the prison, he could do virtually anything that he wished. He lived in a building known as the State House, which boasted twelve "apartments de luxe" for the use of what might be called gentlemen prisoners, his being "a most spacious and pleasing apartment" which overlooked St. George's Fields. The prison was described as "a neat little regular town": there were, along what was known as King Street, rows of shops and stalls; there was a coffeehouse to read the newspaper and smoke a pipe in, and a well-patronized tavern. This last no doubt served both a King's Bench Wine Club and a King's Bench Beer Club. And there were in addition, should they enhance enjoyment, a tennis court, a fives court, and a bowling alley. Wilkes could see any visitors he wished to see and could write as he chose to the public press. Perhaps no one has been less forgotten or been more popular while in prison than Wilkes; indeed, his presence there became more or less the social event of the season. John Almon tells us that he "visited Mr. Wilkes every Sunday morning, during the whole time of his confinement.[1] Temple came now and then, very approving of Wilkes's "dutiful submission to the law, and wise and humane discour-

___

[1] During his confinement, it might be said, Wilkes in November 1768 petitioned the King for clemency but received none, in March 1769 became a

agement of all tumult." Polly came often, sometimes with Wilkes's mother; and from a note he sent to Polly, changing the hour of their visit, we have a hint of how eclectic was his social life: for, says the note, "the beef-steak gentlemen and lord Abingdon are to dine with me, and I believe will stay the afternoon, which will be too numerous a company of *he* creatures for you." Moreover, Wilkes's friends and admirers, whether lordly or lowly, made him a tremendous receiver of succulent goods. From "twenty dozen of wine" at the very outset to a "patriotic leg of pork" a year later, gifts never stopped pouring in—cheese, fish, turkeys, smoked tongues, a brace of fat bucks, a butt of ale from Yorkshire, salmon from Plymouth and Newcastle, baskets of game, hampers of wine, and an assortment of gifts which, said an accompanying note, weighed forty-five pounds. There were also expensive presents—massive silver cups, handsome aldermen's gowns; and from America live turtles and forty-five hogsheads of tobacco—this last large emblematic gift in sympathetic colonial protest against George III. Before Wilkes was a year in prison a newspaper calculated that he had received £2,000 worth of presents. He is also said to have received £100 from the Duchess of Queensberry and another £100 from Lady Elizabeth Germain.

All this, however, by no means exhausted the testimonials Wilkes was given. On his birthday in October he received a somewhat unusual gift from a large number of followers, who "went in a body through the principal streets, breaking windows." Hundreds of people sang "God save great Wilkes our King"; "Wilkes and Liberty!" was roared at George III at the theater and the races; and at a society masquerade, a "Wilkes" appeared, squint and all. A fellow prisoner called Black Bess managed to collect £100 and to toss them at his feet, saying, "If Squire Wilkes wants money, by God he shall have my all." Another fellow prisoner, Lucy Cooper, though empty of purse,

---

Freemason in the prison, and in November 1769 won £4,000 in damages from Lord Halifax.

wished to give her all by sharing her prison quarters with him. Wilkes had any number of women visitors, some from society, some from the streets, some from his past—all of them sympathetic and a great many of them at his service. One of these was Mrs. Barnard, the wife of a Wilkite alderman, who before her marriage had been Wilkes's mistress and at the prison became it once again. She wrote him bubbly letters, now to arrange for a rendezvous, now to tell of encountering Lord Sandwich at Christie's: "He saw I despised him . . . I spoke particularly in your praise, said . . . that if your mind was defiled it was owing to Lord Sandwich, that I was sure you were good at *heart,* as would be seen by your future *conduct.* Perhaps this was going a little too far, for to tell you the truth I doubt you a little in the Primrose Path, indeed I would not have you quit it *yet.*" She can be delicately ribald: "A few words to Little Squib . . . Pray inform him that he has acquitted himself so well, he may be assured of being put into commission the first opportunity. Adieu my sweet fellow."

But a Miss Mary Otto was no such creature. "Feeling . . . as I do," she wrote to Wilkes, presumably in answer to a letter of his, "would it be consistent for me to visit you in the manner you desire? Surely not. Don't, from this, suppose our being alone would induce you to take, or me to suffer, any improper liberties." When she next writes, she is "disappointed in your yesterday's letter. I can't suppose your strong hints have no meaning." With this the correspondence had very likely terminated. On the other hand, demonstrations on the part of the populace continued: to give just one instance, when George Cooke—who had been elected for Middlesex with Wilkes—died, the defeated Sir William Beauchamp Procter stood as Cooke's successor against Wilkes's stanch Serjeant Glynn. The election produced violent disturbances, including the death of a young Wilkite lawyer; but this time it was not Wilkes sympathizers who proved disturbing. "The mob," wrote Walpole, "seems to have been hired by Sir William Beauchamp Procter for defense,

but by folly or mismanagement proved the sole aggressors."
Glynn won easily.

Glynn was one of Wilkes's stream of men visitors at the
prison; others were highborn supporters, City men of wealth,
lawyers and men of affairs with whom Wilkes might have political discussions concerning his plans and his uncertain future.
George III was insisting to his Prime Minister, the Duke of
Grafton, that Wilkes must be expelled from Parliament. Grafton, however, saw no possible wisdom in this and with Lord
Temple's consent privately proposed to Wilkes by messenger
that if he would stop agitating and stop informing the public
of the illegal treatment he had been shown, the Government
would not oppose his being seated in the Commons. But Wilkes,
who had already announced that he would protest the illegality,
refused Grafton's proposal on the ground that he had pledged
himself to the public to do otherwise. His refusal lost him most
of what remained of Temple's friendship and support—if only,
no doubt, from flouting Temple's wishes.

And indeed Wilkes did not intend to let up on the Government concerning its wrongdoings toward him: both personally
and politically he stood to gain by keeping them alive. He also
had advocates: thus on January 2, 1769, he was elected alderman—which meant also a magistrate—for Farringdon Without,
one of the two largest of the City's wards[2]—and on January 10

[2] From a Farringdon election poem (Wilkes speaking from jail, and probably
not the author):

> Your late worthy Alderman now being dead
> I beg to solicit your votes in his stead;
> I have always stood up in defense of our laws
> And would lay down my life for Liberty's cause.
> To the King and his family I have always been true
> And behaved as a dutiful subject should do.
> Religion, indeed, I'll say little about it;
> I find I can always do better without it.

. . .

> Like a bird in a cage I'm now confined here
> But have plenty of turtle and other good cheer
> For which I'm obliged to good friends in the City
> Who look on my sufferings (God bless them) with pity.

a half dozen of his Farringdon supporters dined with him at the King's Bench prison. Through a technicality, the City aldermen who sided with the Government got the Farringdon election declared void, only for Wilkes some three weeks later to be re-elected without opposition.[3] The Government aldermen strove further to keep him out of office, which they doubtless thought they did so long as he was stuck away in prison; but when, by the time of his release from prison, he appeared at the court of aldermen, they either cared not or dared not oppose him and peaceably let him in. At the urging of John Horne, affluent and influential advocates of Wilkes founded the Society of the Supporters of the Bill of Rights, an organization that would help pay Wilkes's political expenses and pay off his debts. An appeal was made for Wilkes as having "suffered very greatly in his private fortune for the severe and repeated persecutions he had undergone on behalf of the public." There was a decided response, prosperous London merchants being particularly generous, and the Assembly of South Carolina voted, through bills of exchange, £1,500 sterling. Indeed, inside a year of its founding, the society had paid off £20,000 of Wilkes's debts—he was also granted a £1,000 annuity—and it had set about promoting a more ambitious objective, the protection and enlargement of "the legal, constitutional object of the subject."[4]

The scene, very soon after Wilkes's election as an alderman

[3] When supporters, for fear of resulting violence, had asked Wilkes not to stand again and he refused them, they said they would have to take the sense of the ward. He agreed, adding that he would take the nonsense and beat them ten to one.

[4] Wilkes's debts were calculated as at least £30,000, much of it the result of extravagance, such as owing £1,000 to Paris jewelers. Some "debts" passed beyond extravagance: it became known that Wilkes, as a trustee of the Aylesbury Foundling Hospital, had, after his duel with Martin, taken to the Continent, and never repaid almost £1,000 of the hospital's money and had also used £800 belonging to the Buckinghamshire militia. Wilkes claimed that Humphrey Cotes had been entrusted with these matters and that the money had been lost when Cotes went bankrupt. Horace Bleackley comments soundly that, though not "wilfully dishonest," Wilkes, besides being notably nonchalant about money matters, felt he was "entitled to live at the public expense" in return for the services he rendered the people.

and the founding of the Supporters of the Bill of Rights, moved to the House of Commons. At the opening of the new session— in part with the hope of rallying the Opposition—Wilkes, from prison, had petitioned the House to consider the whole matter of how he had been treated and to grant him redress; and as he was a Member of Parliament his petition could not be passed over. But the House, in considering it, put so many restrictions on the hearing that Wilkes's counsel could get nowhere and the petition was rejected. Walpole described the situation as "a fair trial between faction and corruption; of two such common whores the richest will carry it." The House, having thrown out the petition, proceeded at once to throw out the petitioner. Constantly prodded by George III, who regarded Wilkes's expulsion as "a measure whereon my Crown almost depends," the Administration set to work toward satisfying their monarch. Their particular basis for expelling Wilkes was, now in February 1769, that he had written and printed a newspaper attack on the Administration's misconduct in the matter of Lord Weymouth's instructions to magistrates in advance of the St. George's Fields massacre. On appearing in the House, Wilkes spoke out on the subject, acknowledging that he had printed Weymouth's letter with prefatory remarks of his own,[5] and he added: "Whenever a Secretary of State shall dare to write so bloody a scroll I will through life dare to write such prefatory remarks . . . I ask pardon that I made use of too mild and gentle expressions when I mentioned so wicked, so inhuman, so cowardly a massacre as that in St. George's Fields on the tenth of May."

He then offered, whenever the House should appoint a day,

[5] "I send you," Wilkes wrote anonymously to the St. James Chronicle, "the following authentic state paper, the date of which, prior by more than three weeks to the fatal 10th of May, shows how long the horrid massacre in St. George's Fields had been planned and determined upon before it was carried into execution, and how long a hellish project can be brooded over by some internal spirits without one moment's remorse."

to prove the truth of all he had said, including the statement that a magistrate named Ponton had received Weymouth's improper original letter. But when the statement bore this out, the House refused to go into the matter; instead, Wilkes was put under fire for publishing the leaflet, and for publishing the *No. 45* and the *Essay on Woman* as well. Thus two things for which he had already been punished were designed to punish him more, and on a political basis. As a result, the Government had three parliamentary groups from which to gain a majority against Wilkes, for, as R. W. Postgate remarks, "it was calculated that members who would not vote to expel him because he had libeled the Government might yet do so because he had libeled the King, and those who resisted both arguments might reject him as an obscene writer." The motion to expel him, moved by Lord Barrington, read

> That John Wilkes Esquire—a member of this House, who hath . . . confessed himself to be the author and publisher of what the House has resolved to be an insolent, scandalous and malicious libel; and who has been convicted . . . of having printed and published a seditious libel; and three obscene and impious libels, and . . . has been sentenced to undergo twenty-two months imprisonment and is now in execution of the said judgment—be expelled this House.

"At three on Saturday morning," wrote Walpole, "after four days of such fatigue and long sittings as never were known together, the House expelled Wilkes by a vote of 219 to 137."[6] Scotland and Wales provided more than half of the 219; and George III collected the names of those "whose vote was unsatisfactory," intending to "intimidate them by being very rude" at the

[6] The great William Blackstone wrote for the ministry that Wilkes's expulsion constituted an incapacity disqualifying him for re-election. But the first edition of Blackstone's famous *Commentaries*, giving nine reasons for disqualifications, did not name expulsion as one of them, which led him to revise what he had stated. Thereafter a popular Opposition toast was *"The first edition* of Dr. Blackstone's *Commentaries!"*

next royal Drawing Room. There had been considerable opposition, from Edmund Burke and from George Grenville[7] among others, with "many who were reckoned Tories" against expulsion; and—though Walpole found Wilkes quite unimpressive and likelier to be crushed in the House of Commons than "anywhere else"—he stressed how little the Government had gained and how extremely much it must pay for it:

> [Wilkes] stands again for Middlesex, to be again expelled; yet nobody dares oppose him . . . Still, there are people so wild and blind, as not to see that every triumph against him is followed by mortification and disgrace . . . As worthless a fellow as Wilkes is, the rigours exercised toward him have raised a spirit that will require still wiser heads to allay.

And indeed Wilkes's defeat was one more victory. There were riots in Drury Lane; in the City there was increased enthusiasm, not least from the immensely wealthy Alderman William Beckford; and two thousand Middlesex freeholders, including men of marked influence, immediately made Wilkes a candidate for re-election. Wilkes, in a handbill, had urged his constituents to assert their right "of naming their own representative" by re-electing him. "If ministers," he wrote, "can once usurp the power of declaring who *shall not* be your representative, the next step is very easy . . . It is that of telling you who [*sic*] you *shall* send to Parliament; and then the boasted Constitution of England will be entirely turned up by the roots." The election, held less than two weeks after Wilkes's expulsion, was unopposed and ended in what were by now the largely stand-

[7] But Grenville, on Wilkes himself, was unfriendly enough to provoke from Wilkes a vituperative reply. Denouncing Grenville as "mean and despotic," Wilkes went on to write, apropos the Grenville connection: "It is time, sir, to put an end to your silly peevish bickerings and uninteresting family disputes. The public has laughed long enough at your girlish quarrels and now expects Lord Temple to take the lead." Temple, however, was much put out when shown the letter and told Wilkes not to send it to Grenville, let alone publish it. When he did, Temple terminated their relationship; they never spoke to each other again.

ardized celebrations and processions throughout London. Not
the least festive celebration was in the King's Bench prison
where Wilkes gave a dinner "in his apartments" to some of his
supporters; the *pièce de resistance* was a "fine large swan." There
was no end of music; there were, sounding their own music,
gentlemen on horseback who rode by Wilkes's window to congratulate him; and at night the prison was lighted up, the occasion ending "with the utmost joy and festivity." Next day the
House of Commons once again threw out Wilkes, with the added
declaration that he was "incapable of being elected a member."
It was even argued that to vote for an "incapable" member put
one in contempt, this making it possible for every Wilkite in
Middlesex to be sent to Newgate. Dr. Johnson contributed,
in support of the Government, a tract called *The False Alarm,* in
which he maintained that the House had an inherent right to
exclude a member permanently, for otherwise anyone expelled
could at any time be reinstated. This was rebutted by asserting
that the House of Commons attempted in a resolution what
could only go into effect as a law, which required the vote of
both Houses. (In this case, as a matter of fact, a law could
have been easily enacted.) At bottom, of course, Wilkes wasn't
being molested and incapacitated by a largely bought Parliament because of his bold talk and defective morals, but because
of the King's great hostility to him; and the hostility was clearly
based on Wilkes's being an obstruction to the King's desire to
determine the political life of Great Britain—to do a great deal
more than just reign. A month later Wilkes was once again
elected, unopposed—a Government candidate withdrew for lack
of finding anyone to nominate him; and on the very next day
Wilkes was rejected by the House of Commons. "But," wrote
Walpole, "lest the county should complain of not being represented, another writ is issued; the Court is to set up somebody,
and a new egg is laid for riots and clamours."

And indeed it was. The three times that Wilkes had, thus

far, been elected were triumphant occasions for his supporters; and the resolutions in Parliament that denied him membership had been incentives for gaudily renominating and re-electing him. If he could not be seated, no more could he be stopped—or even, it would seem, opposed; and with each expulsion his cause gained force and friends. But now, with another election looming which would repeat the previous ones, the Government felt the need to oppose Wilkes in Middlesex rather than—or at any rate in advance of—expelling him in Parliament. Hence it set about finding a suitable opponent. After what might be supposed a substantial canvass of possible candidates, the Administration produced Henry Lawes Luttrell, a twenty-six-year-old army colonel who was also a Member of Parliament, representing the pocket borough of Bosinney, which seat—no doubt because of Government pressure or Government promises—he now resigned. For standing against Wilkes he received "a life insurance at Lloyd's." The two candidates were said to be on very bad personal terms; and Luttrell, like Wilkes but even more, had a reputation for profligate living. He also, but less like Wilkes, was blustering and boastful; was notorious for not paying his women and for having seduced an extremely young girl (his bribed witnesses testified that she was a prostitute). Though he later had something of a military career along with a parliamentary one and, at the death of his father, became Lord Irnham and later Earl of Carhampton, he seems to have had the worst of reputations. His father so much loved him as to challenge him to a duel, which Luttrell refused on the ground that his father was not a gentleman. Before the election, bets were made on Luttrell's life, and for months after it he "did not dare to appear in the streets, and scarce quit his lodging." (Some thirty years later two men were executed for conspiring to assassinate him.) Two other candidates turned up for the election, a Serjeant Whitaker who, it seems, hoped with his "mild Whig" views to profit from opposing two extremists; and a Captain Roche. Once a bodyguard of Wilkes's and as boastful, blustering, and un-popular as Luttrell, Roche was conceivably nominated—to win votes away from Luttrell—by the Wilkites.

At 11 A.M. on April 13, 1769, the polls were opened at Brentford with the Government taking every sort of precaution to prevent or curb disturbances, and with constables, jus-tices and soldiers given specific assignments. Long before elec-tion day Wilkites had menaced loyalists, and their new slogan, "Wilkes and no King," had reverberated throughout London. But what few disturbances there were on election day were minor as well. In the main Wilkes's supporters paraded the London streets, "riding in hundreds past the clubs in St. James's Street," bands playing and colors flying, before they set out for the polls, en route to which all the pubs sold beer cheap "in honor of Mr. Wilkes." Wilkes himself was understandably de-tained elsewhere, and none of the other three candidates made the slightest splash. Indeed, Serjeant Whitaker—owing, it seems, to legal business in Westminster—never turned up at Brent-ford, and Captain Roche had taken leave of it by noon. Luttrell, on his way to the polls, had objects thrown at him and his hat knocked off; and only reached the hustings, surrounded as he was by a hostile mob, because John Horne, Alderman Beckford, and James Townsend, who had been Wilkes's nominators, acted as Luttrell's bodyguard. The polls closed at 3:30 P.M., and the results of the voting were Wilkes 1,143, Luttrell 296, Whitaker 5, and Roche 0. Illuminations followed while church bells rang; and, "attended by several thousand people," a number of horse-men went to the King's Bench to congratulate Wilkes on his success. For the voters, as the *Middlesex Journal* reported, it was a particular success: Wilkes's own close friends had refrained from voting "so that the election was the free and genuine desire of the people," and his election strengthened the voters' cause as well as the victor's.

The next day, however, the House of Commons, in its by

now monotonous fashion, declared Wilkes's election null and void. And the day after, George Onslow, once friendly toward Wilkes but latterly a hostile opponent, moved that Luttrell be seated in place of him. (Actually, Wilkes could not have been seated in the same parliamentary session that voted his expulsion; but seating Luttrell was quite something else.) There was considerable debating—with "the Lobby full of dirty people"— which ended in a vote of 197 to 143 "that Henry Lawes Luttrell, Esq. ought to have been returned a member for Middlesex, and not John Wilkes Esq."[8] Onslow's argument was that any votes for an incapacitated Wilkes must be thrown out, and the candidate with the next largest number of votes must be judged elected. With such an argument George III was far from finding fault and wrote to thank Lord North, who had managed matters, for his "spirit and good conduct."

The Middlesex elections involved two crucial issues: whether the House of Commons, by expelling a member, could disqualify him for re-election during the same sitting of Parliament or could elect, against the will of the electors, someone else in his place. The second of these was much the more important issue, since it deprived freeholders of the right to choose their representatives in Parliament: on such a basis the House, by

[8] A very young Member of Parliament, Charles James Fox, voted for Luttrell with rather eloquent words that he might later wish to eat: "I shall adore Colonel Luttrell to the last day of my life for his noble action; and I will not take the will of the people from a few demagogues, any more than I will take the word of God from a few priests."

"To reject Wilkes and accept Luttrell," wrote Walpole, ". . . will probably make the country quite mad. In short [the Government] have done nothing but flounder from one blunder into another . . . Instead of annihilating Wilkes by buying or neglecting him, his enemies have pushed the Court on a series of measures that have made him excessively important; and now every step they take must serve to increase his fiction, and make themselves unpopular."

And the trenchant, anonymous Junius wrote in one of his printed articles to Grafton: "If such a case can happen once, it can happen frequently; it may happen always; and if three hundred voters can prevail against twelve hundred, the same reasoning would equally have given Mr. Luttrell his seat with ten votes, or with one."

rejecting a winner and "electing" a loser, itself became the electorate. In this particular case the ministry, or one might say the
King, became just that; and if such a procedure prevailed, the
Administration, by always being able to outvote the Opposition,
could ultimately eliminate it. Over this issue the expulsion of
Wilkes and the seating of Luttrell became an object lesson,
and as such—whatever Wilkes's personal faults—it constituted a
charge to support him *politically*, which all enlightened men of
law and politics did, as did great numbers of the poor, the
hard-working, and the ill-educated. Few of these last, to be sure,
had the qualifications to vote; but it was the agitation over
Wilkes, as something of an eye-opener to the multitude, that
became something of a gate-opener for many of its desires and
demands. From this time on, the reform of Parliament and the
extension of the suffrage became vital issues, calling for vigorous
action.

On the very day that George III wrote to North, he was made
uneasy by the protest meetings of Middlesex freeholders and
asked that records be kept of all pro-Wilkite resolutions that
were passed, as well as the names of those "most active in fram-
ing them." The next day a meeting attended by perhaps 2,500
people, with 5,000 more gathered outside, saw carried a resolution, proposed by John Horne, that a committee of 100 draw
up a "bill of grievances and apprehensions" to submit to Parliament. There were constant demonstrations and when, five days
after Luttrell was declared elected, Wilkes—on a matter involving the surrender of bail—went from prison to Lord Mansfield's
chambers, he was cheered by the crowd, who replaced the horses
in drawing his coach; and he was once again forced to hide in a
tavern and get hold of a different coach to sneak off in. Soon
after, the bill of grievances and apprehensions, which had become unwieldy in length, was discarded in favor of a petition
to Parliament; but the petition, subsequently drafted by Lord
Rockingham after consultation with Edmund Burke, emerged

as simply a protest against seating Luttrell in Wilkes's place. When it was presented to the House of Commons, the matter was deferred for ten days. Then on May 8 Wilkes's ineligibility was adjudged legal and unquestionable—for one reason, Wilkes's being in prison when nominated—and by a vote of 221 to 152 Luttrell was declared "duly elected" and formally seated. Inside Parliament as well as out, there was decided opposition, with one M.P. refusing to pay his land tax since Middlesex was illegally represented; and with Burke describing this final rejection of Wilkes's rights as "the fifth act of a tragi-comedy—a tragi-comedy acted by His Majesty's servants, at the desire of several persons of quality, for the benefit of Mr. Wilkes and at the expense of the Constitution."[9]

What happened of real and particular importance was that Wilkes's sympathizers and the Administration's antagonists acted much less like irresponsible mobs who rioted than like purposeful men who joined hands—boisterously on occasion—at public meetings. The meetings might be held to nominate or elect people, or to draw up or pass resolutions, or to sign petitions. A further difference was that where almost all the demonstrations for Wilkes had taken place in or near London, the meetings and petitionings took place in many parts of the country—as far north as Liverpool and Newcastle and in such distant and diversified counties as Cornwall and Yorkshire, Somerset and Durham, Norfolk and Gloucestershire. The King, in seeking counterpetitions and loyal addresses—his best source was Scot-

[9] All this not only menaced Wilkes's rights, but led Opposition groups in Parliament, as Carl B. Cone says in *The English Jacobins*, "to protest vehemently against the threat to the independence of the House of Commons and to warn against the influence of the Crown." The most famous protest touching on this was Burke's famous pamphlet *Thoughts on the Causes of the Present Discontents*. Wilkes set going much petitioning and protesting beyond what was done for him: thus, freeholders of Surrey bespoke the right of free election; freeholders of Middlesex petitioned the King to dismiss the ministry; and citizens of London petitioned the King to dissolve Parliament. "The more dramatic and in the long run the more significant outgrowth of the Middlesex election controversy," says Mr. Cone, "was organized urban radicalism."

land—would seem to have done himself more harm than good, since this caused a great many silent opponents to become vocal and also to sign anti-Administration petitions. In any case, the Wilkite forces were far in the lead, with as many (for those days) as 60,000 signers of petitions asking the King to alter the conduct of the Government. Alter!—the King did not even answer: when Parliament next opened, he spoke about the diseases of horned cattle. The Government retorted on the 60,000 petitioners with the explanation, as set down in the *Annual Register*, that "the majority of gentlemen of large fortunes, of justices of the peace, and of the clergy . . . had not signed the petitions . . . the inferior freeholders were not capable of understanding what they signed," and that farmers and weavers were only drawn into the matter through "seditious and factious men": even should they have signed petitions without such pressure, they were a mere "ignorant multitude, incapable of judging."

Actually, though a very great part of Wilkes's support came from workingmen, and workingmen on strike, and men out of work, a great part of it came also—and very particularly in London—from the middle class—from well-behaved artisans and shopkeepers and from City men of some prominence and affluence, who stood as firm as the immensely rich Alderman Beckford. (Wilkes also gained many merchant-class adherents by his insisting—on occasions when the mob might have rioted—on law and order.) Wilkes had also among his supporters professional men of education and intellect; and he had, as with "Parson" Horne, the support of men with "radical"[10] sympathies. In addition, with the King and his largely bought Government becoming, in thought and action, more outrageous, and unconstitutional, and laws-unto-themselves, Wilkes won over, at least

[10] The word "radical" at just about this time first appeared as a political adjective. It would not become a noun for a generation or more, and it meant, to a great extent, reformist.

politically, a great many men in law and politics. Burke, squeezing himself into a huge packed City election-and-petition meeting at the Guildhall, records that "on the question for the petition there was not [despite anti-Wilkites present] a single hand against it . . . It was carried with all possible triumph and exultation."

After serving all but the last day of his sentence, Wilkes, on April 17, 1770, was released from prison. The occasion seems to have been one of mannerly rejoicing, with no sign of anything boisterous; the fact that it rained may have helped. There were banquets in Bristol; in London, Alderman Beckford's mansion was decorated with the word LIBERTY spelled out in letters three feet high; the Duke of Portland's mansion was ablaze with light; many parties of forty-five celebrators were given; and overseas in Boston the "illustrious martyr to Liberty" was toasted at a public dinner. Prison had done Wilkes's health no harm, though it had been no friend of his waistline, for he had exercised too little and eaten too much, and there were remarks that his appearance quite befitted a City alderman. A further cause of his popularity in the King's Bench was his giving a great proportion of the gifts he received to his fellow prisoners. On the day following his release, this greatest-of-party-giving prisoners published an address to the Middlesex freeholders, stressing his "sufferings of the last two years" and "the many tedious months of his long confinement." He now rented a house at 7 Prince's Court, Great George Street, which he had decorated—the parlor, said Henry Angelo, was "hung with Hogarth prints"—and which was very near Parliament; but it soon appeared that his chances of being seated there were decidedly remote. A good many remonstrances to the Crown had come on the heels of the petitions, but won little response; and in the House of Lords, Chatham—who had taken the enlightened side about the seating of Luttrell—introduced a bill "for reversing the adjudications of the House of Commons, whereby John Wilkes

Esq. has been judged incapable of being elected a member to serve in the present Parliament." In Wilkes's opinion this was one of Chatham's great speeches. On the matter of Wilkes's 1,143 votes against Luttrell's 296, Chatham asked, "What do the House of Commons?" and answered: "Why, they shut the door in [Wilkes's] face and, by a new state-arithmetic, make 296 a greater number than 1,143. Is not this, my lords, flying in the face of all law and freedom?" But Chatham's bill was rejected by a majority of 46. He had said earlier that he looked on Wilkes "merely and indifferently as an English subject, possessed of certain rights which the laws alone can take from him . . . In his person, though he were the worst of men . . . God forbid, my lords, that there should be a power in this country of measuring the civil rights of a subject by his moral character." And, with a foretaste of Lord Acton, Pitt added: "Unlimited power is apt to corrupt the minds of those who possess it." And the upright Sir George Savile, who had risen in the Commons to call the vote expelling Wilkes "the offspring of corruption," when asked next day by Lord North if he hadn't spoken with too much heat, answered with superb straightforwardness: "No, I spoke what I thought last night, and think the same thing this morning. Honourable members have betrayed their trust. I will add no epithets; because epithets only weaken. I will not say they have betrayed their country corruptly, flagitiously, and scandalously; but I do say that they have betrayed their country, and I stand here to receive the punishment for having said so."

Getting nowhere with Parliament, Wilkes, as already a City alderman, set about gaining strength and support in City politics. The City was governed by a common council of rather more than two hundred members, these elected by the livery companies[11] within the City's twenty-six wards, and by a court

---

[11] Whole guild companies entitled to dress in a special way, spoken of collectively as "the livery."

of aldermen representing the wards. The common council members were largely middle-class businessmen—merchants, craftsmen, wholesalers; but among the court of aldermen could be found, if few craftsmen or tradesmen, bankers and future bankers, a governor of the Hudson's Bay Company, and gentlemen of leisure. (Wilkes, sworn in as an alderman "without any opposition," wrote to Polly in Paris ten days after his release from prison that all the aldermen present "took me by the hand and wished me joy with great *apparent* cordiality.") Sitting higher, as it were, the aldermen could be much more accessible to Government influence than were the common councilmen—a situation already deprecated, before Wilkes's release from prison, by the Opposition Chathamite and Whig forces. By the time of his release, Wilkes himself had made considerable gains (over those made when he was sent to prison) in livery and common council support; and he threw himself at once into a strenuous round of political and social engagements. Within a few months, it appears, he became a strong factor in electing a Lord Mayor, Brass Crosby; he headed, with some success, a group of protests against letting City magistrates issue warrants for impressing men into the Navy; and he advocated control of the price of bread in behalf of the poor.

There now arose, however, a more vital issue which would have historical importance and prove notable in Wilkes's own history. From far back—and specifically since 1728—the House of Commons had forbidden the publication in newspapers of parliamentary debates. Such privilege was based on a conception of needed privacy—"Modest, timid members," declared the Speaker, "would never give us their sentiments if they were liable to be misrepresented [in the papers] and made the subject of ridicule and contempt thereby." R. J. White well puts it that the House "took the view that the electorate had no right to know what their representative said." The prohibition had been flouted on occasion, and in very recent years much more so;

indeed by 1771, when Wilkes took up the cudgels, a dozen or more newspapers were regularly publishing reports of debates, enough for an M.P. to bring up the matter in the Commons and contend that the prohibition should be enforced. But this, rather than intimidating the newspapers, led two of them—the *Middlesex Journal*[12] and the *Gazetteer*—to sneer at the M.P. and go right on publishing. The House of Commons thereupon voted, 90 to 55, to summon the publishers of both papers into its presence. Thompson of the *Gazetteer* came as ordered, but both he and Wheble of the *Middlesex Journal* defied the House thereafter, and when the serjeant at arms ordered their arrest, they went into hiding. At first the Commons and the King showed restraint, but when the serjeant at arms reported that neither printer could be found—each of eight calls in one afternoon at Wheble's office elicited the information that he had just stepped out for an airing—the Treasury offered a £50 reward in a London newspaper for each man's arrest. "It is highly necessary," wrote the King, "that this strange and lawless method of publishing debates in the papers should be put a stop to; but is not the House of Lords . . . the best court to bring such miscreants before? as it can fine as well as imprison."

The printers were not acting alone; they were being encouraged by anti-Administration people in the City, who were now inciting other newspapers to defy the prohibition. John Horne claimed to have persuaded the printers to remain defiant, but Wilkes himself would seem to be one of three men—the two others were Lord Mayor Crosby and Alderman Richard Oliver—who concocted a further plan. When a motion was made in the House ordering six additional printers to appear before it, objections were raised that the prohibition of 1728 was ob-

[12] The *Middlesex Journal* was founded in April 1769, just before Wilkes would for the fourth time be elected to Parliament. It was very partisan and was subtitled "the Chronicle of Liberty." *The North Briton,* incidentally, functioned for "some years" after Wilkes's imprisonment; and *The Monitor,* the other Wilkite organ, survived for two years after the *No. 45* upheaval.

solete and that though the printers' offense might be great, "they had offended no law." The Commons, after voting twenty-three times, adopted the motion at 4:45 A.M., and when one of the six printers, John Miller, refused to appear, the serjeant at arms was ordered to arrest him. Of the five other printers, two were forced to get down on their knees while being admonished.

Matters now quickened. Or rather, a little before this, Wheble of the *Middlesex Journal* was apprehended by one of his own employees who was all too aware of the £50 reward. Brought for judgment before Wilkes, who as a magistrate had sat waiting for him, Wheble went free: he was, ruled the magistrate, a London freeman who had been arrested by neither a constable nor a City peace officer. Wheble's employee, on the other hand, was bound over by Wilkes on a charge of assault and was also served with a paper for having apprehended Wheble so that he could claim the £50. Next, a House of Commons messenger tried to arrest Miller, who resisted him, only for a by-no-means-accidental constable nearby to charge the House messenger with assaulting a City freeman within the City's limits. The constable then brought both Miller and the messenger to the Mansion House, where Wilkes now sat with the Lord Mayor and where Alderman Oliver, the third member of the scheming trio, acted as Miller's counsel. The Lord Mayor soon found that the messenger was not a London constable and ordered him to answer charges at the next session; as for Miller, since the Speaker's warrant for arresting him had not been backed by a City magistrate, the Lord Mayor ruled that the arrest had been illegal.

This manner of turning the tables left the Government rather stumped, but the King and some of his adherents felt that it called for stern measures. "The authority of the House of Commons," wrote George III to Lord North, "is totally annihilated if it is not in an exemplary manner supported tomorrow by instantly committing the Lord Mayor and Alderman Oliver to the Tower." Wilkes, declared the burnt-fingered King, was "below the notice of the House." The House, but only after considerable dissent, ordered the Lord Mayor to present himself. One member called what was happening "a matter that may involve the House, the Kingdom, the King on the Throne and his posterity into distress and difficulties," and Burke contended that "this fresh turn with Wilkes is a fresh disgrace to us, but a fresh service to him." Wilkes and Oliver were also ordered to attend, but Wilkes refused, saying that as M.P. for Middlesex he would appear only in that capacity; which very much relieved both the King and Lord North, who didn't want Wilkes to appear at all.

Hampered by gout and cheered by the crowds, the Lord Mayor on reaching the Commons maintained that had he not acted as he did, he would have broken his oath to uphold the City's character; and he bellowed, while being pelted with insults from Government M.P.s, that so long as he was Lord Mayor he would act no other way. He—as did Wilkes and Oliver—had the City behind him with both thanks and money; and the House now postponed action on the Mayor to pass judgment on Oliver. Oliver, asking what he was charged with, was answered by Charles James Fox that it would depend on what he said in his defense. "I shall make no defense," said Oliver. "I shall say nothing. You may do as you please. I defy you." What the House pleased was to send him to the Tower. The gout-beset Lord Mayor was once more summoned to the Commons while, it was said, fifty thousand people lined the streets and the approaches. First Lord North's chariot, and then his less stately carriage, was broken, with North himself injured and frightened. The King was shouted at—"No Lord Mayor, no King!"; Fox was rolled about in the gutter; Burke wrote, "I am totally at a loss what to do," saying, "The Mob is grown very riotous"; and the Lord Mayor was judged guilty of a breach of privilege. Then, refusing "the custody of the serjeant-at-arms," the Lord Mayor half-drunkenly followed Oliver to the Tower. Chatham, though not in favor of the City's actions, was far less in favor of the Court's—"for they have contrived to be guilty of the rankest *tyranny* in every step taken to assert the right."

The two culprits confined to the Tower were well provided with food and maintenance by the City of London; were visited by dukes, marquesses, earls, admirals, and Edmund Burke; on Tower Hill dummies representing the King's mother and Lord Bute were "beheaded . . . and burned," as, a few days later, were Lord Halifax, Lord Sandwich, and Colonel Luttrell; and when the Lord Mayor and Oliver were released from the Tower, they received a twenty-one-gun salute from the Honourable Artillery Company and an escort of fifty-three carriages. As for those who started the whole thing, both printers went unpunished and were presented with £100 each by the Supporters of the Bill of Rights. As for what they started, the printing of debates in the newspapers—though the House would not yield its right to prohibit them—went on undiminished and unchallenged. The Commons was worse off than ever, and only the employee who "arrested" Wheble suffered: instead of £50 he was given two months in prison.

This was a glowing episode, a victory for the Lord Mayor and Wilkes, for the City and liberty alike. (Sheridan would later conclude a speech with: "Give [the people] a corrupt House of Lords, give them a venal House of Commons, give them a tyrannical prince, give them a truckling Court, and let me have an unfettered press—I will defy them to encroach a hair's breadth upon the liberties of England.") The Commons, so far as effective future action went, was pretty well foiled: it summoned Wilkes, who credited himself with having engineered the whole matter, only for him to repeat that he would not appear except as member for Middlesex; and by now the King had come to realize that Wilkes's nonattendance was much the happier outcome. "Have nothing to do," George III counseled, "with that devil Wilkes";[13] and the House, which had lost face, now tried to save it by ordering Wilkes to appear before it on April 8 [1771], while it cleverly voted to adjourn until April 9. More than ever Wilkes could thank the Commons for increasing his influence. Chatham said that "it was solely to the measures of the Government, equally violent and absurd, that Mr. Wilkes owed all his importance"; that "the King's ministers . . . had made him a person of the greatest consequence in the Kingdom"; and that the Commons' treatment of him "made the very name of Parliament ridiculous." Having been outlawed, expelled, imprisoned, he could now congratulate himself for what in the last few years he had come to stand for and to fight against, and could exult in how high he stood because of this: his protests had done wonders for his ambitions and, as time went on, should do even more.

[13] George III seems to have been bedeviled even by his own small sons, who would open the door of a room he was sitting in and call out, "Wilkes and Number 45 forever!"

3

BUT WILKES STOOD too high to avoid being a target for envious or ambitious men within his own world; had politically too much power not to menace or diminish the power of other men; and had personally so much wit and such good manners as to make his inferiors—a number of them City people—ill at ease and even resentful. Despite his good manners, his witticisms were sometimes insults: when at a City banquet one of the diners replaced his wig with a nightcap and asked Wilkes if it looked well, Wilkes answered: "Oh, very well, but it would look better pulled over your face." Wilkes was also selfish and could be self-promoting: in some ways, though not the most important ones, he was distinctly the senior partner in the firm of Wilkes & Liberty. His position during these years was to some degree anomalous: it had the twofold appeal and the double force of someone who both carried the banner of populist leadership and bore the cross of libertarian martyrdom. His own right to demand, and be awarded, justice had grown into a powerful cause and a mounting crusade; the oftener he was denied a seat in the Commons as representing Middlesex, the more he came to represent a great deal besides Middlesex—nothing less, indeed, than great numbers of people all over England. The more his rights were impugned and his claims disallowed, the more he symbolized something beyond what he personally was, and the more he stood opposed to the most formidable of opponents, the King of England. No wonder the populace adored him, or that men in politics resented him, or that his ambitions walked beside him and sometimes led the way.

Among Opposition politicos the intense antagonism was not, of course, toward Wilkes, but toward the King and his satellites; and even when the Opposition forces contrived a kind of brotherly united front, they far from maintained it—it was a matter of too many cliques spoiling the brotherhood. Chatham's right-hand man, Lord Shelburne—who would bear the nickname, which Wilkes had pinned on him, of Malagrida—and Lord Rockingham, the Whig leader, were differing parts of the Opposition rather than partners. Within the Chathamite, or Patriots, faction there was in the City itself disagreement, and this example of divide-and-not-rule would not exempt Wilkes. Shelburne would naturally want to weaken Wilkes's powerful hold on the City, and some of his allies would join up with him rather than with Wilkes. Furthermore, Wilkes was encountering opposition inside one of his own citadels. By the autumn of 1770 the Bill of Rights Society had been having internal trouble: Robert Morris, known as "Bill of Rights" Morris, resigned as secretary, and a little later James Sawbridge—"the best whist player" and "most dogmatic radical in London"—who had long been a Wilkes supporter, differed openly with him at a great meeting that Wilkes presided over. On the issue of having City M.P.s impeach Lord North, Sawbridge thought an attempt at impeachment quite futile: North would have at his back a strong majority made up of Scots, bishops, and King's men; and John Horne, Wilkes's strongest supporter, took Sawbridge's, which was very much the stronger, side. Indeed Horne, whatever his reasons, had become decidedly antagonistic toward Wilkes and was to serve as an ally of Shelburne's against him. So far as the Society of the Supporters of the Bill of Rights itself went, Wilkes had tended to regard it as the Society for the Supporters of John

Wilkes. Horne and others had envisioned the society—besides straightening out Wilkes's finances and regarding him as a great figure and rallying point—in political terms, not personal ones. Indeed, on the society's own resolution it sought, as we know, the protection and enlargement of "the legal, constitutional liberty of the subject," and indeed its developing policies and activities became models for subsequent radical undertakings and societies. Thus, true to its resolution, the "remnant" of the society called in 1771 for parliamentary candidates to pledge themselves for short sessions and for fairer and more equal "representation of the people." Wilkes saw the society in a different light: when its money was sought to help the man who had printed Wilkes's attacks on the Court and who, for refusing to answer questions or inform on his employers, was given a three-year prison sentence, Wilkes refused to allow such aid, saying that he needed all the money for himself. This, it appears, caused a protesting Horne to leave the society[1] and found a Society for Constitutional Information. It certainly caused Horne to show increased hostility toward Wilkes: Horne now made a public attack on him, anonymously at the outset and damagingly in describing Wilkes's Westminster clash with Sawbridge and in accusing Wilkes of having insulted the Westminster electors. But Horne soon cast off his anonymity: when Wilkes announced that he would stand for sheriff, Horne, in a succession of open letters, brought a number of serious accusations against him. Wilkes, he charged, was jobbing his followers for City posts, which the followers as well as Wilkes futilely denied. Horne further charged that Wilkes was afraid the Supporters of the

[1] Despite the schism, and despite Wilkes's attitude that the Supporters of the Bill of Rights existed for him alone, he became wise enough to admit that he had no claims on it, and the society was loyal enough to pay his debts for many years and to give him his annuity. If, after the break, there were fewer supporters, there were a number of affluent ones; and such Whig grandees as the Duke of Devonshire, the Duke of Portland, and Lord Rockingham annually dropped £100 each into Wilkes's purse.

Bill of Rights would give up being "his creature" in an effort to win "the public confidence." Horne stood against Wilkes at a meeting of the Supporters, losing on the issue before them by twenty-four votes, but gaining a number of wealthy backers for the Society for Constitutional Information. Horne seems to have racked his brain to run Wilkes down: he accused him of embezzling foundling hospital funds, of cheating his moneylender, and of swindling French jewelers. He also said that, on leaving prison, Wilkes took a house at only £50 a year that he might lay out some hundreds on its repairs; at the same time he "took a country house at 60 guineas the season" and sent Polly to Paris "to see the Dauphin's wedding." At this point Wilkes refused to carry on his correspondence with Horne, out of entire indifference "to a thirteenth or a thirtieth letter." The rather comic side of Horne's accusations charged Wilkes with having drunk claret while in prison, with having a staff of six servants (three of them French), and with having pawned some rather splendid clothes he had entrusted Wilkes with in Paris. When Wilkes proved that the clothes were deposited with a Paris banker and emerged unscathed, Horne challenged him to a duel, which Wilkes waggishly refused. "Wilkes," wrote Walpole, "seems destined to confound all his adversaries. He carries the palm triumphantly from Horne, who has proved a very dull fool . . . Wilkes maintains his empire over the mob . . . Wilkes's canvass for Sheriff stands in place of a considerable horse race."

Wilkes's standing for sheriff had against him not only Horne, but James Townsend, the Shelburne forces in the City (with Townsend as leader), and Richard Oliver, whom Wilkes had sought as a running mate.[2] Rockingham expressed a preference: "In regard to the great quarrel now subsisting between Mr.

[2] Oliver, from the Tower, had answered Wilkes: "I am determined not to share the office of Sheriff with you because I really do not think from your own declarations that your political aims are similar to mine." Nor, doubtless, Wilkes's economic aims: Oliver knew he would have to pay Wilkes's campaign expenses along with his own.

Wilkes, and Mr. Horne and Js Townsend &c., I own my partiality is toward Mr. Wilkes . . . If in the end Wilkes get the better, he will be a great power but perhaps not so dangerous as the others would be . . . probably, too, *Wilkes single* in the end would be easier to manage than a whole pandemonium." Rockingham also thought, or hoped, that the clashes would destroy both parties. The election in July 1771 saw Wilkes lead the polling with 2,315 votes and his running mate, a rich merchant named Bull, come second with 2,194; Oliver, running on his own, came last with a mere 245. Burke exulted in Wilkes's victory, calling Shelburne's Patriots "treacherous"—and properly punished for thinking that, having succeeded *with* Wilkes, they could also succeed against him. "Wilkes is another Phoenix," commented Walpole, in the amplest of his ironic encomiums. "Does not there seem to be a fatality attending the Court whenever they meddle with that man? . . . What instance is there of such a demagogue . . . maintaining a war against a King, ministers, courts of law, a whole legislature, and all Scotland, for nine years together? . . . Wilkes, in prison, is chosen member of Parliament and then alderman of London. His colleagues betray him, desert him, expose him, and he becomes sheriff of London. I believe if he was to be hanged, he would be made King of England." And added: "I don't think of Great Britain." In their shifts and turnabouts the Patriots did however, by allying themselves with the Court and the Rockingham forces, succeed in electing a new Lord Mayor, William Nash. Nash ran against two better men—Sawbridge, whom Wilkes would have done well to support but did not, and Brass Crosby, who with Wilkes's help was seeking a second term. Nash's victory, besides delighting the King who judged it a good omen,[3] loosened to a certain extent Wilkes's hold on the City.

[3] The King had need of a good omen, for he was about to have family as well as political troubles. He had already been concerned over his libertine brother,

As sheriff, however, Wilkes with his fellow sheriff Frederick Bull, made strenuous efforts to administer justice and to season it with reformist mercy. Their attempts included ordering bailiffs to treat debtors humanely (they dismissed a bailiff who failed to); abolishing the practice of making prisoners, who during their trial are presumed innocent, appear in chains; and abolishing the sale of places at court and the collection of fees from the public. The sheriffs also toured the jails regularly to see that prisoners were treated properly; they prosecuted and saw put to death an officer who dealt in blackmail and other criminal practices; and at the end of their year of service, when they were thanked by the livery, they made an appeal to the citizens of London which "remained unanswered for forty years." Their appeal asked whether the citizens might not find it expedient "to instruct [their] representatives in Parliament . . . to move for a revision of those laws which inflict capital punishment for many inferior crimes."

At the end of his year as sheriff, Wilkes decided to take the plunge: he would be a candidate for Lord Mayor. He had lost ground in the City, partly from losing some of his most valuable supporters who had in turn allied themselves with his opponents. But his great enemy was still the King who, during this five-man election for Lord Mayor, kept tabs on what was going on by way of Lord North. At first the two Court candidates pulled a good many votes, but eventually Wilkes and James

---

the Duke of Cumberland, whom Lord Grosvenor had named as corespondent in his divorce suit against his wife and from whom Grosvenor won £10,000 in damages. Now George III's sister, married to the "half demented" King of Denmark, was arrested for adultery and sent to prison; Lady Grosvenor's Duke of Cumberland married a sister of Colonel Luttrell; and the King's brother, the Duke of Gloucester, married the illegitimate daughter of Horace Walpole's brother. These fraternal misalliances made the King insist on a Royal Marriage Act, which forbade the sons of a king to marry without the sovereign's consent. Charles Fox defined the act as "[a measure] giving the Princes of the Blood leave to lie with our wives, while forbidding them to marry our daughters." (The King himself had come very close to marrying Fox's nonroyal aunt, Lady Susan Lennox.)

Townsend came out first and second, and in informing the King, North's best, or only, sop was that "there is the greatest reason to believe that many of [Wilkes's] votes are illegal. The strange ragged forces whom he brought up today were such as were never seen at any poll before, except at his own when he stood for Sheriff." This led to a recount of the votes—a mere waste of time since there was no change in the results; but there was a decided change in what followed. Lord Mayors were chosen by the votes of aldermen from the two candidates who stood first and second on the list,[4] but it was virtually automatic for them to elect the man who had the greater number of votes. Wilkes had it—2,301 to Townsend's 2,279; but on this occasion the aldermen chose Townsend, with whom Wilkes was on unfriendly, not to say hostile, terms. An explanation of the aldermen's action is that Richard Oliver, as sheriff and as Townsend's friend, had rounded up a number of anti-Wilkes aldermen to cast a vote before most Wilkite aldermen appeared; but recent research has thrown doubt on this, and in any case Wilkes had lost. Townsend took office on a day that ended with a crowd of three thousand people disturbing the peace in robust Wilkite fashion; riots went on into the small hours, leading to a good many arrests. Subsequently, we are told, Townsend as Lord Mayor fell far short of the office; was called a cheat and a liar, a bootlicker of the Court, a creator of mobs to disturb City processions, a coward whose grammar was bad and a bully whose table manners were worse.[5]

[4] Parties customarily put up two candidates, hoping to gain representation from one or the other.

[5] Townsend also thrashed a six-year-old trespasser on his land, crying "I'll cut you to death!" as he persevered until the boy's "backside was as red as your waistcoat, the weals on it as big as [the boy's mother's] fingers." Soon after Townsend took office, Wilkes put through a City remonstrance to the King supplicating His Majesty, by virtue of his powers, to dissolve "the present Parliament" and remove its "evil counsellors." It became the Lord Mayor's duty to present the remonstrance, which Townsend shuddered at—"he," said Wilkes, "will be undone at St. James's if he presents it, and stoned by the mob if he doesn't." Wilkes stayed away, on a plea, first, of being *non grata* and secondly, that any

Beaten, Wilkes was not one to despair—he dined out, according to his diary, a hundred times during Townsend's year in office—and a year later, in 1773, he stood once again for Lord Mayor. This time he chose as a fellow candidate his old fellow sheriff Frederick Bull, whose loyalty was unquestionable. And this time the contest was against the Shelburne connection only, their nominees being Sawbridge and Oliver. Wilkes and Bull came out far ahead, Wilkes a bit in the lead. When the court of aldermen voted, there were nine votes for each man, whereupon Townsend, who had voted against Wilkes as an alderman, now broke the tie by voting against him as Lord Mayor. Bull became Lord Mayor; and Wilkes, unseated in the City as he had earlier been in the Commons, buried *déjà vu* under *en avant,* making plain that he would continue to stand for Lord Mayor while choosing his running mate, so that should he not win, someone he approved of would.

Accordingly he stood in 1774: this time Sawbridge, who had been somewhat reconciled with Wilkes, refused to stand, eliminating the Shelburne faction; and Wilkes, who again chose Bull as a partner, had only two ineffective Court candidates opposed to him. Again Wilkes and Bull came out far ahead, Wilkes again a little in the lead, and again the aldermen were ready to choose Bull. But at this point an act of common council of the reign of Henry VIII was read to them—an act forbidding the election of the same man for Lord Mayor for two consecutive terms.[6] As a result, for the first time since his troubles began, Wilkes was allowed a major office he had been elected to. In the first flush of victory he said that had the King sent

slightest disturbance would be laid at his door. George III, having heard from Lord North that the remonstrance "exceeds in violence, insolence and falsehood any that have gone before" and that Wilkes drew it up to put Townsend down, took North's advice not to be angered by it and reduced Wilkes's plan of revenge to a mere sniffy royal rejection.

[6] Postgate alone brings up the act of the reign of Henry VIII; other versions just have Wilkes chosen Lord Mayor with three dissenting votes. (Could what they were dissenting against have been the act?)

him when he was in Paris a pardon and a thousand pounds, he would have accepted them, "but I am obliged to him for not having ruined me." And Walpole chimed in on his usual note: "Thus all the power of the Crown, all the malice of the Scots, all the abilities of Lord Mansfield, all the violence of Alderman Townsend . . . all the treachery of his friends, could not demolish him." The City's response outdid all previous celebrations. "The joy of the populace," said the *Gentleman's Magazine*, "was so great that in the struggle for the honour of drawing [Wilkes's coach] to the Mansion House[7] one man lost his life and another was much hurt." There was a traditional Lord Mayor's show of stately barges on the Thames which drew Wilkes's largest crowd. It was succeeded by a great banquet, although "their Royal Highnesses the Dukes of Gloucester and Cumberland, the Lord Chancellor . . . the Secretaries of State and most of the nobility were suddenly *taken ill*" and could not attend. It so happened that Wilkes was really taken ill, thanks to a strenuous long day and the raw November air. He sat, and even danced, the banquet out, but went home—where he remained for a week—a victim of ague. There was rioting too—the very last rioting inspired by Wilkes.

[7] According to H. B. Wheatley (*London Past and Present*), the Lord Mayor has within the City the right of precedence over even the royal family.

THE RISING CLASS

The son of a prosperous distiller, Wilkes was born into a class that would decidedly prosper during the eighteenth century.[1] And though a number of men, Wilkes to a large extent included, might rise to an upper-class level as merchants and bankers, as men in the professions and in politics, class lines for the most part still held. The commercial classes, whose great stronghold was London, stood socially apart but politically exercised great power. They voted, held office, owned property, and so overwhelmingly ruled the City that it was a considerable risk for a politician to ignore, or a statesman to override, their interests. Exemplifying their power at its strongest was that vast creditor of the nation itself, the Bank of England; but at lower levels the smaller shopkeeper and the smaller manufacturer were increasingly conscious of their independence and alive to their opportunities. Though they might look to a higher place, they knew their own and accepted it; but they were not to be pushed about or imposed on, even in their own interests.

London for the most part was a middle-class world run on middle-class standards. In the eighteenth century it was quite as great a port as it was a metropolis: the Thames, for miles,

[1] Gibbon said: "Our most respectable families have not disdained the counting-house or even the shop." Nor, far into the eighteenth century, was being "in trade" derogatory: Lord Fermanagh's nephew, Lord Townshend's brother, and many younger sons of the upper class became merchants and the like, at no cost to their social standing.

was crammed with ships and shipping—a foreigner said "one can scarcely see the water"—and merchants traded as vigorously with the West Indies and American colonies as with the East. These same merchants and traders dominated the City and controlled the most affluent of its ninety-one companies, while the smaller merchants and shopkeepers lived, as well as made their living, in the City. But London was not predominantly a middle-class world simply because of its commercial greatness. Its aristocrats spent much of the time away from London: when summer came with its heat or when the Houses of Parliament were not in session[2] they made off to their real homes, to their country houses. Moreover, when they *were* in London the aristocracy grandly shut themselves in, while the poor, from what mattered most to them, were shut out. It was the people in between who moved constantly around, shopping or sightseeing or on business, who insured the success of the coffeehouses, filled the theaters, built sturdy Nonconformist churches, and stayed winter and summer in London. They had little craving for travel and vaguely disapproved of it; they had rather throng London's places of amusement, save their pennies while their betters squandered their pounds, and go, very many of them, to bed at night in comfortable rooms over their shops. They largely made their livings off one another and in the main had the same politics and something like the same religion.

As the century advanced, however, London itself did not remain the same nor did certain middle-class customs. Physically, the City—often described as having a head too big for its body—changed a great deal. As the actual City became increasingly commercialized and the fashionable world moved west, and farther west—all the way from Covent Garden to Grosvenor Square and beyond—the more wealthy merchants aped the gentry. They moved from living over their shops to houses in new

[2] Even when Parliament was in session many aristocrats made for the country during the long parliamentary weekend, which Sir Robert Walpole had established so that he (and they) could have their fill of fox hunting.

and smarter residential areas, while acquiring a carriage and a footman; and a very few, which is to say the *very* rich, might leave their places of business for seats in Parliament. It was an age of building, both north and south of the Tyburn Road, which itself would soon be called Oxford Street. In 1737 London Bridge was the only completed one, and it was full of three-story houses half leaning over the water. But the houses would soon be removed from it; in 1750 Westminster Bridge would be opened (for some reason, at midnight); in 1757 London Bridge was widened; and in 1769, Blackfriars Bridge was made available to "wheeled traffic." During the 1760s the City's gates were taken down; then or earlier the streets were better paved, and the old contested custom of trying to walk next to the wall (there was less danger of being spattered or pushed into the street) was replaced by "every man keeps to the right." The streets were also better lighted, making less mandatory Dr. Johnson's injunction to "sign your will before you sup from home." The shops with their bow-fronted windows became more and more enticing —though often in the better shop windows not merchandise but a single hat or pair of riding boots appeared, to indicate the special nature of their wares. "The magnificence of the shops," reported a foreigner, "is the most striking thing in London"; and certainly their finely engraved tradesmen's cards could not be more elegant. The shopkeeper was expected to be all things to all customers, and not least to those who merely looked around. A fancy "gold and silver lace" shopkeeper was expected "to speak fluently . . . to entertain the ladies; and to be the master of a handsome bow and cringe"; he should also hand a lady in and out of her coach[3] without being "seized with a palpitation" on seeing "a well turned and much exposed limb." He must remain in good humor even if asked to unfold a hundred bolts of material, must offer to send a two-shilling purchase to

---

[3] Or her sedan chair: upper-class or affluent ladies were carried in comfort and security from one shop to another and followed into the shops by a footman.

the other end of town, and must invite anyone spending several pounds to a cup of chocolate or a glass of wine.[4]

However better paved and lighted, the streets remained unbearably noisy, as they remained unendingly crowded. During the 1780s it was said of the "thronging crowds" that "more people are abroad" at midnight in London than in many continental cities at noon. Indeed, the streets themselves were something for people to set forth to look at, however frightful they might be to listen to. The racket of rumbling carts, the clang of cart bells, the shrill street cries, "the thunder of iron-shod wheels and the clatter of hooves" provided hideous cacophony: to get away from such blare, said the rustic young Wordsworth, was like escaping from an enemy. The streets were also congested with traffic, alive with fights and footballs, and afflicted with pickpockets and wig snatchers. Far more attractive, and quite as popular, was the promenading in the parks. The Mall in St. James's Park was dubbed "the walk of the century," whether for fashionable people who went there to stroll or for cits who went to stare.[5] The cits also went to the sights and places of amusement—to the Tower of London with its wild animals, particularly the lions which became so much the rage as to coin the phrase "to lionize"; to the great fairs, with their booths and sideshows—tightrope walkers, acrobats, merry-andrews, and Indian rope dancers; to the Lord Mayor's show, which in 1774 was John Wilkes's—all parades and pageantry by day, all boisterousness by night; to those great pleasure haunts and "grand seminaries of luxury," Ranelagh and Vauxhall; to the suburbs, among other things to drink

tea on summer afternoons
At Bagnigge Wells with china and gilt spoons,

[4] Among the shopkeeper's merchandise could be the countless mugs, punchbowls, and handkerchiefs containing Wilkes's portrait which were sold, when he was a hero, everywhere.

[5] Not very surprisingly, the parks by the 1760s had acquired a reputation for misbehavior, with letters of protest flooding the newspapers.

and to the pleasure gardens—"of every degree of exclusiveness or promiscuity"—where cits might play at skittles, or a bat-trap-and-ball, or possibly at cricket, and where a dinner could cost as much as eight shillings. There were also such forms of entertainment as "a fight between two women stripped to the waist, each woman holding half a crown in each hand," the first to drop money losing the contest. Cits loved the theaters, where the audience could hiss as well as applaud, and even hiss the King when he appeared, for having put through an unpopular tax.[6] Sundays, despite a German's comment that they were all "cold meat and hymns," were a great day for stepping out—an American found the number of amusements "inconceivable"— and inns and alehouses struggled to give enjoyment to the crowd. Like their betters, cits gambled inordinately and made outlandish bets: one such man gambled his wife away, and another bet was that six old women from Lambeth could drink a gallon of scalding hot tea faster than six old women from Rotherhithe.

For a great part of the century the most prominent of middle-class male social habits was the coffeehouse. In the earlier part, when coffeehouses achieved their peak of popularity, there were three thousand of them and they were at once the most dominant and the most democratic of London institutions. They existed at all levels and catered to all tastes; aristocrats mingled with businessmen and engaged writers in talk; merchants clutched at crumbs of news from politicians; nobodies could gaze at the great and dullards eavesdrop on the brilliant. For a penny, the not very well off could warm their bodies by the fire and their bellies with a "dish of coffee"; there were newspapers to read, and all sorts of gossip. Soon enough particular

[6] Yet many people stayed away from the theater for fear of the danger in going home. The same fear led proprietors of pleasure gardens to hire Foot Guards to escort their patrons home; and in the village of Kensington, bells rang through the night to collect groups to be taken back to central London. The two Fieldings partly succeeded in getting London a police force, but it was not till 1805 that a permanent horse patrol came to exist, and during the Regency, London seems to have been as lawless as under Queen Anne.

coffeehouses became identified with men who had kindred interests—thus, scholars frequented the Grecian, medical men went to Batson's, musicians to the Smyrna, and businessmen to Lloyd's[7] where ship news was brought in and merchandise auctioned off "by the candle"—i.e., an inch of one was lighted when the bidding began, and the last bidder before the wick went out was declared the buyer. Somewhat later in the century a great change had come about: the aristocrats, who had walled themselves in at White's chocolate house proceeded to turn it into a very exclusive club, and other fashionable clubs—Arthur's and The Cocoa Tree, like White's, had been chocolate houses— soon sprang up, leaving the coffeehouse to lesser breeds. To all such, coffeehouses continued to be important. Here businessmen came even before breakfast, sometimes in dressing gown and slippers, to read the news; here came reporters in quest of news; here politics were aired and argued over, and men talked shop. Here, too, young newcomers to London could strike up acquaintances and pick up information; and people of uncertain whereabouts could call for their mail or tell people where they could be found. The coffeehouse differed decidedly from the tavern, to which as time went on it lost ground, being rather a place of convenience than of pleasure and aiming at decorum—gambling was banned, swearing and quarreling were fined, and though liquor as well as coffee was served, taverns were the places for getting drunk. "A tavern," wrote a contemporary, "is a little Sodom," and he lists the types who come there: libertines, "to drink away their brains"; aldermen, "to talk treason and bewail the loss of trade"; gamesters and sober knaves who "walk with drunken fools"; sots and beaux, bullies and spendthrifts.

The social and domestic life of middle-class people differed very much as their purses did: affluent bankers and merchants

[7] At Lloyd's, when it became known for underwriting, a number of speculative insurance policies were made about Wilkes, whether on his being elected M.P. for London, M.P. for Middlesex, or on his "life for one year."

might have incomes of £2,500 a year and might, by providing suitable dowries, marry their daughters into the upper classes; small shopkeepers made do with around £150. Foreigners spoke well of how clean and well kept were the more prosperous middle-class houses, where the family might be commemorated in a conversation piece hanging on the wall. Foreigners objected, however, to the custom of letting the servants they brought along get as drunk as they did; and objected perhaps even more to have to tip their hosts' servants scandalously, even if they had come for just a single meal.[8] (Visitors to London, foreign or English, lived almost always in lodgings—hotels lay in the future, and the coaching inns were boisterous, bibulous, and decidedly ungenteel.) Servants were no less complained of by their employers, for demanding much too high wages, for constantly throwing up their jobs to go elsewhere, and for their insolence and their thieving. "Jemmy Pelham is dead," wrote Walpole, "and has left to his servants what little his servants have left to him." The servant problem, however, was scarcely as pressing as the servants' plight, all too many of whom were badly overworked, badly lodged, and in general not well treated. Middle-class people tended to overeat and to have bad table manners—sticking their knives and forks, for instance, into the food on platters or rinsing their mouths from finger bowls.

Middle-class plumbing was for the most part still primitive—aristocratic Bedford House installed two water closets in 1758, but was infinitely more the exception than the rule; while slops thrown out of an upstairs window was a very common sight. The household's daily routine differed greatly from today's: thus Fanny Burney writes: "We breakfast always at 10 . . . we dine precisely at 2, drink tea about 6—and sup exactly at 9."

[8] At a higher level, a guest leaving a dinner party offered the waiting cook a crown, to be told: "Sir, I do not take silver." "Don't you?" said the guest. "I do not give gold."

Breakfast was not only late (most people were long up, and some people had paid calls, by ten); but breakfast was also lean, consisting of tea with either bread or rolls and butter. Tea was consumed in huge quantities, particularly by women, though Dr. Johnson, among others, was an insatiable tea drinker. Small beer was the usual everyday drink, though earlier in the century the lower-class craze for gin had increased the drinking of hard liquor elsewhere.[9] The Englishman, not least the English merchant, had taken to drinking port and getting gout in order to hold on to the Portuguese and Brazilian markets. Woolens were very much a leading product, with prohibitive duties on foreign cloth; and cotton manufacturing went from a million pounds a year at the beginning of the century to twenty-two million in 1787, this before Whitney's invention of the cotton gin. Many possible projects inspired Britain's energetic technological mind: submarines and horseless carriages; airplanes born partly of the new functioning balloon; a robot who played chess, an electrical cure for St. Vitus's dance, and "a composition for shaving without razor, soap or water." Meanwhile, at the highest level of middle-class finance, there were the great trading companies, the vast trade with the Americas and the Far East, the Royal Stock Exchange, and the Bank of England itself. The bank was founded in the 1690s when England was at war with France—a war the English Government was too strapped to finance. Established simultaneously was the National Debt, from the Government's borrowing large sums at guaranteed interest (though with no promise to repay the principal). A great loan of £1,200,000 was raised, and the bank was incorporated with a prominent merchant at its head and with twenty-four directors. It proved extremely successful "and rendered a service to the public which even exceeded that given to the state." It reduced the

9 Almost no one, which includes the poor, drank water; and it was not till cheap cotton goods were introduced that the poor—who wore leather and woolen clothes for years on end—could have their clothes washed.

The murder of Allen during the "massacre" of St. George's Field.

"Chairing the Member,"

"The City Charters," engraving after a drawing by John Collett.

John Wilkes (second from right) points to Lord North who offers a bribe, while North America bursts into flame.

level of interest, created an acceptable paper currency, kept gold coinage in better condition, made hoarding unnecessary by providing the safe deposit, and improved foreign-exchange operations. Curiously, the terms of the Bank of England's foundation "forbade Parliament to create any other bank," a ban that lasted into the nineteenth century, with even the Bank of England establishing no branches. The bank very well symbolized an eighteenth century whose dominating thoughts, as L. B. Namier put it, were "property, contract, trade and profits."

Perhaps not quite such dominating thoughts, but very serious ones, were those about sickness and medicine. Epidemics with fatal results were so frequent that there were said to be no true third-generation Londoners, the population being maintained by the people who moved to London. The epidemics resulted from fevers with any number of first names: spotted fever, putrid fever, intermittent fever, relapsing fever—and names for what today is typhoid—brain fever and low fever. (Sir D'Arcy Power suggests that some of these fevers have become unknown having died out when better hygienic conditions prevailed.) Though the death toll was greatest among the poor, from their almost never being seen by a doctor, the fevers persisted at higher levels. Yet in the course of the century the plague had become a thing of the past; better hygiene had reduced that other sibling, jail fever; and Jenner, by discovering vaccination, had mastered smallpox, which curiously seems to have been a disease of the well fixed and the upper classes and, during the first half of the century, chiefly a children's disease. During the entire century there was apparently no effective treatment of mental disease. We glimpse this in the haunting—and very representative—last episode of Hogarth's *Rake's Progress:* madmen, generally, were "chained, whipped, starved" by the lowest class of keepers.

There was great improvement in surgery; earlier, the surgeon's barber pole had indicated his inferior status. In a pre-

anesthetic era, the patient undergoing surgery was seldom
drugged, but usually given something like a glass of brandy; and
wasn't bound, though assistants were present to keep hold of him
if need be. Patients reported afterward that the pain was intense
but not insupportable and that though they sweated fiercely,
they did not faint. (Many people died under surgery—indeed,
before being operated on, patients had to post burial money in
case they should die.) It was the famous John Hunter who converted surgery "from a trade into a science," learning much about
the procedures and passing it on to devoted pupils. Apothecaries
acted something like general practitioners, while also selling
their patients medicine. After examining a patient, the apothecary sought out an M.D. at a coffeehouse for advice and written
directions. Except in very serious cases, the physician might
never see the patient; his *visiting* fee was a guinea, or if he went
a distance, two-thirds of a guinea per mile. "Barber-surgeons,"
with no hospital appointments, stood to the surgeon much as the
apothecary to the doctor. There were also countless quacks: one
such, who called himself "Optholmiator Pontifical, Imperial, and
Royal," actually treated a number of monarchs; and an ignorant
woman got £5,000 out of Parliament for her secret for curing
the stone—a mixture, it turned out, of (among other things) soap,
calcimined snails, and eggshells.

Eighteenth-century London saw a tremendous improvement
in communication. Very early in the century came the London
penny post, which made letter writing cheap and deliveries regular and frequent. The first London daily newspaper, the *Cour-
ant*, appeared in 1702; by the 1720s there were three daily, five
weekly, and ten thrice-weekly papers; and by 1773 "53 newspapers circulated in London alone."[10] *The Gentleman's Magazine*, founded in 1731, introduced a form of reading matter that

[10] For a very small sum, newspapers could be rented by the hour, the delivery-
man on his return sounding a horn as he approached the client, who had to
have the paper folded and ready when he knocked on the door.

by mid-century became the fashion and by the end of the century, the rage.[11] Reading in general greatly increased, as would bookshops and circulating libraries; and middle-class education increased also. Shopkeepers' sons and the like, though not sent to the great public schools, had more and more at their disposal the low-tuition London day schools or such famous free schools as Westminster, the Merchant Taylors', Greyfriars, Christ's Hospital,[12] and St. Paul's. The curriculum for boys stressed arithmetic and mathematics, English, French, Latin, Greek and Hebrew, history, geography, and accounting.

The curriculum at schools for girls was often fantastically genteel: pupils were taught, among other things, to japan, or paint on glass, or raise paste, or make waxworks, or make sweetmeats and sauces. There were two other very popular endeavors: penmanship and stenography. However educated, middle-class young men were often not inclined to marry, there being too much temptation elsewhere; and to marry off their girls middle-class fathers had to go to a good deal of trouble and expense, with the marriage settlement often a much greater bone of contention than the young man's bachelor reputation. Weddings, moreover, were seldom fussed about or elaborately celebrated; there was much more ceremony with funerals.[13]

Extending as it did from what today would be called a very affluent upper middle class to a very indigent lower one, this

[11] Apropos of what Wilkes strongly fought for, *The Gentleman's Magazine* in 1736 was the first periodical to reproduce parliamentary speeches, and its publisher was threatened with trial proceedings. He thereafter published what he called "Debates in the Senate of Lilliput" and altered the speakers' names—William Pulteney, for example, became Wingul Pubrub.

[12] Christ's Hospital pupils, however, groaned over their meals: "Sunday, All Saints; Monday, All Souls; Tuesday, All Trenchers; Wednesday, All Bowls; Thursday, Tough Jack; Friday, No better; Saturday, Pease soup with bread [and] butter."

[13] All corpses had to be wrapped in woolen, as a concession to the woolen trade; many deceased tradesmen, we hear from Oliver Goldsmith, were propped up by the undertaker "in a proper place to receive company"; and the fear of being buried alive had so much persisted from the Great Plague of 1666 that bodies were "generally kept for a week or more."

heterogeneous population, with its many inequalities and un-likenesses, yet had a certain character which left a decided stamp on a later England. This was a world of businessmen and their employees who at bottom were neither a very imaginative nor a very emotional people. At the highest level were men of great ambition and ability who rose to wealth and power. But for the most part, businessmen, though eager to exploit their opportunities, were less given to contriving new ones; and though they jealously guarded their rights, they struggled much less to enlarge them. As Wilkes's supporters, a great many of them were insisting on their rights, and their liberties as well, and were setting the City, so to speak, against the State; but there was no liberalistic philosophy or propensity behind this. As a result, they became the backbone and safety valve of England. Most of them would welcome a clearly defined and somewhat walled-in life: as upper-class manners grew suaver, theirs grew more fixed; as upper-class morals grew more pliant, theirs became more strait-laced. Yet from this class would emerge many of the names that in the nineteenth century helped dominate England.

4

WILKES MADE a good Lord Mayor; yet the first occasion that he could exult in came from outside his mayoralty. In 1774 there was a general parliamentary election, with a good many Wilkite candidates, and with Wilkes himself one. All the Wilkites signed a five-point parliamentary program which Bull had set forth the previous year: shorter Parliaments; the exclusion from Parliament of pensioners and placemen; a more equal parliamentary representation of the people; the redress of grievances and securing of popular rights in Great Britain, Ireland, and America; and a refusal, on the parliamentary candidate's part, to take Crown money in any way. Even Oliver signed, saying that his hostility to Wilkes was personal, the result of "pernicious and detestable practices." To the five-point program Wilkes—and Glynn, who also stood—added a sixth: a pledge to seek parliamentary repeal of recent acts affecting the American colonies. In the election George III made strenuous efforts to find candidates of some strength to oppose Wilkes; but on election day at Brentford, no opponent turned up. His election uncontested, he appeared at the House of Commons to claim his seat as member for Middlesex. Lord North "opposed no obstacle" and Wilkes's claim went unchallenged. (Luttrell had shied off, though he forty years later claimed that George III had promised him a seat for life.) Wilkes would now continue to sit as member for Middlesex during the next sixteen years.[1]

As Lord Mayor he would serve for one year only. George Rudé calls Wilkes's mayoralty "as brilliant, as popular and as lavish as that of any of his predecessors," adding at once that Wilkes entertained the Archbishop of Canterbury and other prelates at dinner. This tribute would seem to speak only for the social Lord Mayor, the bon vivant, the hospitable spendthrift, the well-mannered man of the world; and something more will be said of the Lord Mayor in his robes and more stately roles. But it must needs be added that his one-year mayoralty did not lack achievement, and that as Lord Mayor he was a Wilkite as well as a worldling. Within the City he had great power, which could be exercised at the expense of those outside it, even the Houses of Parliament. The Houses, to be sure, had decided reciprocal power: when, four years before, Crosby as Lord Mayor had flouted the wishes of the House of Commons in a murder case, the House retaliated by passing a bill that cost the City £40,000. Yet Wilkes flatly opposed the House of Lords when a City man named Randall was accused of using "disrespectful" language toward their member Lord Lyttleton. When the lords ordered Randall's arrest, obtaining no warrant and arranging no trial, Wilkes sent constables to guard Randall's house and warned Randall to stay inside it. When the lords sent an official emissary with an escort to arrest Randall, the emissary tried several times in vain to enter the house, Wilkes warning him that if he did not stay outside, *he* would be arrested, on a Lord Mayor's warrant, for annoying a citizen. The emissary withdrew, went

[1] In the 1774 election that reinstated him in Parliament, however, Wilkes lost adherents or candidates who would generally vote his way. Thus Crosby was beaten by Oliver, and Edmund Burke, who had thought of standing when Wilkes promised his support, withdrew when Wilkes pulled back. The mere dozen M.P.s who were pledged to support Wilkes he called his "Twelve Apostles."

back to the House of Lords and told his story; and there the matter ended.

But Wilkes did more than maintain the rights and dignity of the City; he worked, as he had done earlier, for the welfare of its citizens. As alderman he had successfully fought profiteering; as sheriff he had successfully fought for prison reform. As Lord Mayor he would drastically reduce the price of bread, punish tradesmen who gave short weight, clear the streets of prostitutes, and strengthen the weakened power of the workers' guilds. On market days he sent the City marshal to Smithfield to prevent "ubiquitous practices," in particular "the barbarous treatment of cattle"; in court matters he established a table of court officers' fees and stopped beadles from holding up warrants indefinitely. What he could not do for the City was police it properly. Bribery abounded and then as now it was the custom for marshals "to receive compliments from those who kept houses of ill fame." But Wilkes remained a great figure in the City—his portrait its figurehead, his name its battle cry, his words its Magna Charta. Where there was agitation over issues, rights, privileges, it might have been said of Wilkes, as earlier of Marlborough, that "he rides in the whirlwind and directs the storm."

But he could also ride in the Lord Mayor's coach and give dinners and banquets, with an elegantly bred Polly, now in her mid-twenties, acting as hostess at the Guildhall;[2] and he could play the leading role in processions, and go on state visits, and receive important visitors. (Oddly, soldiers, who conceivably were among the visitors, could not pass through the City without the Lord Mayor's written permission.) There was also, with

[2] At the 1775 Easter party, we are told that the "food was much warmer than commonly is the case at these great dinners" and that "in the ballroom taste and magnificence prevailed." The Duke of Leinster and the Lady Mayoress (Polly) opened the ball; there were "minuets, cotillons, allemandes and country dances" till three in the morning. Present, along with a number of lords and ladies, were Prince Pallavicini (the "late Pope's nephew") and Mr. Boswell, who, on finding a seat for someone, said, "See what it is to have a Scotchman for your friend at Mr. Wilkes's table."

Wilkes, much informality and rather conspicuous amour. As Lord Mayor he displayed his latest mistress, Marianne Geneviève de Charpillon, whom we shall meet again. Wilkes himself, once "thin as a shotten herring," continued to display "a belly truly aldermanic." And seasoned man of the world though he was, he seems in his social role to have made a decided blunder. Or rather to have repeated one: accused, when sheriff, of being a French agent—perhaps for having in the Chevalier d'Éon a French secret agent for a friend—he defensively forbade serving French wines at official dinners; and he forbade it again on becoming Lord Mayor. The upshot was that guests, including the Archbishop of Canterbury, had to drink heavier wines—sherry and port—and wake up with heavier heads next morning.[3] Yet City men, it appears, preserved Wilkes's custom of sherry and port; and when at length they abandoned the custom, they made matters worse: a twentieth-century wine expert was informed on good authority that the worst claret in the world was that served at the Mansion House.

On ceasing to be Lord Mayor, Wilkes found himself heavily in debt. The office of mayor, like that of a modern ambassador, called for a man of means, for he would have to spend far more than he earned.[4] The spendthrift in Wilkes may in some degree have moderated itself, but his "brilliant" administration was also judged "lavish." In any case, he was "steeped in poverty to the very eyebrows," owing money on all sides; and on all sides he was threatened with arrest.[5] In so tight a fix that he was

[3] In his own house, however, Wilkes is said to have served his guests "excellent claret."

[4] Wilkes's estimated revenue as Lord Mayor came to £3,575, his set expenditures to around £2,760. Had he spent less than £1,000 for entertainment he would have become a byword for stinginess; he in fact spent £5,460 for entertainment and became for some a model of hospitality, for others a synonym for extravagance. Actually, it was not his expenditures that were out of line with those of previous Lord Mayors; it was his income.

[5] Wilkes's financial troubles were hardly helped by his receiving no salary as an M.P.—any remuneration there was for all M.P.s had to come from the con-

"often in want of a guinea" for the merest maintenance, Wilkes
saw a way out when the office of City chamberlain suddenly
fell vacant: it paid very sizably and was close to a sinecure.
Unhappily Wilkes had years earlier sniffed at the office when
it was suggested for him, going so far as to write, "I will never
accept it"; and these five words were now placarded all over
London. The point was also raised that a man frightfully in
debt was scarcely one to deal with the City's finances. All this
induced the Court party to provide their own candidate, an
aging, miserly family man and rapacious man of business named
Benjamin Hopkins. When Wilkes's supporters exploited Hopkins' shortcomings, the Court twisted Hopkins into someone all
sobriety, thrift, and virtuous living. The Court also hit out at
Wilkes with posters reading "No French whores, No French
servants, No French wines," and with such statements, suppos-
edly from Wilkites, as "Foundlings, soldiers, Jews, Parisian Taylors and Jewellers solicit your vote . . . for the immaculate John
Wilkes Esq." Another statement began:

> Your Vote, Poll and Interest are desired
> for John Wilkes, Citizen and Joiner,
> to be Chamberlain
> He having more creditors than any other person.

Hopkins, to Wilkes's angered surprise, was elected. Wilkes continued to contest the office at annual elections, only to be beaten
far worse than the first time—for traditionally, the chamberlain
was never opposed for re-election on any grounds but misconduct.

At about the same time that Wilkes first lost to Hopkins,
he suffered another substantial loss. His former bedmate and
King's Bench prison mate, the wife of Alderman Barnard, driven
by a guilty conscience and an upsetting midnight dream, had

stituencies they represented. Not until 1904 were annual salaries paid in the
House of Commons.

come screaming to her husband—one of the wealthiest and loyal-est of Wilkes's friends—to confess on her knees her relations with Wilkes. The alderman wrote Wilkes a very stern letter, receiving one in return that talked of "conscious innocence" withstanding "envenomed shafts of malice and falsehood" and of Mrs. Barnard's doubtful sanity. But Barnard was too much shaken by his wife's confession to be moved by her lover's pro-test and sent a copy of his will to Wilkes—leaving him £8,000 "and the whole of his library, paintings and prints"—to say that the bequest had been canceled. Wilkes, in hopes of forgiveness, is said to have sent Barnard "a very fine hare"—certainly a not very tactful choice—"from an old friend." He had indeed lost, as Barnard wrote, his "most affectionate and disinterested friend"; and what he may well have regretted more, an extremely gen-erous one.

Seated at last in the House of Commons, Wilkes failed to impress it. Doubtless it had resolved not to be impressed; and doubtless Wilkes remained, when let in, as impudent as when locked out. He certainly survives as one of the greatest of prank-sters and jokers among parliamentarians; and he had scarcely set foot in the House before he scared and appalled the entire body with a rumor that he planned to nominate for Speaker an ex-waiter at a London club who had grown rich and somehow been returned for a corrupt borough. "Be as impudent as you can," Wilkes told parliamentary lawyers, "and say what comes foremost to your mind"; and when a Major Scott was summoned before the bar, Wilkes said to him: "I give you joy. I am glad to see you in full dress." "Joy?" moaned the major. "Why, I'm here to be reprimanded." "But that's why I congratulate you," said Wilkes. "When the Speaker has finished, accuse every one; and then you'll be sent to Newgate or the Tower, and then you can be member for Middlesex or Westminster." In a very early speech—aimed, with malice prepense, at George III—Wilkes contended that the thirtieth of January, the date on which

Charles I was beheaded, should be "celebrated as a festival, as a day of triumph, not kept as a fast." Wilkes went at George III in one pert way after another. The civil list was a favorite target: when matters had to do with Parliament's paying the King's debts, Wilkes carefully scrutinized the accounts, asserting that they were "loose, unsatisfactory, perplexed and unintelligible," and adding that the nation suspected that by just such payments the Administration bought its majorities in Parliament. Because of his intense dislike of the young Prince of Wales—the future George IV—Wilkes withheld himself from the family rows against the King; but he set about making royal pensioners of the King's brothers, the Dukes of Cumberland and Gloucester, whom the King was on bad terms with.

One of Wilkes's feats, the nature of which no one could attack, was his public congratulations on His Majesty's ability to propagate. "The greatness of this House," he said, ". . . increases every year with the fortunately prolific annual increase of the royal offspring." (George III sired twelve children in sixteen years.) "We triumph," Wilkes continued, "in those endearing pledges of our monarch's love, and in the public felicity which an all-bounteous Providence continues to bestow on this particularly favored nation. The Kingdom at large contemplates with rapture His Majesty's numerous and still, I hope, increasing progeny." Two of Wilkes's better known plays on words are also at his monarch's expense—his saying that he "so loved his King that he hoped never to see another," and his reply when asked to take a hand at whist: "I am so ignorant that I can't tell a king from a knave." (As a matter of fact, gambling—though perhaps the greatest passion of the day—was the one worldly diversion that Wilkes had no taste for.) A third play on words is technically in the King's favor. When at a party at Carlton House, the Prince of Wales's residence, the Prince asked for toasts, Wilkes responded: "The King—long life to him!" The Prince, who detested his father even more than Wilkes detested the Prince, growled: "Since when have you been so anxious about my parent's health?" "Since," answered Wilkes, "I had the pleasure of your Royal Highness's acquaintance."

But his wit was more than part of his attractiveness and his social success; it was also part of his wiles. He wanted to keep annoying and embarrassing the Administration, which in the past had caused them to behave fatuously, to retaliate fatally, and to make very costly mistakes. His jests and gibes also gave him a publicity he courted and kept his public ardent and expectant. In much the same way, his pranks were actually part of his politics. Though he could make a good speech on occasion—he made some forty speeches in the first six years after he was seated[6]—he was not regarded by Commons standards as an at all successful speaker and was even less of one in an age that boasted the elder Pitt, Burke, and Sheridan; nor was he a good debater in an age that boasted Charles James Fox. What perhaps most told against him in House of Commons esteem was the impression of insincerity he created; he wasn't clever enough to realize that he could be too clever. Nor was he much in favor with the Opposition: politically, even the most progressive Whiggism lagged well behind Wilkite objectives and demands, such as the reform of Parliament; and personally, most Whig leaders would have nothing to do with him. Moreover, he could hardly hope, however eloquent, to persuade a House of Commons dominated by the King and Lord North—a House whose members the King had all too often bought. Wilkes's best serious hopes, as well as his best showmanship, lay in being a gadfly. And being much oftener an actor than a statesman, his strength lay not in leading a party but in attracting a vast public.

Yet the gadfly and the actor did not oust the politician and the people's friend. In his criticism of the civil list, Wilkes had

[6] Wilkes wrote out his speeches and got them by heart; and their being unspontaneous on top of being virtually inaudible, hampered him further. He perhaps often cared less to be heard than to be read and, one more of his innovations, he sent advance copies of his speeches to the press.

said: "The Crown has made a purchase of this House with the money of the people";[7] and their money, their rights, their place, their troubles formed a large part of his speechmaking. Perhaps his best, and certainly his most important speech, delivered a little over a year and a half after he took his seat, was very much concerned with the people's rights at every level. This speech was also a motion for the reform of the House of Commons and on terms never heard before. He pointed out the highly unrepresentative composition of the House: thus, the County of Middlesex, including the City of London, paid over a seventh of England's land taxes and had eight representatives in the Commons; the Duchy of Cornwall paid a seventieth of the land taxes and had forty-four representatives. Wilkes also attacked the "representation" of rotten boroughs: "What a happy fate, sir, has attended the boroughs of Gatton and Old Sarum, of which, though *ipsae periere ruinae* [the very ruins have perished], the names are familiar to us, the clerk regularly calls them over, and four respectable gentlemen represent their departed greatness . . . The little town of Banbury . . . has, I believe, only seventeen electors, yet gives us in its representative [Lord North] what is of the utmost importance to the majority here, a first lord of the Treasury and a chancellor of the Exchequer." Wilkes then looked to the voting of the House: he found that 254 votes sufficed for a majority and that, out of Britain's population of many millions, the 254 M.P.s could be elected by 5,723 persons. He went on to declare that the bill he proposed would everywhere—Scotland excluded—get rid of rotten-borough representation,[8] enfranchise new large towns,

[7] In the Parliament of 1774, seventy peers and 170 M.P.s "held profitable posts or contracts from the Ministry." In the 1774 elections Lord North bought seats in Parliament by flat payments of £2,500 to £3,000 each, and bought votes at from £7 to £8 a man.

[8] Corrupt boroughs could be offered up for sale, to be owned by one man, shared by two or three, or held by the Crown; and seats in Parliament could be bought much as they are bought today on the Stock Exchange. In the early 1780s pocket boroughs went for £5,000 or £6,000 each.

and give the vote to "the meanest mechanic, the poorest peasant and day laborer . . . Some share in the power of making laws . . . should be reserved even to this inferior but most useful set of men." The motion, after receiving "very jocular treatment," was straightway rejected without even being voted on. The bill itself, in its proposals, went farther than the Reform Bill of 1832.

Among other resolutions that got nowhere during Wilkes's early years as a seated M.P. were two which (in different years) moved that his 1769 expulsion from the Commons be expunged from its records. At the first of the two motions, both of which Wilkes introduced and both of which were defeated, James Luttrell said that he had never approved of his brother's candidacy; and another M.P. asserted that Wilkes had been found guilty of blasphemy. Having proved that this was not true, Wilkes said, loud enough to be heard, "Does he think I don't know blasphemy better than he does?" Some time later Wilkes would support resolutions easing the status of frowned-upon religions—first in behalf of Dissenting ministers and schoolmasters; not long after in behalf of Roman Catholics; and not long after that, in behalf of tolerance generally: he would not, he asserted, "persecute even the atheist." Wilkes's own feelings about religion are not very clear: he seemed sympathetic to Deism, which he extolled in the House as having "almost become the religion of Europe." Yet he once wrote to Polly that he would "keep to my good orthodox mother the Church of England to the last moment of its legal establishment"; and though apparently no clergyman came before he died to administer last rites, he was given Christian burial. And Hume, in 1764, wrote from Paris: "I never see Mr. Wilkes here but at Chapel, where he is a most regular, and devout, and edifying and pious attendant." Such attendance smacks more of public relations than of prayers; in any case, Wilkes was certainly more impolite than respectful toward religion, and he perhaps spoke plainest when he said of Dr. Johnson that "the word *liberty* is as ridiculous in his mouth as *religion* in mine."

But there loomed an issue of much greater importance for the Wilkes who took his seat in the House of Commons at the end of 1774—one that had recently and strongly engaged him when he was Lord Mayor and that had roused him much before then. This was the matter of the American colonies, whose open unrest, protestation, and rebelliousness harked as far back as the early days of Wilkes's troubles; indeed, conceivably the two most prominent Anglo-American battle cries of the century—"Wilkes and Liberty!" and "No taxation without representation"—resounded almost simultaneously on both sides of the ocean. The issues they bespoke constituted, historically, the two greatest blunders of a man who was King—if at times in name only—for sixty years.

5

In however peculiar a fashion, Wilkes and George III were not just the protagonist and antagonist but a kind of hero and villain of the long-drawn-out drama that began with the publication of *No. 45*. Junius, in a letter to the King, had written: "The destruction of one man has been now, for many years, the sole object of your Government." Neither man qualified personally for so antithetical a role, but Wilkes's audacity, courage, and devotion to a cause that came to equal, if not exceed, his own plight and his own self-interest, not to mention his popularity with the masses, had some of the stuff, and much more of the effect, of a hero; and George III's pigheaded actions and resentful behavior, his venal methods, his essential stupidity, his corrupt practices and autocratic ambitions might suggest the performances of a villain. If George III can invoke pathos by virtue of his limitations, he also, by virtue of them, sought all possible power. Brought up to the sound of "George, be King!" he never grasped how much tumult a *bad* king could cause. And a bad king he proved to be, not least for the colonies he lost.

We know that before there was any colonial crisis George III, very new to the throne, had rather naïve intentions of purifying politics and of getting rid of corrupt and immoral legislators. This, to be sure, would prove a tremendous undertaking: "As to honesty," he wrote, "all sorts of men seem equaly [*sic*] to have thrown that aside." He did not feel equal to the under-taking and turned for counsel to a man who in his opinion had no equal, Lord Bute. "Had I always acted," he told his counselor, "on your advice, I should now have been the direct opposite from what I am." Yet George would not "be a cypher" and—a common reaction—from being very unsure of himself, became immovably stubborn. And from being politically very unsophis-ticated, he was given to misapprehensions and made serious mistakes. Thus he thought all the bad men should be got rid of as a united tribe, with no realization that, just for being bad, they were often opposed to one another. George in his way was honest, but it was a way that came to depend on dishonesty, a way that increasingly sought after power and came to rely on corruption. And it was a way that mishandled situations—Wilkes and the American colonies prominently among them—that called for sane, unemotional tactics.

The origins of the American war lay not in political troubles, however much they might eventually enter in, but in economic ones, in the mercantilist policy of the times, particularly as applied by mother countries to their colonies. The Americans had to import either English-made goods or foreign goods by way of England; and they had to export their own goods either to England (when they did not compete with the English market) or nowhere at all. As a result, the colonists had resorted with considerable success to contraband trade which—no doubt more because it was successful than because it was contraband—angered the mother country. Moreover, as we know, after 1759 the strongest ties that bound the colonies to Great Britain—the fear of a French invasion from Canada—were much loosened, and the remaining ties were imponderable ones. It required, however, the 1763 Peace of Paris, which left England's finances very shaky, to produce a crisis. George Grenville was then George III's new Prime Minister—a man of integrity, a careful man of business, an adherent of parliamentary traditions, but a dullard even to the King. And where it was felt that a Pitt, had *he* dealt with America, would have invested "a gigantic commercial enterprise with the aura of a patriotic . . . crusade," the cautious man-of-business Grenville, being neither a diplomat nor a statesman, took shortsighted action with explosive results. In 1765 he sought new revenues in America by means of the Stamp Act.

Theoretically, there was a fair amount of justification for such a tax: Britain, at the end of the Seven Years' War, was £140,-000,000 in debt, and the British themselves were being overtaxed. Legally, moreover, Britain had a right to tax because of a long-standing decision that taxes could be imposed on the colonies, not only by their own representatives but by the British Parliament. But for many reasons it was wrong for Britain to exercise her right. At the lowest level, Britain itself had for years profited much less than had colonial British revenue officers from having their palms greased over smuggled merchandise (it appears that to collect £2,000 worth of custom duties in American ports cost Britain £8,000). But the issue or irritation, as seen from the colonial side, was now much less economic—thanks in part to the successful smuggling—than political. The better-off and influential colonists wanted self-government and were qualified for it; in many ways, indeed, they already practiced it. The colonial governors that England sent over were frequently out-at-elbows gentry—"nonentities, rakes, bankrupts, and discarded courtiers." The colonial governing bodies hugged their power of the purse, just as in crises England's House of Commons did. Moreover, in 1765 the colonies were still fretting over a 1764 Sugar Act which forced them to buy British molasses at a high price. A stamp tax on printed matter, bonds, warrants, affidavits, and the like was now certain to be resented, possibly to the point of being rebelled against. Enacting it was a huge tactical and psychological error—ill-reasoned on the ground that it was legal, and, because of what had gone before, decidedly ill-timed.

The resentment and opposition to the Act extended to England. City merchants worked up a national campaign and, thanks largely to the effort and energy of Edmund Burke, many commercial centers such as Bristol, Liverpool, and Glasgow put pressure on the new Rockingham administration, a far from exemplary one but far better than Grenville's. Pitt denounced the Stamp Act with great eloquence, enough for the colonists to erect statues to him as "the Saviour of Britain and the Redeemer of America"; and the Act was repealed, R. J. White tells us, "after an all night debate in a House besieged by an excited crowd of merchants trading with America."

The Act, which set going strong emotions and actions that would culminate in rebellion, had a life span, 1764–65, that closely corresponds to a year of strong emotions and actions associated with Wilkes. Thereafter the Americans and a Wilkes who had warmed to the American cause would have in George III more and more of a common enemy and a strong fraternal feeling among themselves. We know how, as time passed, George III, by his obstinate hostility toward Wilkes, was made to suffer at the hands of Wilkites; and we know of the growing protest from enlightened men in politics and the law. Accordingly, George, whenever possible, ducked the issue he had devised and kept his hands out of the hot water he had boiled. During the same years his sentiments toward his American subjects would be irritated and indignant, and his estimate of their strength less alarming than his awareness of Wilkes's. The colonists, however, had profited from Wilkes's example quite as much as George III failed to profit by Caesar's or Charles I's. The repeal of the Stamp Act, done very much against George III's wishes, had greatly displeased him, and he was in a mood to be retaliatory as well as repressive in his dealings with the colonists. Many of them were now, however, in a rebellious mood in their dealings with the King. Wilkes as, so to speak, the colonists' London correspondent lent encouragement and perhaps ammunition to their procedures; and when a later tax, on tea, offended them, a number of men dressed up as Indians, climbed onto a tea ship in Boston harbor and dumped its cargo of tea chests into the water. This most famous of tea parties, only challenged by Alice's in Wonderland, gave the King of England—at times a blood relation of Alice's Red Queen—considerable pleasure. That is to say, it made him feel entitled to reciprocate with a far bitterer drink than tea.

By this time—the early 1770s—the King had a compliant Prime Minister in Lord North;[1] and for the wetting he got in Boston Harbor George, by way of North, promptly had an act passed that shut down the port of Boston and forbade all trading and transporting of goods. He had another act passed that rescinded the character and constitution of the Massachusetts Bay province and that reduced its legal and judicial rights. He had a third act passed which authorized the governor to shift cases for trial to a different colony or even to Great Britain. He had passed a fourth and final act—known as the Quebec Act—which, by broadening the scope of Britain's new province of Canada, by restoring French laws there, and by legalizing Roman Catholi-

---

[1] Americans have made a rather sad figure—or at any rate created a rather false image—of North, though the fault is very largely his own. He was for twelve years George III's Prime Minister—a title he would let no one use of him—out of a strange sense of duty and a repeated refusal on the King's part to let him resign. What is to be chalked up against North is not just the egregious and disastrous policy he pursued but the fact that he for the most part disbelieved in it, so that his submissiveness is often unforgivable, and the American view of him—accentuated by blunders like retaining the tax on tea and introducing the Boston port bill—is pretty much justified. But he was by nature no mere mouthpiece: he could be a brilliant debater, proved to be a first-class Chancellor of the Exchequer, and was personally humorous, sweet-tempered, and honorable. After Cornwallis' surrender at Yorktown and the motion to no longer prosecute the war, he determined to resign and did, with George III reputed to have "parted with him rudely without thanking him." Still, there had been compensations—George had given North's children very nice sinecures, had made North's brother a bishop, and North himself was made chancellor of the University of Oxford, lord lieutenant of Somerset, and a Knight of the Garter.

cism, would provide the military manpower that George III could call upon, should New England colonies resist, to subdue them. In pursuit of this, Britain's General Gage led out four regiments to enforce all these new decrees, with Gage himself named governor of Massachusetts.

George had supposed that his resolutions would leave the colonists "meek." Instead, all the colonies except one—perhaps because it was named Georgia—got together in resistance and flooded England with protests, while Massachusetts defied the rulings, ignored the governor, and organized its own militia. When early in 1775 this alarming news reached England, there was much opposition to the treatment of the colonies, with Wilkes, as both Lord Mayor and M.P., a doughty champion of their cause. For commercial as well as political reasons, he had the City behind him; and virtually all of Britain's biggest cities —Bristol, Glasgow, Liverpool, Birmingham, Manchester, Norwich—drew up petitions. The City and its Lord Mayor petitioned both Houses of Parliament and thereafter, in very strong language, the King:

> We . . . beg leave to declare our abhorrence of the measures which have been pursued, and are now pursuing, to the opposition of our fellow subjects in America . . . [We] plainly perceive that the real purpose is to establish arbitrary power over all America. It is therefore with the deepest concern that we have seen the sacred security of representation in their assemblies wrested from them; the trial by jury abolished, and the odious powers of excise extended to all cases of revenue; the sanctuary of their houses laid open to violation at the will and desire of every officer and servant in the customs; the dispensation of justice corrupted by rendering their judges dependent for their seats and salaries on the will of the crown; liberty and life rendered precarious, by subjecting them to be dragged over the ocean and tried for treason or felony here where the distance, making it impossible for the most guiltless to maintain his innocence, must deliver him up a victim to ministerial venge-

ance . . . the Habeas Corpus Act and trial by jury have been suppressed; dutiful petitions for redress of these grievances, from all your Majesty's American subjects, have been fruitless.

The City and its Lord Mayor furthermore asked that the King be presented with the petition while "sitting on the throne." Indignant at so impudent a stipulation, George answered: "I am ever ready to receive petitions and addresses, but I am the judge where." The City refused to give in, and the Lord Mayor gave as its reason that petitions to the King, put into the hands of a lord in waiting, were never answered and very likely never read: if they were read in the King's presence, one knew at least that the King had heard them. Both sides were unyielding until after some months the King agreed to be seated on the throne while listening to a new petition pretty much like the first one. His chief objection to this "new dish of insolence" seems to have been his feeling ill at ease about encountering Wilkes in the flesh; and in giving in, he had a courtier make clear to Wilkes that the King would not speak to him. "The caution," Wilkes answered, "is needless. I didn't expect the honor." The occasion arrived: Wilkes could at least look at a King; the King received the petition, refused the plea it made, and the occasion was over. The King remarked to his courtiers, however, that Wilkes was a very well-bred man and Lord Mayor. But a little later, when the livery informed the King that he was seeking autocratic power over the colonies and that Parliament was bribed, he refused to receive the livery on the throne; in return the livery published its comments in a newspaper.

The powerful voice of the City helped gird the colonies for action, and they were fervent in their thanks to the City and the Lord Mayor. A letter of thanks from a representative of "the City and County of New York" reported that the colonies were so roused by oppression that a shock felt anywhere among them was felt by them all. Wilkes received a letter from John Hancock, as president of the Continental Congress, which read in part:

> My lord,
>
> Permit the delegates of the people of twelve ancient colonies to pay . . . the just tribute of gratitude and thanks for the virtuous and unsolicited resentment you have shown to the violated rights of a free people . . . North America, my lord, wishes most ardently for a lasting connection with Great Britain on terms of just and equal liberty; less than which generous minds will not offer, nor brave and free ones be willing to receive. A cruel war has at length been opened against us and whilst we prepare to defend ourselves like the descendants of Briton, we still hope that the mediation of wise and good citizens will at length prevail over despotism, and restore harmony and peace on permanent principles, to an oppressed and divided empire . . .
>
> By order of the Congress.

But George III, with Lord North as his reluctant mouthpiece, was not of a mind to listen to mediators, or orators, or the voice of reason; and the permanent principles on which he would restore harmony were his own. Having blundered once, he felt that he, or Great Britain, must back the blunder up: give in now, the argument ran, and you must continue to give in. Possibly there was truth in this but it did not augur success; it prefigured ultimate failure. To be sure, the King and his ministry allowed themselves to think that if it came to war, England could whip the rebels hands down; and so, by way of Lexington and Concord, it had come. At the outset the King and the ministry had the bulk of the nation behind them, had all the vast army of mediocrities whom Burke excoriated for speaking smugly of "*our* subjects in America; *our* colonies; *our* dependents."

But enlightened England, conservative as well as liberal, realized the folly and injustice of the King's attitude and of the

North ministry. Burke, in the most famous of pleas, the "Speech on Conciliation" had said, "The question with me is not whether you have a right to render your people miserable; but whether it is not in your interest to make them happy." Horace Walpole saw that victory over the Americans was sure to rivet English chains at home—as Lord Morley would say long after in his *Life of Burke,* "The ruin of the American cause would have been also the ruin of the constitutional cause in England"; and Charles James Fox, now converted to liberal views, would speak, when the English scored a victory over the Americans, of "the *bad news* from Long Island." Actually, the House of Commons, which ordained the calamitous turn of events, was during these years the seat of eloquent objection and protest. Next perhaps to Chatham, whom George III called "the trumpet of sedition," Wilkes was the colonists' best friend, just as he was, in the Commons, their most vigorous champion next to Burke. The war, he declared in October 1775, was "unjust, felonious and murderous"—this in a speech where he asked: "Who can tell whether in a few years the independent Americans may not celebrate the glorious era of the Revolution of 1775 as we do that of 1688?" He also said, more pungently, "We are fighting for the . . . unconditional submission of a country infinitely more extended than our own, of which every day increases the wealth, the natural strength, the population . . . Success, final success, seems to me not equivocal, not uncertain, but impossible. However *we* may differ among ourselves, they are perfectly united." Soon after, Wilkes supported a motion to ascertain just which persons had instigated the proposal to tax America without her consent. And he remained as stanchly pro-American after July 4, 1776, as before. This was not true of a great many other Englishmen, not necessarily mediocrities, who became more pro-English out of loyalty to king and country in times of war; or because of the numerous war materials that made for profit, not to mention profiteering; or what was perhaps most persuasive, the feeling that the colonies would be easily and speedily licked. The colonies had so far suffered defeat, and Wilkes and other sympathizers were sent letters offering nothing but bad news. And when General Howe, acting for the Government, suggested a negotiation about peace in a letter to "George Washington, Esq.," it went back unopened with the comment that unless Washington was addressed as "General" he would touch nothing sent to him. An adjutant of Howe's found an amusing solution through writing to "George Washington &c. &c. &c.," which both the General and Howe found acceptable by way of interpreting "&c. &c. &c." as they chose. But, after consulting the Congress, Washington "with the utmost politeness" rejected the terms—involving a pardon for guilt—as out of the question. Defeats of the Americans continued, and their English advocates became more and more dismayed.

In the Commons, however, Wilkes went on speaking loud and clear for the colonies—first in 1777, against the suspension in America of both habeas corpus and the common law; again, with a plea for "an immediate cessation of arms" and a declaration that the accounts of continuing British victories were not credible; and urging for a third time that all acts having to do with America since 1763 be repealed. But prosperity and optimism prevailed in England and won converts for the King (a buzz of talk that General Burgoyne had been defeated at Saratoga was officially rebutted as a most trifling matter[2]). The Government had indeed gained so much strength and popular approval that it decided to topple the most powerful of antiwar fortresses: the City. The leaders of the Government's subsequent assault were prosperous contractors who controlled a great amount of City employment, and when their candidates lost, the men who had not supported the Government's nominees

[2] Knowing how serious a defeat it had been, Wilkes called for "an immediate cessation of arms"; for, if the powerful confederations of colonies continued, "I own I shall tremble for the fate of Canada . . . as well as for Nova Scotia, the two Floridas, and even the West Indian islands."

found themselves out of work or in some other way losers. In such fashion the Government in 1778 got its candidate—himself a prosperous contractor—elected Lord Mayor; and, swollen with success, the Government next proposed having the City of London raise a volunteer regiment to be sent to America.

Though Wilkes insisted in Parliament that this required the consent of the City, the high-riding Government went into action without it. But when the new Lord Mayor called a court of common council to approve the Administration's regimental project, Wilkes and his supporters went into action also. At this point, a different sort of proposal was made—to look into the Lord Mayor's financial dealings, as a contractor, with the City; and this, when added to his unpopularity, subtracted from his strength. The regimental project was by a very large majority voted down; the City thereafter resumed its strong opposition to the war, and in the next year, 1779, showed its formidable approbation of Wilkes. His old opponent Benjamin Hopkins having died, Wilkes stood for City chamberlain and was elected by a large majority. He had had to stand during five Middlesex elections before being seated in Parliament and during five City elections before becoming chamberlain.

In America, too, the situation changed, with a string of victories for the colonists, while France and Spain went to war against England and waged it outside America, with France also helping inside.[3] In economic terms, England's prosperity slowed down and ceased; in political ones, the Government had failed and was being fled from; and the too complaisant Lord North stayed on only because the King insisted on it. There

[3] Early in 1778 the United States and France signed a treaty of alliance; Wilkes (knowing how late a stage it was) called for a federal union with America with "immediate cessation of arms and recall of troops." But in vain. By mid-March England and France were on the verge of war; soon after, Wilkes recommended "endeavoring to detach the United States from France, by an acknowledgment of their independence and . . . a treaty offensive and defensive with the Mother Country." But acknowledging their independence was more than Chatham would allow.

were petitions and resolutions against the Government's performance, particularly against the ill-spending of money.[4] Burke,
in February 1780, brought motions before the House that would
materially reduce George III's financial ability to buy and bribe
M.P.s; but the motions were defeated. However, in April 1780,
by 233 votes to 215, John Dunning's famous motion was passed
"that the influence of the Crown has increased, is increasing,
and ought to be diminished."

By 1780 Wilkes's own activity and status in Parliament had
diminished. He stood in September for re-election at Brentford
and was returned without opposition; but now he spoke much
less often to a much less responsive House. He had never been
a very effective speaker, in part because of his feeble voice, in
part no doubt because of his unpopular views.[5] And by now
the drama he had made of the American war was as apparent
as the mess the King had made of it. By now Wilkes had no
personal grievances to make drama of; no *Sturm und Drang*
to thrive on; no inflammatory causes to ignite.

Almost at once, however, there was to flare up a vicious episode of *Sturm und Drang:* the most explosive of the century's
mob reactions, loosing the most bigoted of its battle cries and
the most destructive of its riots. Two years before, in 1778, Parliament had passed a Catholic Relief Bill which removed some
of the disabilities to which Roman Catholics were subjected—
those concerned with freedom of worship and the removal of
penalties that made property liable to forfeiture, but nothing

[4] Wilkes had earlier in Parliament raised the matter of the King's debts and
the reason for them: "The nation, sir, suspects that regular ministerial majorities are bought; that the Crown has made a purchase of this House with
money of the people. Hence the ready, tame and servile compliance to every
royal edict issued by the Ministry." Wilkes denounced Dr. Johnson for being
on the pension list; and also whacked Hume, as Chenevix Trench puts it, for
"being pensioned for writing against Christianity, and Beatty for writing
against Hume."

[5] John Nichols said that in 1785 Wilkes "began to print a handsome and
complete edition of his 'Speeches in Parliament' . . . now from its extreme
rarity, a great bibliographical curiosity."

concerned with political rights. Soon groups all over Britain formed associations in defense of Protestantism, and a crackpot Member of Parliament, a brother of the Duke of Gordon, became their spokesman. The Government, needing Lord George Gordon's seat for its own purposes, arranged with his brother the Duke, in exchange for gaining it, to make another brother Lord *William* Gordon Vice Admiral of Scotland; and this exchange the crackpot Lord George saw as a Popish plot aimed directly at himself. The mischief began when on June 2 Lord George led to Parliament a group petitioning to have the Catholic Relief Bill repealed. A huge sympathetic crowd had unexpectedly gathered, which forced incoming members of the Lords and the Commons either to shout "No Popery!" or be molested. At the same time, inside the Parliament Lord George darted hysterically about, haranguing his supporters with "No Popery" orations and denouncing Edmund Burke, among others, as no proper Protestant. In addition, members of both Houses stationed themselves with drawn swords, in case the rioters should come at them. The Commons, in due course, rejected the petition, and the mob at length dispersed, only for large numbers of it, after dark, to destroy the Catholic chapels of the Sardinian and Bavarian ambassadors. After laying off for a day, the rioting reappeared and grew worse—mobs pillaged and burned Catholic houses and shops in all parts of London. The next day was worse than the previous one: the mob, while turning loose Newgate's prisoners, set the prison on fire, this the first of many burning prisons, among them the Fleet and the King's Bench. Mobs also wrecked and set fire to a large Catholic-owned distillery, the gin from its huge vats pouring through the streets, catching fire, and causing hideous deaths for men first made drunk from the liquor and then so helpless from it as to be destroyed by the flames. More people, said Dr. Johnson, were killed by drinking than "by ball or bayonet."

During all this time the Lord Mayor, partly from fear of

being harmed by the mob, was refusing to call out troops, and the City magistrates were carefully making themselves scarce. The next day Wilkes, who had so far displayed a passive attitude, came out for action toward restoring law and order; that night he took charge of the defense of the assaulted Bank of England, when for the first time the rioters were checked. "Wilkes claimed to have fired on the rioters and to have killed several," says J. C. Long, who says also that Lord George Gordon turned up, approached the captain in charge, and offered to try to disperse the mob, but the captain would have nothing to do with him. The next day, equipped with a Lord Mayor's draft for troops, Wilkes took the offensive; he and his party repulsed the mob—some of the mobsters, we are told, being thrown into the Thames. The Government at last took action, with George III and Wilkes singled out as the only people in London who had not failed of courage.

By June 10—when Wilkes broke up a mob at a Fleet Street printing house, seized treasonable documents, and had the owner, William Moore, committed to prison—the rioting was put down, Lord George was sent to the Tower,[6] and the Gordon Riots were over. They had caused tremendous damage, with as many as thirty-six fires simultaneously encrimsoning the midnight sky, and they saw 285 people killed and 160 brought afterward to trial. Nothing quite like them had flared up during the entire century: they had exploded without forewarning, they spread little, if at all, outside London, and they were without any real

[6] Lord George's career was destroyed by the riots. After eight months in the Tower, he was tried for high treason and acquitted; thereafter he sided with the Protestant Dutch in their quarrel with the Emperor of Austria; accused Marie Antoinette of persecuting Cagliostro; denigrated British justice; and—in both cases found guilty of libel—he was sentenced to five years in Newgate. Meanwhile he had become a convert to Judaism and in Newgate conformed in all respects to Jewish ritual, along with giving dinner parties every day and a ball every two weeks. Unable, at the end of five years, to pay the largish securities for his release, he had to stay on in Newgate and died there of jail fever "after singing the Ça ira."

leader; in addition, a great many of the rioters, though anti-something, were not anti-Catholic.

Wilkes's role in the riots has been subject to numerous interpretations and to varying degrees of condemnation and approval. It was so conspicuous a reversal of his precedent role as to carry into future generations the appearance of an expedient about-face, and it certainly suggested a watershed in Wilkes's career. Obviously there are quite ironic aspects to it. The very mobs that Wilkes was shooting into, or was having shot down, contained not just Wilkites for political reasons, but many veterans of the actual mobs and demonstrations that had championed Wilkes. They also contained great numbers of rioters who did battle far more out of protest than out of Protestantism—men without jobs or exploited in whatever jobs they had. Wilkes in a literal sense was firing into his own ranks and seeming to betray his own tenets. Moreover, such former stanch allies of his as Brass Crosby and James Sawbridge had somehow become chief aides of Lord George Gordon, with City members petitioning the Commons to *repeal* the Catholic Relief Bill; the William Moore whom Wilkes committed to prison for destroying a house and printing "seditious and treasonable" papers had also printed *The North Briton;* and the house Moore was charged with destroying was Lord Mansfield's. But even more ironic was Wilkes's issuing a warrant for the apprehension of all idle and disorderly persons in his ward of Farringdon Without[7] which, as Chenevix Trench shrewdly remarks, "must have been a fairly *general* warrant."

So much irony comes almost to smack of conspiracy, almost to give Wilkes every chance to betray every tenet he stood for and every person who stood up for him. What further casts a

[7] Sir Nathaniel Wraxall thought that had Wilkes been Lord Mayor he "would unquestionably by his vigor have prevented many or all of the disgraceful scenes which took place in the capital." (Wraxall also said, "If any man ever was pleasing who squinted, who had lost his teeth, and lisped, Wilkes might be so esteemed.")

shadow is his own reputation, as so much more self-seeking than magnanimous, as so exploitative a friend, so opportunistic a demagogue, so fervent a publicity seeker. And much of this he was. But, with the Gordon Riots, much of this is letting past sins condemn the present, is damning Wilkes with guilt-by-reputation. On some counts, moreover, Wilkes's reputation was excellent. He had undisputed courage; he had come to believe in the things he fought for; though not truthful, he never claimed to be a Wilkite; and, if somewhat for tactical reasons, he had consistently supported law and order. Indeed, however often in his career he had cheered mobs on, only once—at the head of a crowd going to present a petition—did he lead a "mob." And as for mobs and rioting, there were two vital differences between the past and the present ones. The first difference was the objectives of the mobs: the past ones in behalf of important civil and constitutional rights, the present one in bigoted and punitive opposition to the rights of a large religious group. Wilkes, moreover, had always detested and opposed religious intolerance and had said of Catholics: "It would do honour to our Church to treat with tenderness all who are unhappy enough not to be in our bosom." The second crucial difference is the behavior of the mobs, the Wilkite riots being always at the level of misdemeanors, using rowdy but never terrorist tactics, the Gordon Riots being criminally violent and viciously destructive. On any realistic as well as moral basis, Wilkes acted in character and acted right. If a cynic might argue that Wilkes no longer needed mobs himself, he could be answered that Wilkes had not needed to place himself in the thick of the Gordon rioting and to risk—one sniper's bullet would have been enough—being killed. He was perhaps the only prominent Londoner who took that risk.

Actually, the role he played was in some sense symptomatic of the attitude and direction he had for a number of years been taking. Having been extremely successful as an embattled John

Wilkes, he was more and more subsiding into the personal and social way of life he had always most enjoyed. Having now no problems about being re-elected to Parliament or seated in it, no immediate causes to fight for in the Commons—the American war was all but over—and, with one exception, no personal grievances to air or ask redress for, he was increasingly slipping out of political life and was a much reduced figure in it. He would remain in Parliament for another ten years, but as a backbencher and a back number. The "demagogue" had become more and more of a diner-out; the spokesman for the "middle and inferior sort of people" had become more and more the companion of affluent and superior ones; and in the raging conflagration of the Gordon Riots Wilkes's own fire had been burned away. He was truly an extinct volcano. The one grievance that still ached, and by 1780 had all but passed from indignation into habit, was that his earlier expulsion from Parliament had not been expunged from the records of the House. Six times he had moved that it be and six times he had been defeated. Again in 1781 he would be defeated; but a year later his motion was carried, 115 to 47, and his grievance came to a happy if, by now, an uneventful end.

Part Three

I

IF WILKES had all but ceased to make himself heard in Parliament and had quite ceased to matter there, elsewhere he was not so inactive. As an alderman in the City, he had still a considerable position, and he was the City's chamberlain, which made him its treasurer. The livery liked their chamberlain and re-elected him annually until his death: after Wilkes's service during the Gordon Riots the ministry had no reason to back a rival candidate who they also had no reason to think would win. There were, of course, a good many mutterings about a City treasurer notorious for extravagance and debts and about a man with a reprehensible foundling hospital past, who now was in charge of the City orphans' money. Far from resenting or being disturbed by this, Wilkes was amused and good-humored. When an indignant friend asked him whether he had seen "an infamous libel" against him in the morning paper, he said, yes he had and had just written asking another paper to copy it; and when a political opponent accused him in public of all sorts of misdeeds, Wilkes smiled and answered in a pleasant voice: "What a wretched memory you have! You've forgotten all about the Foundling Hospital." Impudence was as often as wit the basis of his retorts.

As chamberlain, however, he was extremely conscientious and scrupulous, keeping his accounts in perfect order if only from knowing how many people would distrust him and insist that the accounts be gone over—something which a Scot named Cowley did regularly for years but without finding anything amiss. When an old friend, Sir Watkin Lewis, asked for his salary in advance, Wilkes refused him, saying, "If the salary isn't paid on the day it becomes due, the Chamberlain would be highly culpable"; but he added, "If [the Chamberlain] paid it the day before, he would also be highly culpable." As chamberlain, Wilkes every morning, except when on vacation, presided over a magistrate's session having to do with apprentices and their masters; and while spectators in the court looked on he, as their legal guardian, would take action for apprentices or admonish them. A boy who complained of having been thrashed by a master for idleness told in later years, when he had become the famous actor Thomas Dibdin, of Wilkes's making peace between the two. "While the worthy magistrate exhorted Sir William he appeared to be looking full at *me*; and while he admonished *me* his eyes seemed fixed on Sir William." (A pleasant story, but we must not forget that the worthy magistrate squinted.[1]) As chamberlain, Wilkes had also, which he enjoyed, a number of ceremonial duties, among them a formal address whenever someone was given the freedom of the City. On such occasions he began his speech by reviving the old salutation: "I give you joy," a phrase that gave him pleasure.

His duties as chamberlain, which were never arduous, gave him considerable pleasure of another kind: the office paid well. Although Wilkes's salary as chamberlain was only some £500 a year, there were perquisites which ran to more than £1,500. This, supplemented by rents from his East Anglian property, produced an income that at least came within sight of satisfying his luxurious inclinations. In 1781, less than two years after

[1] M. Dorothy George, in *London Life in the Eighteenth Century*, cites cases where Wilkes appears to have done less than he might have for the apprentices, and less when they were from poor families than from well-off ones.

he became chamberlain, his mother's death provided him with an additional property in Middlesex. In later years, partly because her other children had died, or proved unattractive, or come to nothing, but chiefly because of what John had stood for and become, his mother grew as proud as she was fond of him and was extremely fond of Polly. Despite the marriage that she had thrust upon John and how often he had differed with her, he seems to have been a devoted son. His devotion presumably survived her remonstrances and reproofs; concerning one of his liaisons she wrote to him in 1771:

> May I not flatter myself that the near connection with a dear son will supersede apologizing for the free contents of this billet? My duty and affection will not suffer me silently to lament your present very obnoxious conduct in making so frequent visits to the *infamous* Mrs. Gardiner, unhappily situated in my neighborhood. A late visit in your sheriff's chariot (which has been repeated) . . . has been severely censured, but not more than such an insult upon public decency merited . . . The populace that was gathered . . . hissed you, as a detestation of your entering a bawdy house . . . Many of the middling class of people . . . see vice countenanced by a magistrate with double abhorrence . . . Let me now conjure you, with the most ardent parental affection, to bid a final adieu to all infamous and ruinous connections, and this in particular.

Three years after his mother, Wilkes's wife died. Though husband and wife had not seen each other for almost thirty years, in the years following his hostile mother-in-law's death they themselves had shown each other no ill feelings. Much of this was due to Polly who often visited her mother with her father's approval—which, it appears, led her mother to speak kindly of her father. But any coming together could only have parted Polly's parents the more; they had nothing in common and much that would make for contention. "Mrs. Wilkes died" is all that John wrote in his diary on the day of her death; yet, perhaps for Polly's sake, or perhaps for decency's, he went into various forms of mourning. He told Polly that he would wear black as long as she did, adding that he thought six months fitted "modern standards." This particular observance far outran any social ones he made: he gave up having people to dinner for four days after his wife died and did not go out to dinner for fourteen. Mrs. Wilkes's death made Polly, now thirty-three years old, a wealthy woman, with an income said to be more than £2,000 a year.

The tremendous affection and devotion that existed on both sides between Polly and her father offer something almost fictional—a kind of saving grace, of compensating goodness—in a father's history large with domestic turmoil, financial distress, boastful debauchery, self-seeking ambitions, and political strife. What is really saving, and quite special, is that this stainless devotion operated at a decided level of worldliness. Not only had Wilkes, from Polly's childhood, wanted her to have—and seen to it that she was given—an elegant, highbred, upper-class education, much of it more French than English, more expensive than expedient; but, with a certain nicety, he also made her aware of the facts of life, of his own life not least. No i's were dotted about the world's or Wilkes's dissipations; but also no eyes were shut. As earlier in his life, so to the very end of it, each of the two counted most to the other.

Kindly, cultivated, poised—versed in the *usage du monde*— Polly never married. This was not because of devotion to her father on her part or of possessiveness on his; apparently she was "very plain," not to say homely, in appearance—there, too, very much her father's daughter. But where he, as he boasted, could win over any woman in half an hour, she for all her endowments failed to win a husband—or needed it to be a suitable husband?—in a score of years. She lived with her father in Prince's Court, and though an indifferent housekeeper—it seems to have been Wilkes himself who oversaw household details—

she was his urbane and well-liked hostess at home, as earlier she had been his Lady Mayoress at the Mansion House. Wilkes delighted in giving dinner parties, the guests "not more than the Muses nor less than the Graces." There seem, however, to have been servant problems, particularly with male servants who got female ones pregnant, who then did nothing about it financially, and who finally threw them, for their lyings-in, on the parish. Wilkes had one such man in his household arrested and made to pay the woman's expenses. Such subject matter recalls a play on words made by someone else's servant and another one made by Wilkes. When a friend of Wilkes's, having just rented a house, jovially asked the housemaid, "Are you to be let also?" she answered, "No sir, I'm to be let alone." And when Wilkes, on a fine day, was walking on the promenade at Brighton, a pretty young girl said, "Good morning, Mr. Wilkes. As you see, I've come here for a little sun and air," "I think, my dear," he answered, "you'd better find a little husband first."

Though Wilkes often went on shortish journeys to such places as Brighton or Bath—and in due course had a summer cottage on the Isle of Wight—in his later years he did no real traveling and never went to the Continent after returning from there in 1768. This seems somewhat strange, particularly in a man who, to go no farther, so much enjoyed Paris during an era when, among people of rank and achievement, visits there were frequent and fashionable. Yet if in decline as a public figure, Wilkes led a quite full private life. Where ladies were concerned, age did not weaken him nor carnality stale. Mrs. Gardiner, whom in 1771 his mother had beseeched him to break with, had been a rather brief connection; and after a period of not very noteworthy or intense amours, he met Marianne de Charpillon, mentioned in passing during Wilkes's year as Lord Mayor. She was then, and for several years after, *maîtresse en titre*. Wilkes might very well have valued her for having rejected a more famous libertine than himself: Giacomo Casanova. Marianne's relationship with Casanova, in his own account of it, was decidedly lurid. She had come to know him, then an Italian adventurer seeking his fortune in England, in 1763 when she was seventeen and very beautiful, and he at once pursued her, aware though he was that she was out to dupe him and that he had already been duped over some jewels by her far-from-spotless mother. Nor would Marianne, a quite vicious minx, sleep with him: when at last she agreed, she met his embraces by lying in the dark in a tightly wrapped nightgown with her arms crossed and her chin pressed against her upraised knees. He fought her and beat her and got nowhere; again and again, at the crucial moment, he got nowhere; and, a superlatively successful rake unused to being thwarted, he stormed into a fearful rage to the point of smashing everything in sight and of having her run shrieking and naked into the street. Taken before a judge, he was sent to Newgate for trying "to disfigure a young and pretty girl," but quickly released when friends spoke up for him. He subsequently said that from the day he met her he "began to die"; and he trained a parrot to say, "The Charpillon is an even bigger whore than her mother."

When Wilkes met the Charpillon she was past thirty but tall, graceful, and alluring, with wonderful blue eyes and a child-like look of innocence. Behind her was not just her own career as a courtesan; she was part of a dynasty, and Wilkes, it seems, took on Marianne's mother and her mother's sisters, all of these ladies, as Olga Venn puts it, endowed with "solid professional talent." The older ladies' attainments had taken them in their day to the capitals of Europe and into the arms of diplomats and noblemen. Marianne, in England, had fared less well in spite of enticing the brother of a duchess, and when Wilkes met her, the dynasty was pretty much on its uppers.

Wishing of Marianne someone akin to a wife, he set her up (with her elders) in a commodious house and provided numerous gifts as well as money. Straitened circumstances had made her tactful and wary and, helped by her charms and her pretense of submission to Wilkes, she delighted him and ruled over him. Although she never met Polly, she praised her—"si accomplie et si perfectionée"—and Polly in return was all politeness. In this pseudo-marital arrangement Wilkes dined frequently and liter- ally *en famille* at Marianne's house; and it was while he was there in 1777 that the two of them came to blows, with Marianne revealing her essential self and reviling Wilkes like a common whore. His susceptibility was by then wearing off: Marianne's need to be elegantly maintained had become increasingly ex- pensive, and his debts were getting out of bounds. He broke with her the morning after the row, writing that the last words she had honored him with were "For me, monsieur, you have become as odious as my mother." She subsequently apologized and was forgiven—he even sent her presents—but they soon stopped seeing each other for good.

Marianne's rather prompt successor, Amelia Arnold, was a very different type, countryfied and with agreeable country looks, who became devoted to Wilkes, seeking above all to please him and bearing him in October 1778 a daughter whom they named Harriet. Mother and daughter continued to play a solid role in Wilkes's life, whatever his engagements else- where; and we shall continue to meet them. Early in 1778, how- ever, Wilkes during a visit to Bath had met at a dinner party a woman named Maria Stafford. Pleasant to look at and enjoyable to listen to, with well-bred graces and a touch of the bluestock- ing, she at once greatly attracted, indeed inflamed, Wilkes, and all the more when he found she was separated from an unfaith- ful husband. She in turn was delighted by the attentions of so famous a man, who had spent the whole evening at her side making unabashed love to her. Though he had to return at once to London, he laid passionate siege by letter while showering her with presents. A lady who valued her social position, she was not of a mind—knowing all too well his reputation—to invite social ruin. But she was plainly fascinated, and she temporized—she rebuked but never rejected him. "Why," she wrote, "will you oblige me to be angry with you? I have more than once entreated you would send me neither letters nor presents . . . Death has deprived me of my natural protectors . . . infidelity of my legal one." "Make me your Protector," Wilkes not very cleverly wrote back: "I shall have a happier lot than Cromwell. I dare not be more explicit, and I trust I need not." This she answered very reprovingly, stating that as both of them were the property of others, "matrimony is out of the question" and "the bare idea of any connection less durable and innocent" had "something in it too horrible to be hinted at." This time the author of the aborted history of England cited James II in reply. "We all agree that James *abdicated and deserted*, and that the *throne* thereby became vacant. I say that Mr. [Stafford] *abdicated and deserted* and that the *throne* of love is hereby become vacant."

But though Maria Stafford always wrote back reprovingly, she always wrote back; indeed she displayed considerable artful nay-saying. Wilkes pursued her with a poem, "Four in the morning—Maria hath murdered sleep"; he began to call her by her first name; he let her know that he was coming to Bath to lay siege. She kept the fire burning by pretending to put it out—she couldn't see him because of a previous engagement in the country; she had a cold; she would only open doors by opening them to "toute [sic] le monde." But Wilkes came and saw his "adorable Maria" tête-à-tête, though he got no further. She did, however, accept a bouquet of roses and asked him to frank a letter for her; and she met him at a concert where "she talked freely of her matrimonial misfortunes." He then gave her a huge bouquet of violets, along with a ticket to another concert, and there was also a possibility of their meeting at a ball. He was clearly gaining ground. A woman who was Maria's close friend and confidante happened, however, to call on her, catch sight of the violets and the ticket, thereupon ask Maria who had sent them, be refused an answer, and learn who by questioning the servants. Astounded, she wormed out of Maria her relations with Wilkes, read her a stiff lecture, made clear the notoriety and ostracism she was courting, forbade any more flowers or letters or meetings, and insisted that she and Wilkes return each other's letters. Awakened and disturbed, Maria wrote to Wilkes, coldly breaking off the relationship.

Her letter left him desolate; but a month later he could write to her that nothing was more ridiculous than a "whining lover," adding, "I know your female friend, and in common with the rest of mankind I thoroughly detest her, but I adore my charming Maria." (One wonders, indeed, how Maria could put up with such a friend.) But though she had shown amour the door, Maria in the next week wrote three times to Wilkes, chiefly to forbid their writing to each other, yet hinting that they might meet now and then in public. But they did not meet while Wilkes was still in Bath; and when he returned there many months later—not having heard from her, or written to her, in the meantime—he found that she had put her house up for sale and left town. A few months after she left town, moreover, she had rejoined her husband. Wilkes, whatever the depth of his feelings for her, was man of the world enough to trade love for friendship, conceivably hoping for better luck in the future. He paid the Staffords a visit; Mr. Stafford he described as "a puppy of a husband," though also a Wilkite. Maria, Wilkes wrote to Polly, "behaved with grace, elegance and ease. She laughingly asked me what salary I would give her to be secretary to the Chamberlain. I said 'You may name your own terms. I have only one condition to insist on, your constant residence.'" This new relationship between Wilkes and Mrs. Stafford was, it became plain, the only possible permanent one, and it proved successful. Wilkes was often the Staffords' guest at Bath and at their country place not far from there; and they were his at

Prince's Court, with Polly playing hostess. Maria was pleased to have so famous a friend; it was all scrupulously platonic; she even returned his expensive presents. He remained Maria's true admirer, though as years went by he found that even being a Wilkite could not redeem the husband.

It would be tedious to report, were it possible to assemble, Wilkes's briefer liaisons and amorous overtures, which certainly extended to late in his life. When he was seventy the gossip columns gave out that he was making "a last Essay on Woman in the neighborhood of Soho." Curiously, despite his charm and his access to good society, he seems never to have had what might be called a Mayfair conquest or an affair with a woman in high society. In the early 1760s Wilkes did, however, write to Charles Churchill: "I wish you could . . . go with me to Lady Vane's house, where you would spend the evening (and dine first apparement) as you like." The Viscountess Vane, who had earlier married a duke's son, "was the finest minuet dancer in England," noted for her extravagance and notorious for her profligacy; and she may have been the exception with Wilkes, or too déclassée to count as one. Wilkes's attachment to Amelia Arnold went on for many years, she not just his mistress, but the mother of a child he grew very fond of. He installed Harriet and her mother in a "lilliputian home" in Kensington Gore and spent much time there, particularly when Polly was not in London; now and then he even gave dinner parties, bringing servants from Prince's Court to wait on table. Although as Mrs. Arnold grew older she grew plainer, having never boasted great looks, Wilkes remained devoted to her and took considerable interest in Harriet's education. Though he voted a childhood letter of hers "very well written" he corrected her spelling and grammar:

> A bad road is spelt rough—an adjective;
> The bird is a ruff—a substantive

For "we have had four or five days of fine weather and I hope *they* will last" read: ". . . and I hope *it* will last." Meaning the weather.

Harriet was to be brought up to become a good housewife, not a social butterfly. Hence Wilkes instructed her to send him regular reports on the Arnold household, garden, and servants. She grew up, like her country-bred mother, loving pets—the house was full of dogs, cats, and birds. "The peroquets," Harriet wrote to her father, "present their compliments to their master and hope his cold is better . . . as for their young mistress, she is as pert as ever." Pert Harriet was indeed—Wilkes called her Miss Riot—and often disrespectful: twice in one morning, for example, she flatly contradicted her father in the presence of various Wilkeses. "If she goes on as she has done of late," Wilkes wrote to Harriet's mother, "she will be a plague to her parents instead of a comfort and blessing"; and after further reproofs, he suggests letting "Harriet read the above more than once, and then burn it." But he remained a loving and indulgent father. Harriet, and Polly who was close to thirty years her elder, apparently never met and were unlike in many other things than age. For all her sweetness and goodness of heart Polly was very much an elegant and perhaps somewhat fussy spinster: this might have awed Harriet, but from what we know of her as a bright, sassy, self-reliant child, she might have found Polly a bore and shown it. But Polly was wise enough, rather than come to know Harriet and her mother, to ask after them, pay them compliments, and send them presents.[2]

Harriet grew up to marry well. Her husband, a lawyer named William Rough, though often in ill health, in need of money, and at odds with his superiors, rose to become Lord Chief Justice of Ceylon and to be awarded a knighthood. He was also something of a radical (in the milder meaning of the word) and a

---

[2] Polly, it is said, tried unsuccessfully to get Harriet, who called herself Wilkes, to change her name.

well-known writer, a friend of Hazlitt, Coleridge, Godwin, Wordsworth, Lamb, and distinguished men of law. The diarist Henry Crabb Robinson described Harriet, after her marriage, as "a woman of some talents and taste, who could make herself attractive." The Roughs had four children, their descendants being Wilkes's only known ones.

Wilkes had also an illegitimate son, Jackie Smith, born in 1763, whose mother had been Wilkes's housekeeper. Toward Jackie, Wilkes showed considerable fatherly interest, seeing a good deal of him as he grew up and intending for him the education and manners of a gentleman. Designated Wilkes's nephew—at least to Polly, who at times looked after him and must have early guessed the truth—Jackie was sent to Harrow and then to an academy in Paris. Spending four years there, he came back to London far more French than English, indeed scarcely able to speak English. Wilkes at once put him in the care of his friend, the great fencing master Angelo, who by way of the gymnasium and the riding school re-Anglicized Jackie, only for Wilkes to plan a year or two in Germany for the boy. At this period Jackie seemed most interested in horses and his father's mistresses—his Gallic manner made him a pet of Mlle. de Charpillon; and when, later, the question of a career came up, Jackie so much loved horses as to ask to become a cavalry officer. Aware that in the late 1770s the British cavalry would not welcome a bastard of John Wilkes's, Wilkes got Jackie into the Hessian cavalry, with the understanding that he could not be sent as a mercenary to America. There were difficulties for Jackie at the outset, but in due course English visitors to Germany spoke of him as "well educated and well behaved" and as also a nice young man—but who now seemed terribly German. Wilkes accordingly withdrew him, sent him back to the academy in Paris, and eventually, with the help of his nabob friend Warren Hastings, got him a cadetship in the Bengal cavalry. But Jackie failed to get very far in India. He changed his name to

John Henry Smith—there were so many John Smiths, he wrote, that he never received his mail—and he begged Wilkes for letters of recommendation, for otherwise he would be left behind. He was still begging for them a year later; and still, it would seem, to no avail. Interestingly, all his letters begin "My dear uncle," except the last one in 1792, which begins "My dear sir." But, as he fades out of history with this last letter to his father, he says "I assure you there is not a happier man in India than I am."[3]

[3] As for other relatives of Wilkes, his brother Israel (1722–1805) eventually settled in New York and had a number of descendants. A grandson of Israel's, Charles Wilkes, was the United States Navy commander who overhauled the British mail steamer *Trent* in 1861 and took off it by force the Confederate commissioners James Mason and Charles Slidell, which created a very famous contretemps with Britain. Later Charles Wilkes got into trouble over similar exploits, was court-martialed, found guilty on several counts, and suspended from duty; but he was ultimately made a rear admiral on the retired list. A sister of Charles, born in New York, married Francis, Lord Jeffrey, a famous Scottish judge in his day but perhaps most famous for founding with Sydney Smith and others the *Edinburgh Review,* and frequently contributing to it.

2

KNOWN, whatever their opinion of him, to all literate Englishmen and many foreigners of his time, Wilkes came to know personally a great number of distinguished and famous ones. In his early days, when he was both something of a political and of a social climber, he fell in, as we know, with a good many aristocratic people, whether through fraternizing with titled fellow rakes or through meeting politicians and Members of Parliament. By the time he got into trouble he was on a certain political footing with several powerful men of state and a number of patrician ones, great Opposition dukes among them. But Wilkes, beyond this, came to know, on social grounds and in terms of friendship, many notable contemporaries in the arts and professions—a relationship that pays tribute to his charm, his wit, his adaptability; indeed, to his being a man of considerable cultivation.[1] Churchill, the man who seems to have meant most to him was, as we know, a talented poet and satirist. Wilkes's boast that given half an hour he could talk away his face, seems to have applied, for different reasons, to men as well as women, even to such doughty opponents as Dr. Johnson and George III. And in his later years, when he was no longer

[1] It may seem surprising that Wilkes never belonged to any of London's more notable clubs; but in view of his middle-class background, of his years of outlawry and jail, and of a reputation bad enough to invite numerous blackballs, his non-membership seems well accounted for.

Wilkes and Polly, 1779, after oil painting by John Zoffany.

Wilkes' "villakin" on the Isle of Wight.

John Wilkes wearing scarlet coat of a colonel of militia,
caricature published on Wilkes' death, 1797.

an idol of mobs, or the most courted of prisoners, or an unseated Member of Parliament, he could be sure of a seat at superior dinner tables. The last fifteen or more years of Wilkes's life are devoid of conflict and very much in character with his inherently social self. He was a diner-out by temperament and only by circumstance an agitator, and infinitely more of a womanizer than a Wilkite. In his later years he did not so much betray his better self as merely revert to his born one; the absence in his life of a perturbed third act and the presence of constant enjoyment bear out that the turbulent second act was indeed something of an accident.

It is not always easy to judge the degree of Wilkes's friendships, particularly with people in the arts. He certainly knew Joshua Reynolds early, when indeed his name appears in Reynolds' records of social engagements oftener than anyone else's. "John Wilkes, with his brother," says Reynolds' biographer Derek Hudson, "was a regular companion at Reynolds' card table in 1755"—this a slight challenge to the belief that Wilkes never gambled, though, this early in life, the occasions doubtless ran to sociability and low stakes. But this is also solid evidence that Wilkes and Reynolds saw a good deal of each other. Hudson says, fifteen years after the card-table days, that Wilkes "had long been one of Reynolds' radical weaknesses"; and as no one could be more circumspect than Reynolds or more conscious of the proprieties, Wilkes must have charmed and amused him.[2]

[2] If Wilkes was one of Reynolds' "radical weaknesses" he could also have been for Reynolds a possible source of artistic strength. In 1777 Wilkes proposed the establishment of a "national gallery" to be set up in the British Museum, this at a moment when Sir Robert Walpole's pictures—"one of the first collections in Europe," as Wilkes described them—were up for sale. Wilkes wanted Parliament to buy them and argued that "a noble gallery ought to be built in the garden of the British Museum for the reception of this invaluable treasure." He also spoke in the Commons for reviving a scheme to have Reynolds and others decorate the interior of St. Paul's. Nothing came of either recommendation, and Walpole's pictures, as is well known, were bought by Catherine the Great and went to the Hermitage in St. Petersburg. Wilkes and Reynolds might also have

When in 1770 or 1771 Reynolds wrote his *Journey from London to Brentford*—a parody of Giuseppe Baretti's *A Journey from London to Genoa*—he spoke of Brentford as a place "renowned in History" and remarked: "This extensive City was formerly inhabited by two Kings who successively dethroned each other . . . The King of England has a chateau directly opposite the town, where he constantly resides, and it is said that if this precaution had not been taken, Don John Alderman Wilks [sic] would certainly before this have been elected King of Brentford. This Don John is the idol of the inhabitants of the town, his name is wrote on every door, window, shutter and dead wall."

F. W. Hilles, in his edition of Reynolds' *Portraits*, remarks that Reynolds frequently "misspells the names of his most intimate friends (e.g. Burk . . . Wilks)." This is the one direct statement of Reynolds' intimacy with Wilkes that I have encountered, and it gains credence from being listed with Burke, who was indeed Reynolds' intimate. And Boswell writes: "With Sir Joshua in his coach to Mr. Wilkes's at Kensington Gore [Mrs. Arnold's house] where we had an excellent entertainment" and where Wilkes brought only rather special friends. On the other hand, Reynolds seldom, and only passingly, mentions Wilkes in his letters; and his only published letter to Wilkes himself thanks him formally—"Sir Joshua Reynolds thanks," etc.—for a book. This was very possibly standard usage in those days, but the date, around 1790, may argue that by then a solid friendship had begun to melt.

Wilkes, it would seem, knew David Garrick better. While in exile he let his Paris apartment to Garrick; Garrick was also on friendly terms with Polly—"A letter from Garrick," Wilkes writes to her from Brighton, "to invite you and me to Hampton and venison." In a letter from Garrick Polly is expected to see

_____

seen each other at the foundling hospital, which was something of a London art center, with its own collection of pictures by superior painters.

"the new play" in Mrs. Garrick's box and Wilkes is welcome
too. "I am much yours," Garrick signs off, "but Miss Wilkes's
more." In 1772 Wilkes saw a good deal of Garrick and his wife
during a visit to the Isle of Wight. "Indeed," Wilkes informs
Polly, "the Garricks gave me many most agreeable hours." "Mrs.
Garrick," he writes, "is as usual the most captivating of the whole
circle"; and he calls her elsewhere "the first woman in England."
Oddly, Wilkes wrote a very damaging epigram about her
husband:

> He comes prepared by nature and by art
> With half a head, but not quite half a heart;
> Half cowardice, half courage to dispense,
> Half modesty, half pride, half wit, half sense.

Wilkes also commented on Garrick's well-known penny-
pinching—thus, apropos someone's small beer, Garrick "would
have made the small beer still smaller"; and there is the famous
actor Samuel Foote's remark that Garrick "walked out with an
intention to do a generous action; but, turning the corner of a
street, he met with the ghost of a halfpenny, which frightened
him." For two reasons in addition to the epigram, Wilkes's friendship with Garrick might have suffered—the lesser reason that
Wilkes was not much of a theatergoer, preferring to be "where
he was able to talk";[3] the more serious reason, that Garrick,
because of his stinginess, refused the hospitality that Wilkes
once asked him for. Garrick died, to be sure, in 1779, just before
Wilkes acquired a good income as chamberlain and before he
displayed his pre-eminently social self. In any case, the two

[3] Wilkes, in one of his less creditable moods, contrived to keep other people
from the theater also. In 1770 he headed a cabal to kill off after two nights a
"capable comedy," Hugh Kelly's *A Word to the Wise,* simply because Kelly
had written in support of the Government. The lethal ploy, it seems, was to
prevent an announcement from the stage of further performances of a play; and
if this could be done on a first or second night, the author received no benefits
whatever and the copyright was valueless. Organized author-baiting and play-
damning was, as with Wilkes's cabal, a common practice.

men during their lifetime were linked in one particular way. "Nothing," said Dr. Johnson's Mrs. Thrale, "is so fatiguing as the life of a wit. [Garrick] and Wilkes are the two oldest men of their ages I know; for they have both worn themselves out by being eternally on the rack to give entertainment to others."

Laurence Sterne and Wilkes, the one so ribald, the other so rakish, could hardly not have known each other; but they seem to have known each other best, and most suitably, in Paris. Writing in the spring of 1764 to Churchill—who had admired Sterne in print and would have enjoyed Sterne as a third in their revels —Wilkes says: "Sterne and I often meet and talk of you. We have an odd party for tonight at Hope's: two lively, young, handsome actresses; Hope and his mistress;—Ah! poor Mrs. Wilkes!" And Sterne wrote later concerning himself, Wilkes, and some others, "We have lived (shag rag and bobtail) all of us, a most jolly nonsensical life." Rumors of Sterne's and Wilkes's friendship soon reached England, the Birmingham *Register* announcing, "We hear that Mr. W[ilkes] and Tristram Shandy, both now at Paris, are going to make the tour of Italy, &c. together"—but what they heard was quite untrue. In the autumn of 1765 Sterne wrote to a friend from southern France: "If Wilkes is at Paris yet, I send him all good wishes." Soon after this Horne wrote to Wilkes: "I passed a week with Sterne at Lyons . . . Forgive my question, and do not answer it if it is impertinent. Is there any coldness between you and Sterne? He speaks very handsomely of you, when it is absolutely necessary to speak; but not with that *warmth and enthusiasm* that I expect from every one that knows you." (In his biography of Mrs. Montagu, Reginald Blunt says that "Sterne's Eliza flirted with Wilkes"— not much, if there *was* a coldness, to go on, unless Eliza went farther.)

This, very inconclusively, concludes the knowledge of the two men's relationship prior to Sterne's death; afterward, however, Wilkes received a number of letters from Sterne's daughter. Speaking also for her mother, she wrote in 1769 to Wilkes, then in the King's Bench prison, hoping he would, when not "better engaged," name an hour for them to visit him. Sterne had died penniless and in debt, and in the letter Lydia Sterne begs Wilkes to ask his friends to subscribe to the three volumes of Sterne's sermons which she and her mother were publishing "in hopes of raising something for our future comfort." Later Lydia wrote rather fulsomely, at staggering length, all about an unsentimental journey of hers in France; and then reminded Wilkes that he had promised to write, or collaborate on, "a life of Mr. Sterne." Three months later, having had no answer, she begs Wilkes for "3 lines: a promise of writing Tristram's life for the benefit of his widow and Daughter would make us happy." A little later she asks him to send her a single line, "I will perform my promise," which will replace their sorrow with joy.

Far from writing the "life," Wilkes never wrote a single line. He and Sterne's friend John Hall-Stevenson, the Eugenius of *Tristram Shandy,* had (according to L. P. Curtis, the editor of the definitive *Letters of Sterne*) agreed to write a biography for the benefit of Sterne's widow and daughter. Apparently Hall-Stevenson did not respond to Lydia's exhortations either; but he *had* published a continuation of *A Sentimental Journey,* to which he added a sketch of Sterne's activities. Wilkes in any case did nothing at all. Some time later, in 1775, Lydia, now married to a Frenchman named Médalle, was editing her father's letters. When, in answer to an inquiry of Wilkes, she heard that he had destroyed all letters from Sterne, she—"inheriting a wayward unscrupulousness from her father"—suggested that if Wilkes would write a few letters imitating Sterne's style, "it would do just as well" and she would insert them "in the volume she was editing"! Could Wilkes, if he did destroy the letters, have done so because they were unfriendly ones, having to do with the "coldness"?

Wilkes started off in David Hume's good graces. When contesting the Berwick-upon-Tweed seat in 1754, and when he was not yet anti-Scottish, Wilkes had a very pleasant letter from Hume, sorry not to have seen him on his return from Glasgow, talking of this and that, and saying that he would be "proud to cultivate a Friendship and Acquaintance" with Wilkes. This, Hume followed up a week later with a letter to accompany a copy of his *History of England,* "which I beg you to accept of." He also entreats Wilkes, despite their not being very well acquainted, to let him have his criticisms of the book. Some ten years later they met in Paris where they were apparently on friendly terms, for all of Hume's making fun of Wilkes's excessively pious churchgoing. But earlier Hume had thought Wilkes's anti-Scottishness ill-mannered and ungenerous, and later he came to outright disapproval of him. "No more noise of Wilkes and Liberty," he writes in 1768. "Lord Mansfield said to me, that it was impossible for him to condemn [Wilkes] to the pillory because the Attorney-General did not demand it." The next year Hume wrote: "This madness about Wilkes . . . exceeds the absurdity of Titus Oates and the popish plot"; and in 1771, "It is a pleasure . . . that the Wilkites and the Bill of Rights-men are fallen into total and deserved contempt." High Tory that he was, Hume saw "disorders" as the abuse of liberty: the English "roar liberty, though they have apparently more liberty than any people in the world; a great many, more than they deserve; and perhaps more than any men ought to have." Hume sympathized, however, with the American colonists. Had it not been for politics, which were a blind spot with Hume, the two men, seated in a drawing room, might have got on splendidly; as it was, the skeptical Tory had no use for the cynical patriot.

With Junius, that master of stinging denunciations—Coleridge said the *Letters of Junius* were suited to their purpose and perfect in their kind—whose anonymity has never been pierced, Wilkes carried on a rather considerable correspondence.[4] They both violently opposed George III and sought to reform the House of Commons; "Kings, Lords and Commons," said Junius, ". . . are the trustees, not the owners of the estate"; and Wilkes's erstwhile friend the Duke of Grafton became Junius's chief villain. Junius among other things attacked Grafton for his treatment of Wilkes: writing in March 1769, when Wilkes was still an outlaw, Junius asks Grafton, who had pardoned a murderer: "Has it never occurred to your Grace . . . that there is another man who is the favorite of his country, whose pardon would have been accepted with gratitude, whose pardon would have healed all our divisions? Have you quite forgotten that this man was once your Grace's friend? Or is it to murderers only that you will extend the mercy of the Crown?" And, a month later, concerning the way Grafton had turned against Wilkes: "I am proud to affirm that, if I had been weak enough to form such a friendship, I never would have been base enough to betray it." When at length, much owing to Junius, Grafton resigned as

---

[4] Junius remains one of the great unsolved mysteries of all time. He was clearly aware, indeed had close knowledge, of political matters and of people of importance. Henry Woodfall, the editor of *The Public Advertiser*, which printed the *Letters* one by one, was known to the public; corresponded with Junius; served as go-between for the Junius–Wilkes letters; and was given by Junius all publishing rights and profits. If Woodfall knew the secret, he kept it. He, like Wilkes, was prosecuted for seditious libel and, in a celebrated verdict, was found guilty of printing and publishing only, which was not a legal verdict. At a second trial Woodfall was freed but had to pay the costs. Many people claimed to know who Junius was, some of them while themselves disclaiming that they were Junius. Among the candidates in this two-hundred-year-old guessing game have been Wilkes, whose own candidate was a certain bishop; Lord Temple, Lord Shelburne, William Gerard Hamilton, Colonel Barré, Edmund Burke, and, the most favored, Sir Philip Francis. But none of these men's hands quite fit the glove. Junius is perhaps the only famous man of whom nothing unquestionable is known but his *Letters* (1768–73). He can be glimpsed at his most menacing in a note to Garrick: "I am very exactly informed of . . . the information you so busily *sent* to Richmond, and with what triumph and exultation it was received. I knew every particular of it the next day . . . Meddle no more, thou busy informer!—It is in *my* power to make you curse the hour in which you dared to interfere with JUNIUS."

Prime Minister, Junius said of him: "Sullen and severe without religion, profligate without gaiety, you may well live like Charles II without being an amiable companion, and for ought I know may die as his father did, without the reputation of a martyr." (Grafton was descended from one of Charles II's bastards.)

Though very critical of Wilkes, Junius all in all approved of him—at least as a *faute de mieux*: "You will not suspect me of setting up *Wilkes* for a perfect character," he wrote in 1771 to a now anti-Wilkes Horne: "The question to the public is, where shall we find a man who with purer principles will go to the length, and run the hazards, that [Wilkes] has done? The season calls for such a man and he ought to be supported." And in his next letter to Horne, Junius sarcastically defends Wilkes at his weakest: Should Wilkes wangle a £1,000 pension for thirty years, "he must be supported . . . because it would mortify the King!" Should Wilkes wish to see Lord Rockingham and his friends "once more in administration . . . the public must . . . assist Mr. Wilkes—because it would mortify the King!" Should Wilkes demand the government of Canada, "he must be supported in his pretensions and upheld in his insolence—because it would mortify the King!"

Junius's correspondence with Wilkes himself was "private" (though Junius, a little later, wanted some of it made public). It extended from August 1771 to January 1772—ten letters or notes from Junius to Wilkes, eight from Wilkes to Junius. Writing first, Junius opens with: "I presume, sir, you are satisfied that I mean you well . . . it must always make part of *Junius's* plan to support Mr. Wilkes while *he* makes common cause with the people." His contention is that Sawbridge rather than Crosby ought to be Lord Mayor and that Wilkes ought to support him. Junius was probably right, but Wilkes in reply thought Junius had "too favorable sentiments of Sawbridge," and added, "I allow him honest but think he has more mulishness than understanding" and "is become the absolute dupe of Malagrida's

[Shelburne's] gang." Also, Sawbridge "has declared that if chosen . . . he would not serve . . . because Townsend ought to be mayor. Such a declaration . . . borders on insanity." Meanwhile Junius had written Wilkes a second letter, this time lengthily criticizing the Bill of Rights Society's plan for reforming the House of Commons. Wilkes in answer says that an American, "Dr. Lee . . . was the author of the too long preamble" to the plan, and of other writings to be deprecated, but that it had been too late to revise them. "I am satisfied," he adds, "that Junius now means me well, and I wish to merit, more than his regard, his friendship." "Lord Chatham," Wilkes continues, "said to me ten years ago 'The King is the falsest hypocrite in Europe.' I must hate the man as much as even Junius can." The correspondence continues amiably and admiringly on the same or kindred subjects, though Junius on occasion reads Wilkes the riot act: "Depend upon it," he writes, "the perpetual union of *Wilkes* and *mob* does you no service . . . It is your interest to keep up dignity and gravity. I would not make myself cheap by walking the streets so much as you do." Irrepressible, Wilkes retorted that if he stayed indoors it would be from fear of those "villains out of hell, the bailiffs." Later Junius picked Wilkes to revise his preface and his introduction to his *Letters*, saying that he accepted as much of Wilkes's friendship "as you can impart to a man you will assuredly never know."

James Boswell we have seen with Wilkes during his days of outlawry on the Continent; but despite their differences over religion and their greater differences over politics, along with Wilkes's opinion of the Scots, their friendship persisted for many years. Actually the two men were very little drawn together by their profligacy; indeed, their attitudes toward it differed. "You too like the thing," Wilkes wrote to his fellow rake, "almost as well as I do"; but Boswell, it appears, disliked to talk and laugh about it, which Wilkes enjoyed doing very much. What Boswell chiefly appreciated and admired in Wilkes was his courageous and virile nature and his always being very good company. They were also cultivated men, with almost as much taste for Latin as for ladies; and though Wilkes was much less a snob than Boswell, they both liked knowing wellborn and distinguished people. What Wilkes—who seems to have sought out Boswell less than Boswell did him—most prized in their friendship is less easily isolated; but as Boswell's authoritative biographer, Frederick Pottle says, he was the first person who "assessed Boswell's peculiar gift correctly, and encouraged him to exploit it. Everybody else wanted to make Boswell over, Wilkes saw that he was *sui generis* . . . Long before any one else, he recognized that Boswell's letters and journals were significant art, not the mere exercises that Boswell himself considered them." Certainly very few men would, like Boswell, while throwing up their hands at Wilkes's wickedness, have stretched forth their hands in genuine friendship.

Boswell, in one way or another, wrote a great deal to and about Wilkes. He first saw him in November 1762 at a meeting of the Beefsteak Club. He first met him, along with Charles Churchill, on May 24, 1763, just eight days after his first meeting with Dr. Johnson and soon after Wilkes's arrest and confinement in the Tower. Wilkes he thought "a lively, facetious man," Churchill rough, blunt, and very clever. "They were very civil to me"; but their profane, boisterous manner led Boswell, or gave him the excuse, to call on Dr. Johnson. The next day, however, Boswell, as the most unhesitant of doorbell ringers, speaks in his journal of calling on Wilkes and, not finding him at home, "leave card, with full directions." He had been a faithful reader of *The North Briton*—"There's a poignant acrimony in it," he told his journal, "that is very relishing"—but he stopped commenting before *No. 45* appeared. Boswell himself submitted an essay on British politics to *The North Briton*, but it was never published. (Later, during their Continental talks, Wilkes flattered Boswell as the best person to defend the Scots against his *North Briton* attacks upon them.)

On their getting to know each other, Boswell wrote to Wilkes: "I would carpe diem as much as I can while you and I are near each other." While piling on admiration of Wilkes he can be amusingly tactless: "I have found," he writes, "cheerfulness, knowledge, wit and generosity even in Mr. Wilkes"; and of Wilkes being spoken of in Italy as "Il Bruto Inglese," "It is disputed among your friends and your ennemys," Boswell writes, "whether the epithet ought to be translated 'The English Brutus' or 'The Ugly Englishman.'" (Years later, in a letter to Wilkes concerning Polly, Boswell again jests about Wilkes's looks: "You should have been mon beau père. Ah, qu'il est beau!") And having said in a letter, "I embrace you with joy as a regular correspondent," Boswell next proceeds to lambaste Wilkes with "You did all in your power to stir up jealousy and hatred between the southern and northern inhabitants of Britain, and . . . you treated with indecent irony our worthy monarch, for which I say you deserved to be beaten with many stripes."

Boswell's frankness about Wilkes, about himself, about almost anything, must have amused Wilkes as it has amused posterity. His omniverous curiosity reveals itself in his wanting to see Wilkes (before he knew him) brought out of the Tower; arriving too late, he decided he ought to see prisoners somewhere, so he set off at once for Newgate. Toward Wilkes in the King's Bench prison some years later Boswell showed, though with his usual frankness, more prudence than friendship: "I had a desire to visit the pleasant fellow," he wrote, "but thought it might hurt me essentially." (As for the risk involved in seeing Wilkes, Pottle reminds us that Boswell was at precisely that moment preparing to load the public press with an account of the incredible ass he had just made of himself at the Stratford Jubilee.) For the same prudential reasons, Boswell had a year earlier caught sight of Wilkes in London but "made no attempt to speak to him" or even "wave his hand." In his journals Boswell sets down in rough form talks with Wilkes at some of their Continental meetings. Given to bouts of melancholy, Boswell was given to philosophic speculation also, asking Wilkes, for one example, how he could get through life. "While there's all ancient and modern learning and all the arts and sciences," Wilkes answered, "there's enough for life even if it lasted three thousand years." Boswell protested: "But the problem of Fate and Freewill?" Wilkes spoke three words: "Let 'em alone." Wilkes soon changed the subject: "Dissipation and profligacy . . . renew the mind. I wrote my best *North Briton* in bed with Betsy Green." And the next day Wilkes continued: "Thank Heaven for having given me the love of women. To many she gives not the noble passion of lust."

In postprison years the friendship was resumed[5] and one of the great "differences" between Boswell and Wilkes was somewhat narrowed. The High-Tory and Johnson-exalting Boswell, who had earlier championed Corsican independence, now turned sympathetic, as both man and lawyer, to the American colonists. And in 1776 Boswell wrote an eight-stanza campaign song for Wilkes, who was standing for chamberlain, which Wilkes had printed but to no avail. In 1778 Boswell records a conversation while calling on Wilkes, "the same cheerful, gay, polite, classical man as when he and I were happy together at Naples in 1765 . . . I was in excellent spirits and a pretty good match for him." He also records that Wilkes called him the only Scot he knew with a sense of humor.

From the 1780s on, Wilkes and Boswell were on a very friendly footing. In 1783 Boswell, now the Laird of Auchinleck, invites Wilkes to come to Scotland for a visit. A few years later Boswell gives a dinner party, with Wilkes and Reynolds

[5] Chauncey Tinker, in *Young Boswell*, ranks Wilkes, together with Dr. Johnson and the Corsican patriot Pasquale di Paoli, as Boswell's "three most celebrated friends."

among the guests; Wilkes invites Boswell to a dinner party; later Boswell asks Wilkes, who had said of the *Life of Johnson* that it was "a wonderful book," to confirm this in writing for his archives;[6] and in the last of his letters to Wilkes, Boswell writes that it will be another week before he can repay Wilkes the money he has borrowed.

But of all their meetings and dinner parties, the most famous —indeed one can think of few dinner parties more famous— centers in the presence of Dr. Johnson. Wilkes and Johnson, even more than Wilkes and Boswell, had differed on the subject of politics and religion, not to bring up the subject of morals. At their very first meeting in 1763 Dr. Johnson said to Boswell of Wilkes, "I think he is safe from the law but he is an abusive scoundrel." In 1770 Johnson had written, in his pamphlet *The False Alarm*, of Wilkes: "Lampoon itself would disdain to speak ill of him"; had gone on to call him "a retailer of sedition and obscenity" and to add, "We are now disputing . . . whether Middlesex shall be represented . . . by a criminal, from a gaol." In 1773, during his tour of the Hebrides with Boswell, Johnson, talking of politics, said, "It is wonderful to think that all the force of government was required to prevent Wilkes from being chosen the chief magistrate of London[7] though the liverymen knew he would rob their shops; knew he would debauch their daughters." And, as we know, Wilkes—although he had praised Johnson's *Rambler*—had attacked him, in particular as George

[6] Actually Wilkes had grave reservations about the *Life:* "His book," Wilkes wrote to Polly, ". . . is that of an entertaining madman. Poor Johnson! Does a friend come and add, to the gross character of such a man, the unknown trait of disgusting gluttony? I suspect . . . a mistake in the *dramatic personae.* He has put down to [himself] what was undoubtedly said by Johnson." (That Boswell may have seemed a bit mad is not too hard to believe; but to write thus of Boswell's manner of writing the *Life* is more than a bit mad of Wilkes.)

[7] Wilkes was of course chosen chief magistrate (Lord Mayor) the next year and, said Boswell, "discharged the duties of that high office with great honour to himself and advantage to the City." (On Wilkes's being elected chamberlain, Boswell hurried to congratulate him with "All Scotland, my dear sir, will rejoice at your triumph.")

III's creature, for accepting a pension. Only a Boswell would first have dreamed of bringing the two men together; would then have dared to do it; and would finally have pulled it off. Boswell's delightful account of the meeting must in a greatly abbreviated form be set down; no one familiar with it will, I think, protest:

My desire of being acquainted with celebrated men had made me obtain an introduction to Dr. Samuel Johnson and to John Wilkes, Esq. Two men more different could perhaps not be selected out of all mankind. I conceived an irresistible wish to bring Dr. Johnson and Mr. Wilkes together. How to manage it, was a nice and difficult matter.

My worthy booksellers and friends, Messieurs Dilly in the Poultry, had invited me to meet Mr. Wilkes and some more gentlemen on Wednesday, May 15 [1776]. "Pray (said I) let us have Dr. Johnson." "What, with Mr. Wilkes? not for the world (said Mr. Edward Dilly): Dr. Johnson would never forgive me."—"Come (said I), if you'll let me negociate for you, I will be answerable that all shall go well." DILLY: "Nay, if you will take it upon you, I am sure I shall be very happy to see them both here."

I was sensible that [Dr. Johnson] was sometimes a little actuated by the spirit of contradiction, and by means of that I hoped I should gain my point. I was persuaded that if I had come upon him with a direct proposal, "Sir, will you dine in company with Jack Wilkes?" he would have flown into a passion, and would probably have answered, "Dine with Jack Wilkes, Sir! I'd as soon dine with Jack Ketch." I therefore took occasion to open my plan thus: "Mr. Dilly, Sir, sends his respectful compliments to you, and would you dine with him on Wednesday next, along with me." JOHNSON: "Sir, I am obliged to Mr. Dilly. I will wait upon him." BOSWELL: "Provided, Sir, I suppose, that the company which he is to have is agreeable to you." JOHNSON: "What do you mean, Sir? What do you take me for? Do you think I am so ignorant of the world as to imagine that I am to prescribe to a gentleman what company he is to have at his table?" BOSWELL: "I beg your pardon, Sir, for wishing to prevent you from meeting people whom you might not like. I should not be surprised to find Jack Wilkes there." JOHNSON: "And if Jack Wilkes *should* be there, what is that to *me*, Sir? My dear friend, let us have no more of this." BOSWELL: "Pray, forgive me, Sir: I meant well." Thus I secured him, and told Dilly that he would find him very well pleased to be one of his guests on the day appointed.

Upon the much expected Wednesday, when we entered Mr. Dilly's drawing room [Dr. Johnson] found himself in the midst of a company he did not know. I kept myself snug and silent, watching how he would conduct himself. I observed him whispering to Mr. Dilly, "Who is that gentleman, Sir?"—"Mr. Arthur Lee."—JOHNSON: "Too, too, too" (under his breath), which was one of his habitual mutterings. Mr. Lee could not but be very obnoxious to Johnson, for he was not only a *patriot*, but an *American*. "And who is the gentleman in lace?"—"Mr. Wilkes, Sir." This information confounded him still more. His feelings, I dare say, were aukward enough. But he no doubt recollected his having rated me for supposing that he could be at all disconcerted by any company, and he therefore resolutely set himself to behave quite as an easy man of the world.

The cheering sound of "Dinner is upon the table," dissolved his reverie, and we *all* sat down without any symptom of ill humour. Mr. Wilkes placed himself next to Dr. Johnson, and behaved to him with so much attention and politeness that he gained upon him insensibly. No man eat more heartily than Johnson, or loved better what was nice and delicate. Mr. Wilkes was very assiduous in helping him to some fine veal. "Pray give me leave, Sir;—It is better here—A little of the brown—Some fat, Sir—A little of the stuffing—Some gravy—Let me have the pleasure of giving you some butter—Allow me to recommend a squeeze of this orange—or the lemon, perhaps, may have more zest."—"Sir, Sir, I am obliged to you, Sir," cried Johnson, bowing, and turning his head to him with a look for some time of "surly virtue," but, in a short while, of complacency.

Mr. Wilkes remarked, that "among all the bold flights of Shakespeare's imagination, the boldest was making Birnamwood march to Dunsinane, creating a wood where there never was a shrub; a wood in Scotland, ha! ha! ha!" Mr. Arthur Lee mentioned some Scotch who had taken possession of a barren part of America, and wondered why they should choose it. JOHNSON: "Why, Sir, all barrenness is comparative. The *Scotch* would not know it to be barren." BOSWELL: "Come, come. You have now been in Scotland, Sir, and say if you did not see meat and drink enough there." JOHNSON: "Why yes, Sir; meat and drink enough to give the inhabitants sufficient strength to run away from home." Upon this topick he and Mr. Wilkes could perfectly assimilate; here was a bond of union between them. They amused themselves with persevering with the old jokes. JOHNSON: (To Mr. Wilkes) "You must know, Sir, I lately took my friend Boswell, and shewed him genuine civilised life in an English provincial town. I turned him loose at Lichfield, my native city, that he might see for once real civility; for you know he lives among savages in Scotland, and among rakes in London." WILKES: "Except when he is with grave, sober, decent people, like you and me." JOHNSON: (smiling) "And we ashamed of him."

"I attended Dr. Johnson home," Boswell continues, "and had the satisfaction to hear him tell Mrs. Williams how much he had been pleased with me, Wilkes's company, and what an agreeable day he had passed."[8] Wilkes called on Dr. Johnson, who found him "very amusing," but in less than a year he attacked Johnson in the House of Commons as a "state hireling" whose name "disgraced the Civil List." And Johnson did write, not very successfully, for the Administration, perhaps thinking that he must show gratitude or make plain his Tory views.

In 1777, talking to Boswell, Johnson said: "Did we not hear so much said of Jack Wilkes, we should think more highly of

[8] Writing next day to Mrs. Thrale, Johnson said: "You think . . . what is Johnson doing? What should he be doing? He is breaking jokes with Jack Wilkes upon the Scots. Such, Madam, are the vicissitudes of things."

his conversation. Jack has great variety of talk, Jack is a scholar, and Jack has the manners of a gentleman . . . He has always been *at me;* but I would do Jack a kindness rather than not."⁹

Just five years after they first met, Wilkes and Johnson met at the Dillys' a second time. "No negociation was now required to bring them together," says Boswell; Johnson was "very glad to meet Wilkes again." The two of them made more jokes about the Scots and their poverty; and at one point Wilkes said to Boswell, "loud enough for Dr. Johnson to hear," "Dr. Johnson should make me a present of his 'Lives of the Poets,' as I am a poor patriot, who cannot afford to buy them." Johnson seemed to take no notice, but soon after called to Mr. Dilly, "Pray, Sir, be so good as to send a set of my *Lives* to Mr. Wilkes, with my compliments." And at the end of the evening Boswell "was struck with observing Dr. Samuel Johnson and John Wilkes, Esq. literally *tête-à-tête;* for they were reclined upon their chairs, with their heads leaning almost close to each other, and talking earnestly, in a kind of confidential whisper, of the personal quarrel between George the Second and the King of Prussia." But the honors of the evening, by way of retort, went undoubtedly to Johnson when, earlier, he had asked Wilkes: "Is there not a law, Sir, against exporting the current coin of the realm?" and Wilkes had answered "Yes, Sir; but might not the House of Commons, in case of real evident necessity, order our own current coin to be sent into our own colonies?" "Sure, Sir," said Johnson, *"you* don't think *a resolution of the House of Commons* equal to *the law of the land."* To which "God forbid, Sir!" was all Wilkes could summon in answer.

⁹ Wilkes had some years earlier done Johnson a kindness: when a press gang seized Johnson's servant and Tobias Smollett asked Wilkes for aid, Wilkes got the servant released. Before the *Briton–North Briton* animosity, Smollett had been a friend of Wilkes's. Little more than three months before the start of *The North Briton,* Smollett wrote to him: "Dear Sir: My warmest regard, affection and attachment you have long secured"; also that he hoped to visit him soon. But he was also moved to write of Wilkes as a demagogue, "disgraced by the most dissolute morals and profligate habits."

In 1783 Boswell suggested another meeting between the two men and informed Wilkes that he had found it "would not be unpleasant to Dr. Johnson to dine at Mr. Wilkes's. The thing would be so *curiously benignant*, it were a pity it should not take place." But Johnson regretted: "Mr. Johnson returns thanks to Mr. and Miss Wilkes for their kind invitation; but he is engaged for Tuesday to Sir Joshua Reynolds, and for Wednesday to Mr. Paradise."[10]

[10] Chauncey Tinker thought that Johnson definitely did not want to go to Wilkes's or even write to him; and that, since nowhere in the *Life of Johnson* does Boswell mention the matter, there must have been something of a scene between him and Johnson, which ended with Johnson writing the few lines just quoted and which Johnson furthermore did not himself despatch but made Boswell deliver. And so it might have been, but the note, though brief, cannot be called curt; and surely, had it meant to be, Johnson would have regretted without even speaking of previous engagements, let alone specifying whom they were with.

THE RULING CLASS

THE EIGHTEENTH CENTURY'S aristocracy lived most of the year outside London, but came to it to escape the hardships of deep-country winters, to enjoy the pleasures of a metropolitan society, and, above all else, to rule. For Parliament met there, and the upper classes *were* Parliament, its House of Commons scarcely less than its House of Lords. England's eighteenth-century middle class, with its increasingly greater economic power, had a considerable voice in all that went on; had, often indeed, the deciding vote. But though it might get its desires voted into law, unless it had backing from the upper class—as Wilkes originally had—it very seldom voted itself into Parliament. The Commons might champion the freeborn Briton's cause or further the London merchant's or Bristol shipowner's welfare; but it was still very much a gentleman's, if not always a gentlemanly, club. With modest exceptions, the House of Commons was composed of people with at least some claims to birth and with usually some affiliations with the House of Lords, if only because most seats in the Commons were in the disposal of affluent peers, blooded landowners, or nabobs in the East India Company. Many such M.P.s were jackbooted and muttonheaded country cousins, connoisseurs of little else than horse-flesh; or were henbrained fops, whose forte was lace ruffles or clouded canes. They enjoyed patronage and in many cases not just seats in Parliament but pensions and sinecures and, under George III, bribes. They might be the King's Turnspit or even the King's Cock Crower; and unless this was so, the Administration could not feel sure of the worst nonentity's vote. Of its disproportional representation—its private ownership of a number of seats, its pocket boroughs frequently up for sale—and of the power of the great Whig grandees who long ran England, we are well aware.

It was not, however, the long summer of the Whig ascendancy that gave Parliament its historic eighteenth-century luster, but rather, for all the King's pigheaded blunders, the subsequent age of George III with its large issues and great oratory. Earlier—as in some ways always—a highborn Parliament failed to provide highbred conduct. Far from displaying a starched elegance, M.P.s would joke, eat, suck oranges and crack nuts, stretch out full length and snooze, or cough down boring or bungling speakers. But there were also great speakers, as there came to be great occasions for them. The elder Pitt, with his lordly presence, sonorous voice, and dramatic delivery, was as impressive an orator as the House would ever hear. Soon after his resounding victories of 1759 there opened an age of oratory which would extend from one epoch-making upheaval to another, from Burke's plea for conciliation with America to his warnings about the revolution in France. After the elder Pitt came Burke, Fox, Sheridan, and Pitt the Younger—no group more famous, or more formidable, in parliamentary annals. The year 1788 saw the opening in Westminster Hall of the trial of Warren Hastings, which with its heraldic splendor, its roll call of crimes, and its magnetic orators, was hardly so much an indictment, as a valedictory of the old order.

To be sure, the *opening* of the Hastings trial was mainly a social event in a lustrous age of society. For as the eighteenth century had moved forward among the Georges, the life of the ruling class had undergone change, with, dominating its tastes, a conscious striving after elegance or at any rate elegant frivolity; and with the fine brushwork of Gainsborough and Reynolds commemorating its distinction. The great London site and symbol of this patrician world had by now emerged—which is to say that fields behind Piccadilly known as May Fair had become streets and squares and town houses constituting Mayfair; and along Piccadilly itself great mansions were rising. In those years the withdrawing room, whither ladies withdrew to leave the men at table, became that other symbol of urbanity, the drawing room (though it seldom became that center of wit and formal talk, the salon).

In other ways, however, society *was* French, or frenchified, enough; for ever since Charles II's return from exile in 1660, it had been fashionable to ape the French courtier's manner and out-peacock the French fop's clothes, just as no English words were so indispensable as such French ones as *goût* and *ton*. As a model of good form there emerged yet another lasting symbol, Lord Chesterfield. Even in his own day he seemed more statue than man, and in his famous *Letters* was certainly more schoolmaster than father, warning his son against every conceivable social blunder, even that it was vulgar to laugh and lowbred to play the violin. Such implacable elegance could only produce glacial sociability; but happily Chesterfield was too severe a model to become the mode. Much more frequent in upper-class society were rakes and bullies on the one hand and mincing coxcombs who scented themselves and went in for girls' names on the other. The *ton* itself was to be defined as "taking no notice of things, and never seeing people . . . and never hearing a word . . . and always finding fault; all the *ton* do so."

The aristocracy became more and more of a fixed caste. For one thing, what with the increase in middle-class wealth, there was more clamor for admittance to society and less willingness to admit. In Queen Anne's day aristocrats could safely condescend to the bonhomie of the coffeehouses; a half century later not only had society become more rigid, but the most sociable of institutions had become the most snobbish: the coffeehouse had given way to the club. Membership in White's, or Boodle's, or Almack's, which later became Brooks's, could be greater proof of status than membership in the House of Commons. The two most celebrated clubs were political adjuncts of the House, White's being rather augustly Tory, Brooks's rather dashingly Whig.

Not the ballot box, however, but the dice box was the real emblem of the clubs. The most famous Whig at Brooks's, Charles James Fox, was also its most famous gambler, who once boasted of losing £200,000 (some $6,000,000 in today's money) in a single night. But Fox's was an epidemic vice: the betting books of the clubs abound in stiff wagers on virtually any subject, such as which of two pregnant women would have a child first ("N.B. Miscarriages go for nothing"). One member quit Brooks's in disgust for having won only £12,000 in two months.

The decanter pretty well kept pace with the dice box. The English jested that water is very good to bathe in (though there is no great evidence that they bathed in it: Norfolk, the premier duke of England, was notorious for neither washing nor changing his linen). What is more, the English did not greatly favor light wines; they might indeed have been heeding Dr. Johnson's famous prescription: "Claret is for boys, port for men, but he who would aspire to be a hero must drink brandy." Dr. Johnson himself once drank, without budging, thirty-six glasses of port with a lump of sugar in each glass. The younger Pitt's addiction to port enabled him, as he put it, "always to see two Speakers when addressing the House." It was mandatory to be a three-bottle man at a sitting (though the bottle, by today's standards, was small); Sheridan, the chief dramatist of the age, was said to drink six, and Richard Porson, the chief classical scholar, having drunk all he could get, would go round draining what was left in other men's wineglasses—and, if necessary, it was said, would swallow ink. From their getting less exercise, men of fashion could be even worse "soakers" than the country gentry. The drinking not only ruined and shortened lives, it menaced many other people's; for though most men drank well, many men did not and while in their cups would quarrel, play barbarous practical jokes, assault women, and come to fatal dueling. The wellborn, like their inferiors, lurched and sprawled in the streets: certain hackney drivers virtually lived off cruising about late at night to pick up swaying gentlemen and carry them home.

Even those who could keep steady on their legs might lose the use of them, for the upper-class consumption of port brought on the upper-class affliction of gout, punishable by gout boots, wheeled chairs, and bed. Huge heavy meals were as common among the rich as was heavy drinking; and dinner—which, from being served around two in the afternoon early in the century, had reached six at the end—was usually supplemented by supper and late hours. (Indeed, one great lord's cook threatened to give notice, from being worn out preparing suppers at three in the morning.)

But not in gambling, drinking, and eating alone was this age of elegance also one of excess. In the way of costume, probably no other modern period can rival the second half of the eighteenth century, whether for being gorgeous or *outré*. Dress swam with color, with sumptuous fabrics and gold lace. Every gathering suggested a fancy-dress ball—or a mad dream of one, for men as well as women might circle the ballroom in high heels, and women generally wore ten-foot towers of false hair so that, driving in carriages, they were forced to sit on the floor. The male fops or macaronis wore suits costing £500, and a fop who committed suicide left a wardrobe that fetched £15,000 ($450,000 today) when auctioned off. Surviving today as symbols of the age, men would rap their snuffboxes and women rattle their

fans. Too often elegance could only shake its head at extravagance, and fashion goggle at the *dernier cri.* Yet inside a generation sobriety would have the last word for good and all. The
French Revolution set so high a tax on hair powder that the
supreme emblem of the expiring age—powdered hair—expired
with it. So did dress swords and knee breeches and silk stockings
for men; men took to trousers while buckles gave way to "the
effeminate shoe-string," and umbrellas were no longer unmanly.

Although, as the century advanced, sexual morality grew more
and more straitlaced, the aristocracy was affected least. Not only
were many great lords notable rakes, but many great ladies were
among their conquests. If early in the century Horace Walpole
was thought not to be Sir Robert's son, and a child of Henrietta
Duchess of Marlborough was almost certainly Congreve's daughter, late in the century the ménage of the Duke of Devonshire
sported a nursery of many fathers, and Dr. Johnson called the
aristocratic Lady Diana Beauclerk a whore. Yet in the course of
the century not only did wild oats and wantonness decline, but
the flaunting of loose morals gave way, with the help of middle-
class morality, to a hypocritical decorum. The theater, always
something of a barometer of behavior, keeps bearing this out.
It is enough to compare Sir John Vanbrugh's bawdy *Relapse,*
produced in 1697, with Sheridan's stainless *School for Scandal,*
produced in 1777; but it is even more telling to compare *The
Relapse* with *A Trip to Scarborough,* the cleaned-up play Sheridan made from it.

But however innocuous the trip to Scarborough, London's
own famous pleasure haunts added risk to recreation. It was a
sufficiently democratic recreation, which could equally serve lords
and aldermen, housewives and hussies. Vauxhall, on the Surrey
side of the river, dating (under another name) from the Restoration, was purely for summer frolics, being visited by everyone
from "the Duke of Grafton to the children of the Foundling

Hospital." There music played, barges went "swan-hopping,"[1] tea was drunk and reputations were torn to shreds, or expired amid the shrubberies. By 1763 the "dark alleys" had to be railed off; by 1764 the railings were all in pieces.

Ranelagh, across the river in Chelsea, was opened in 1742 and though available to all breeds—the opening was described as "much nobility and much mob"—it seems to have become, with time, more fashionable and more "discreet" than Vauxhall; it was indeed said to be so quiet and orderly "that you could hear the whishing sound of the ladies' trains as the immense assembly walked round and round the room." In due course Horace Walpole announced that the newest fashion was to go to Ranelagh "two hours after it is over . . . The music ends at ten, the company goes at twelve." There was strolling and strutting, there were royal families and rustic ones, there was tea drinking, fireworks, and regattas; much music, and masquerades that cast reflections on Ranelagh's morals.

The Pantheon in Oxford Road, designed by the very gifted James Wyatt, was described as "the most beautiful building in England"; but its patrician masquerades came to be denounced with such allegations as that Lady Grosvenor, "a fine woman," was there "lost to all sense of modesty." At another Pantheon entertainment Miss Elizabeth Chudleigh, who would soon bigamously marry a duke, appeared almost naked. Masquerades, generally, became such social villains, so mongrel and lax, as to go out of style and drive their entrepreneurs out of business.

There was also a more private society life, a *grand monde* whose houses commanded the services of Gainsborough and Reynolds and whose drawing rooms and ballrooms and supper rooms might claim a Gainsborough's elegant grace, a Reynolds's complacent distinction. One change in upper-class life, as the century moved forward, was the much greater social min-

---

[1] Actually, swan-upping, which meant marking the swans (many of them at that time privately owned) on the Thames.

gling of the sexes, this despite the advent and permanent ascendancy of clubs. One reason was the advent of many fine town houses, a number of them bearing historic names. These palatial dwellings became showcases for hospitality. Among the great houses were Burlington House, boasting "the most expensive piece of wall in England"; Devonshire House, which would be sneered at as "spacious—but so are the East India Company's warehouses"; Lansdowne House, possessing fine books, splendid pictures and statuary; and, enjoying a longer and more literary fame, Montagu House, where the best-known of the century's bluestockings was hostess to Wilkes. Much talked of was its Feather Room, for the adornment of which Mrs. Montagu sought birds' plumage of all her acquaintance, even the "tails of partridges," but in maintaining which Mrs. Montagu proved no match for moths.

The "tone" of Montagu House, and of certain less sumptuous sister houses, was seldom one of fad or feathers. Small talk was outlawed and the card table unthought of, while discussing scandal was itself judged scandalous. In other drawing rooms there was more wit if less intellect. By the 1780s Devonshire House was presided over by a lady of different stamp but dazzling aura, by that Duchess whom Reynolds painted three times —once by herself, once as a child with her mother, once as a mother with her child. Despite a by no means immaculate life, Georgiana Duchess of Devonshire still goes swathed in glamour, she who, to win votes for Charles James Fox, kissed the most plebeian lips and whom the Prince of Wales called "the best-bred woman in England."

Her Grace evoked a resplendent world of powerful Whigs and of brilliant and witty personalities. The wit, now whimsically and now waspishly social, was the champagne of clubs and country houses, very little of it displaying a Swift's acid bite or a Hogarth's forthright fist. Chesterfield's wit could be impeccably iced, as in describing a certain marriage: "Nobody's son has married Everybody's daughter"; but oftener, as with mere society wits like George Selwyn, the effect lay half in how the remark was drawled, and the remark itself died with the occasion. Even Sheridan, who in his own age held primacy of place, administered gentle flicks, as when an old maid, whom he avoided taking a walk with on the plea that it was raining, informed him that the rain had stopped. "Yes," said Sheridan, "it has stopped enough for one person to go walking, but not for two."

This was also an Age of Reason which could yet be glitteringly streaked with eccentricity; with *sui generis* bordering on *non compos mentis;* with nonconformity that had great panache. And it is this bold impress, this pungent infusion of personality, that often saves what is Augustan about the eighteenth century from being arid; and that saves from being sordid what so often is licentious and decadent. Certain figures, certain chroniclers stand out. Horace Walpole, for example, is—in books dealing with eighteenth-century England—probably the most quoted of all writers, and was indeed the century's greatest, if most gossipy, social historian. Yet this son of Sir Robert's, as elegant and feline as Sir Robert was hearty and bluff, did much more than exhaustively chronicle his times. He enlivened and embellished them, if only with trifles and toys. There was his sham-Gothic house, Strawberry Hill; his pioneering neo-Gothic novel, *The Castle of Otranto.* But far more serviceable were his anecdotes of people, which stud his letters and other people's books; and there were his cynical *touchés,* such as "Virtue knows to a farthing what it has lost by not having been vice." All this, and a polished style, have given the rococo dilettante a lasting fame: right in our own generation a word derived from him— *serendipity*—has taken root.

Lady Mary Wortley Montagu survives, like Walpole, as a superb letter writer; but was unlike him in almost everything else. As against his squeamishness, fussiness, elegant birdcage cosmos, she was the unfettered aristocrat for whom privilege meant participation, whether with the patrician's assurance, the bohemian's adventurousness, or the barbarian's feudal appetites. A duke's daughter who became an ambassador's wife and a Prime Minister's mother-in-law, Lady Mary penetrated the harem in Constantinople and brought back to England the Turkish custom of inoculation against smallpox. When just past fifty she left England and her husband and for over twenty years roamed up and down Europe, meeting all manner of the great, turning her back on pointless proprieties and on a worthless son, being named in scandal and called a freak. She grew stingy and slovenly—told at the opera that her hands were dirty, she said, "You should see my feet"—and at length, looking more witch than woman, she crept back to England to die.

Lady Mary's restless, unladylike years on the Continent call to mind that more classical Continental visit prescribed for young gentlemen: the Grand Tour. Perhaps first conceived by Queen Elizabeth—though it is certainly something she never embarked upon—it became in the eighteenth century a uniquely English requisite of culture and status, with Paris introducing the young English "milord" into a world of sophisticated fashions, and with Italy, that second home or Heaven for the English traveler, providing a cultural feast not ungarnished with amour. The Low Countries, a few German duchies and principalities, and (as the taste for romantic scenery grew) the Alps could also form part of the tour which, with long sojourns in various capitals, might last for several years. Among many young tourists none saw so much, met so many, stayed so long, or behaved so oddly as James Boswell, Esquire.

The presumed purpose and the parental conception of the Grand Tour was to polish the young visitors' manners, widen their horizons, and deepen their aesthetic awareness—though the more realistic parent might also envisage an accredited courtesan or an obliging contessa or two. And indeed a great many young gentlemen came home chiefly as finished rakes, or depleted gamblers, or perfumed fops; in fact it was remarked

> How much a dunce that has been sent to roam
> Excels a dunce that has been kept at home.

The young men's well-off elders also traveled, with many of them given to collecting, particularly in that vast picture gallery, Italy. They bought so madly and indiscriminately that the Romans said, "If the amphitheatre were portable, the English would carry it off." Throughout the century there was constant traffic and mutual gain between London and Paris. However often France and England might be at war, Paris remained a pleasure ground for England's aristocrats. At first glance this seems truest in the way of fashions, of the need for French clothes and jewels, French lady's maids and valets, French cosmetics and perfumes, French wigs and wines, French fencing masters, dancing masters, and, as we know, French turns of phrase. Yet at times there was an even greater passion in France for things English. To be sure, in order to visit England the French often needed, as with Voltaire and Rousseau, the spur of unpopularity or exile; but the French delightedly opened their doors to English aristocrats and equally to people of reputation rather than rank—to a Sterne, a Hume, a Gibbon, a Wilkes, an Arthur Young. But by the end of the century the English were playing host on a different basis to French aristocrats, who were seeking refuge from an uncongenial revolution.

3

Though from the early 1780s on, Wilkes as a Member of Parliament and a symbol of causes was indeed an exhausted volcano, he not so much exhausted his politics as scrambled them. To be sure, the politics of the first half of the 1780s were very much scrambled themselves: Lord North finally got George III's permission to resign; then, in 1782, the death of Lord Rockingham put an end to the coalition ministry that bore his name; and, as the King's choice, Lord Shelburne took over, with Pitt the Younger as Chancellor of the Exchequer leading the Commons, Fox and Burke having resigned from the ministry. Early in 1783 Shelburne resigned, both Lord North and a twenty-two-year-old Pitt refused to form a ministry, and what followed was the astounding creation, under the nominal premiership of the Duke of Portland, of a Fox-North coalition. When in December 1783 Fox's India Bill was defeated in the Lords, the coalition resigned, and Pitt became Prime Minister and, as Chancellor of the Exchequer, the only Cabinet member in the Commons. All this took place within two years.

Wilkes, who had consistently supported Fox since he had changed "from hot Toryism to savage opposition" and become a liberal Whig, now turned against him for having trampled on Whig principles. Fox had, to begin with, opposed removing Wilkes's expulsion from the records of the Commons, a personal as well as political slap; Fox, disapproving of Shelburne as Rockingham's successor, had resigned in a huff just when peace terms with America and other countries were about to be made; and Fox, in joining North, had not only split the Whig ranks but had himself linked arms with a former Tory Prime Minister and King's mouthpiece—with a man he had denounced as the villain of the American war and the corrupter of the English Parliament. This Fox-North alliance had shocked the nation, and Wilkes was justified in being outraged by it: he called it a "monstrous, unnatural union," only understandable as an alliance to divide "the public spoils." And, as someone else would put it, Fox and North had not a single thing in common, but between them they had a majority. Fox, moreover, had successfully courted the young Prince of Wales who, it was said, might now as a convert visit the fat, slovenly Fox and see him "wrapped in a foul linen night gown" and "rarely purified by any ablutions." Wilkes of course detested the Prince of Wales, and thus might all the more disapprove of the Prince's new master, who had become the ally of George III's former slave.

But Wilkes, in such a situation, was not confused as to where to turn. Where he turned might ten years earlier have seemed like turning inside out; in allying himself with Pitt and George III, he might certainly seem to go the Fox-North coalition one better. Pitt was a king-chosen Prime Minister; and Wilkes, standing at that time for re-election for Middlesex, had for his running mate not, as previously, a Wilkite but one of the "King's Friends." (He had no trouble winning, nor did the King's Friend; Wilkes's campaigning for short Parliaments and a reformed Commons still proved effective, and the Friend, in order to win, expediently spoke out for Wilkite theories of parliamentary reform.) Pitt himself, however, very much favored parliamentary reform; indeed, was pledged to it. In May 1782 his motion for "a moderate and substantial Reform" of Parliament

had dared to say that the House of Commons did not represent the people of Great Britain—a motion rather narrowly defeated, 161 to 141. Pitt spoke thereafter for bills to shorten the
length of Parliaments and to put down bribery at elections.
Indeed, on becoming Prime Minister he started off well ahead
of his time—as virtually a liberal Whig favoring (though also
failing at) not only parliamentary reform, but the abolition of
the slave trade and Catholic emancipation. Foiled as a reformer,
Pitt became a very notable administrator, stabilizing British
finance. He also, as an administrator, got rid of eighty-five
sinecures, tried to abolish rotten boroughs, and considerably
reduced corruption. The French Revolution and the subsequent
war with France made English reform unsound for Pitt: he stood
behind statesman William Windham's argument: "Who would
repair their house in a hurricane?" Pitt's coldness and haughti-
ness of manner, his connection with George III, and the later,
inferior, essentially Tory years of his administration have dented
his substantial claims to greatness.

For Wilkes another of Pitt's virtues was his being the son of a
man who had helped to raise Wilkes up as well as let him down, a
man who had thundered on the righteous side where causes were
concerned. When, soon after becoming Prime Minister, Pitt
was given the freedom of the City of London, it was Wilkes's
duty as chamberlain to deliver the official speech. It appears to
have been a successful one, known to have brought tears to the
speaker's eyes: "The administration of your father," said Wilkes,
"gave us security at home, carried the glory of this nation to
the utmost height abroad, and extended the bounds of the Empire to countries where the Roman eagle never flew."

All the same, Wilkes's support of young Pitt as a king-
chosen premier and Wilkes's standing for Middlesex with a
King's Friend did not go down well with many of Wilkes's own
friends; and his new adherence, so redolent of apostasy, became

good copy for satire and caricature. Sheridan is supposed to have written:

> Johnny Wilkes, Johnny Wilkes,
> Thou greatest of bilks,
> How changed is the tune you now sing!
> Your famed Forty-five
> Is Prerogative,
> And your blasphemy, "God save the King."

A newspaper epigram, labeled "Political Consistency," hit much harder:

> What Liberty Wilkes, of oppression the hater,
> Called a turncoat, a Judas, a rogue and a Traitor;
> What had made all our patriots, so angry and sore,
> Has Wilkes done that which he ne'er did before:
> Consistent was John all the days of his life
> For he loved his best friends as he loved his own wife;
> In his actions he always kept self in his view:
> Though false to the world, to John Wilkes he was true.

Actually, Wilkes was in no way so culpable as he was held to be. Pitt in office had a real tie with Wilkes in standing for reform, and in April 1785 he again brought in a motion for it, to be again defeated. But Wilkes by now spoke so seldom in Parliament that his opinions were almost those of a private person. As for his apostasy, it was to George III of all people that in a famous phrase he disavowed it. The two men, now in some ways on the same side, had encountered each other now and then; and, talking to Wilkes at a levee, the King mentioned Wilkes's friend, no longer living, Serjeant Glynn. "Sir," said Wilkes, "he was no friend of mine. He was a Wilkite, which I never was." Though ungratefully rejecting here an old friendship, Wilkes spoke truth about his politics at bottom; indeed, as he said elsewhere, he was "a patriot by accident." By nature,

Wilkes leaned far more toward grandeur than toward power; and as his literary executor, Charles Butler, put it, "he would much rather have been a favorite courtier at Versailles than the most commanding orator at St. Stephen's." What Wilkes had become was somewhat of a true-blue Englishman with imperialist leanings, an inheritance from his admiration of the elder Pitt. When in November 1783 Fox had introduced his India Bill in the Commons, Wilkes had voted against it. The notably sound purpose of the bill was to lessen, indeed stamp out, the corrupting power of the East India Company and the nabobs, this by shifting the government of India from the court of directors and the court of proprietors to a board answerable to Parliament. Actually, with its patronage, its bribes, its use of extortion, the existing regime made India "the paradise of the fortune hunter" and made England "a sink of Indian wealth." If anything could justify the Fox-North coalition, it was the India Bill. Burke, who had instigated it, supported it in one of his greatest orations, while eulogizing Fox: "He has put to hazard his ease, his security, his interest, his power, even his darling popularity, for the benefit of a people whom he has never seen . . . He may live long, he may do much, but here is the summit. He never can exceed what he does this day." The bill was approved in the House of Commons by a margin of 114. But the King, who like Wilkes opposed it but lacked the courage to refuse it royal assent, managed to have the bill defeated in the House of Lords; and a week later, at midnight, he dismissed Fox and North.[1]

It was said that Wilkes strongly opposed the India Bill because it might prove harmful to the City with its rich traders and merchants; and this may well have influenced Wilkes's vote. What may also have influenced it is that rightly or wrongly

[1] This provided the famous anecdote of George III's messenger arriving at Lord North's house in the small hours with an order that North surrender his seals. Dragged in his night clothes out of bed and a deep sleep, North is said to have muttered, "Why don't you come in and see Lady North too?"

Wilkes saw in the bill Government interference restricting Anglo-Indian liberties, as earlier it had restricted colonial American ones. In any case his Pittite imperialism persisted long enough to bring forth in the Commons his one great latter-day vocal effort, acclaimed as the best speech of his career. He rose on May 9, 1787, to defend Warren Hastings, not the less well for being his friend. "The late Governor General of Bengal," said Wilkes, "has been frequently compared to the Roman Praetor of Sicily: Verres . . . I do not quite comprehend the justness of the comparison: In the impeachment of Verres every city, town and valley of Sicily except Syracuse and Messina . . . concurred. The impeachment of the late Governor General of Bengal has been announced to the public [for] above four years. Where, sir, are the petitions to the House against [Hastings] from a single town or village, or the most inconsiderable body of men, or even an individual, in all Asia? . . . The fact, sir, is that no man was ever more beloved throughout Indostan than Mr. Hastings. His departure was lamented by all the natives and Europeans as a general calamity." The very next day, however, Hastings was impeached in the Commons by Burke.[2]

[2] The character and career of Hastings are too intricate and contradictory to compress even into several pages, let alone a paragraph. As governor general of India he is said to have been "at once mild and dictatorial," "a good, even indulgent master," a sort of "benevolent Indian despot," and inclined where possible to integrate British and Indian policies. But he "worked within a bad system," he tolerated corruption (though insisting there should be "a limit" to it); he committed blunders when encountering opposition, rivalry, and hostility—in particular, in India, from a harshly ambitious Philip Francis, the putative Junius. Most students of Hastings' life and times admire more than condemn him, and his impeachment and dragged-out trial (1788–95), led by a frenzied Burke egged on by a vicious Francis, ended in acquittal on all charges. Steven Watson describes the famous first day of the trial: "Hastings, aged fifty-three . . . dressed in a plain red suit . . . knelt to face his accusers, in the face of the whole of London society which thronged [Westminster Hall] with enthusiasm compounded of delight in prize fights, in politics, in play-acting . . . and in seeing a human soul stripped bare. They were not cheated by the main actors. Sheridan's denigrating eloquence caused experienced men of affairs to collapse into one another's arms [as Sheridan, on finishing, did into Burke's] and society ladies to be removed insensible from nervous exhaustion. What Burke had to

Late in 1788, when George III showed signs of mental ill-
ness—which in our day has been diagnosed as the result of por-
phyria—there arose the possible need of a regency, which made
Wilkes anything but happy. It would establish the Prince of
Wales as Regent and would quite conceivably make Charles
Fox, the Prince's political master, Prime Minister. In view of
Wilkes's relationship with both Fox and the Prince and of his
new adherence to Pitt, Wilkes might very well lose his seat in
Parliament and quite possibly the office of chamberlain: his
only hope was that the Regent should have very limited powers.
While the matter was being debated in Parliament, Wilkes kept
close watch on the King's condition, writing to Polly in Paris,
it has been said, about "each favorable symptom as though he
were announcing the convalescence of a beloved relative." At
moments Wilkes was rather overcome: "The stories of the King,
Queen and youngest princess," he wrote, "are so affecting that I
have not courage to describe them." Pitt finally managed to pass
a bill withholding from the Regent the right to create peers or
grant places (enough of these could have outvoted and hence
ousted the Pitt administration). Fortunately the King recovered
soon after, and Wilkes relayed to Polly the good news.[3]

It was not Wilkes's enemies who terminated his parliamentary career, but rather his old friends. A year after the Regency
crisis, at a meeting to nominate the Middlesex candidates for the
1790 general election, Wilkes was so poorly supported—is it
coincidence or contrivance that says only forty-five hands were
raised for him?—that he refused to contest his seat. His opposition to Fox was not the only reason for lack of Middlesex

say could have been put in a short pamphlet." Wilkes's defense of Hastings is a
good deal less at fault than the Burke-Fox-Sheridan denunciations.

[3] The King's recovery led Lord Chancellor Thurlow, who had ratted to the
Regent's and Fox's side, to about-face to Pitt's and the King's. "When I forget
my King," he told the House of Lords, in a burst of tears, "may my God forget
me!" "God forget you!" Wilkes commented. "He'll see you damned first!" while
Burke contributed: "Forget you? It's the best thing that could happen to you."

support, but it would have been a sufficient one. It came as something of a blow, which Wilkes behaved very well about. One might speculate that what Wilkes, in ceasing to be a Member of Parliament, would most regret was not his being removed from the political center of things, but his no longer having frequent if casual connections with great men and men who bore great titles.

But if no longer an M.P., Wilkes did not want for company, some of it quite distinguished; nor did he wish for a new occupation or a change of scene. He had gone again and again to the Isle of Wight, for many years seeking a house of his own there, but it was not until 1788 that he found one he sufficiently liked. It had formerly been occupied by the Earl of Winchilsea and was actually quite small, just two stories high, and standing alone on downs that overlooked the sea. Wilkes was enamored of the view and of the tiny house which he called his "villakin." He managed to get a fourteen-year lease, took possession at once, and—in addition to other Isle-of-Wight visits—spent two months in every summer there until he died. The house and the four acres surrounding it came to be something of an avocation as well as a holiday retreat, with Wilkes at considerable pains to alter, improve, and adorn them. There was an apple orchard, a fish pond, a grass walk "with seats and arbors here and there," and a Doric pedestal which contained within it (to be shown to guests) a large stock of port wine. On the outside of the pedestal was the porphyry urn bearing Wilkes's Latin inscription in memory of Churchill. There were also two pavilions on the property, one, full of fine china and furniture, dedicated to Polly; the other featuring engravings and Tuscan vases. There were aviaries, and a "pheasantry," and peacocks with their "solemn galanteries," and dovecotes everywhere, and pigeons perched on the housetop or strutting on the lawn. These last Wilkes had had trouble keeping. "I bought my pigeons in England and Ireland and France," he said, "but they all flew away. Then at last I got some from Scotland. They never went back."

Both inside his villakin and out, Wilkes entertained, or had house guests, or received strangers who professed a great interest in the place but came chiefly out of interest in the proprietor. He would show the strangers about, or ride by himself around the island on a pony, or shoot with a neighbor whose family seat went back to the Conquest, or dine out among the residents as they in turn dined with him. Many summers Mrs. Arnold and Harriet would come for a visit, with Polly coming after they had left. The first summer that Wilkes occupied the place he published an edition of Catullus—103 copies from the press of John Nichols,[4] the author of the once-famous 6,580-page *Literary Anecdotes of the Eighteenth Century*. Catullus, at the time, was not fashionable and some people decided Wilkes must have chosen him because he thought they had things in common. Wilkes's edition has not fared very well at the hands of subsequent scholarship—one shudders to think what that merciless classical scholar, the author of *A Shropshire Lad*, would have done with it; but in his own day Wilkes was much praised,

[4] An invitation to Nichols also indicates the nature of Wilkes's social letter writing: "My dear Deputy, I was glad to escape from a crowded Capital to the sweet and grand scenery here, on the first of the dog-days last Friday. I hope to pass all the time of the *canaille* . . . on the borders of old Ocean; and I wish you would come, in pilgrimage with the worthy Elmsly, to see Miss Wilkes and me any part of that time. If you can come by the 30th you will be amused . . . by a grand *sailing match* round the Isle of Wight, by about 50 vessels . . . You will add greatly to your stock of nautical ideas, in which I suspect you are very poor; and at Christmas Wardmote, we will compel the Common Council of Farringdon Without to admit the profoundness of our Naval Skill."

And another friend offers a few details of a visit to the villakin: "I called on Mr. Wilkes . . . His dress, excepting in one instance, was perfectly Arcadian: instead of a crook he walked about his grounds with a hoe, raking up seeds and destroying vipers . . . Wilkes . . . showed me a large pond . . . well stocked with carp, tench, perch and eels 'because,' he added, 'fish is almost the only rare article by the seaside.'" Wilkes said that the *glance* from his eye, as he facetiously termed his squint, had done great execution with the farmers' pretty daughters . . . "But," he continued, "my glance . . . has not everywhere met with a similar success."

not least by the famous people to whom he sent copies. Two years later Wilkes published the first complete edition of the *Characters* of Theophrastus. In this he committed the crime of omitting all Greek accents and breathings, which classical scholars reprobated and which the greatest of then living scholars, Richard Porson, literally pooh-poohed. "Pooh, pooh," he said, "it is like its editor—of no character." Side by side with Porson's cool response to the Theophrastus goes a laudatory note from Lord Mansfield, thanking Wilkes for sending him a copy. And indeed, as an amateur classicist Wilkes would seem no one to sneer at. He also, Nichols reports, urged the literary critic Dr. Joseph Warton to join him in a new edition of Pope, "which," we are told, "Warton soon after undertook, and completed, singly."

Though Wilkes appears to have thrived off his outdoor summers on the Isle of Wight and to have remained in good health, in his later years he came to look prematurely old, his face wrinkled and his figure bent. The loss of youthfulness in his appearance may have owed something to there being no sign of loss in his sex life. It went enough beyond the domesticated liaison with Mrs. Arnold to smack of dissipation—among others, there was a two-year periodic affair with a girl named Sally Barry. In addition, Wilkes lived an active life in London as both host and guest, which meant a great deal of eating and drinking, and a keeping of late hours, even though he did so in relative moderation. No longer much officially engaged, he could go in for considerable social activity; and, always a welcome guest, he constantly added to his acquaintance. Indeed, so ready a Latinist as Wilkes may have mated those two famous essays of classical Rome, *De Senectute* and *De Amicitia,* as the formula for his declining years. In terms of friendship he not only made many new friends but, as we are aware, converted many old enemies— the King, the Great Cham, Lord Bute's eldest son, and Lord Mansfield. "Mr. Wilkes," said Mansfield, "was the pleasantest companion, the politest gentleman, and the best scholar I ever knew." It is a pity that Wilkes and Charles Fox, two of the ugliest men in history, did not come together—a particular pity, because as time went on they more or less reversed their roles. The almost twenty-five-years-younger Fox began his career as a very conservative anti-Wilkite when Wilkes was a quasi-radical and ended his career as a rather fiery Liberal when Wilkes was a quasi-Tory. What seems most regrettable is that their full agreement about the American war did nothing to unite them. (The famous buff-and-blue colors associated with Fox, particularly in the 1784 election, were the colors of George Washington's uniform, which Fox had worn defiantly in the House of Commons all through the war.) Fox, however, did pay tribute to Wilkes when, during the French Revolution, he spoke against the Treason Bill: "I have not the honor of this gentleman's acquaintance nor have I, in the course of our political lives, frequently agreed with him; but now that the intemperance of the time is past, I submit to the House what must be the feeling of every liberal heart in [once having condemned] a person of such high attainments, so dear to the society in which he lives, so exemplary as a magistrate." And Wilkes, in opposing Fox's India Bill, had spoken at least as generously of Fox. They had both, he said, fought against North and for the Americans "and in all the spirited struggles against the too great power of the Crown. I have frequently been in rapture from the strains of his manly eloquence, the force of his reasoning, and the torrent of his oratory. So perfect a Parliamentary debater this House has never known." But Wilkes went on to say, "I am indignant when I see [Lord North] brought back to power and caressed by the very man [Fox] who undertook to impeach him as the great criminal of the State, the corrupter of Parliament, the author and contriver of our ruin." R. J. White says that Wilkes "had most of the virtues and the vices of Charles James Fox," which in a certain sense is true,[5] and not less so for Fox being said to have the virtues and vices of his great-great-grandfather Charles II. And when a Frenchman spoke of how an immoral Fox had greatly influenced a moral English people, "Ah!" said Pitt, "you have not been under the wand of the magician."

The French Revolution roused Wilkes for perhaps the last time, but in a reverse fashion. At the outset in 1789 he saw it as the bloodless upheaval that had visited England in 1688 and approved of it accordingly, as he did somewhat later of a French limited monarchy. But so soon as there were signs of violence he became horrified and hostile, and even so early as July 1790 he was writing to Polly, "The late barbarities in France exceeded those even of their own Bartholemy." By 1792 he could say: "I scarcely think that the history of mankind can furnish scenes more truly horrid"; and he waited for the "bloody savages of Paris" to be condignly punished.[6] Though he had no respect for so indolent a weakling as Louis XVI, he sympathized romantically with Marie Antoinette, though with French workingmen on the other hand he seemed quite unsympathetic. As has been often pointed out, he failed to realize the ancestral role he played in the French Revolution, for "Wilkes and Liberty" meant to the American Revolution what in some degree the American Revolution meant to the French one. Wilkes reacted understandably to the violence and bloodshed, but not at all to what caused it or what it might have been shed for. In this he can scarcely be called a turncoat, for at heart he was never a radical: he had become a tremendous symbol, but the symbol had never coincided with the self. Late in life he dismissed his agitated past with a certain humor, consigning it to what by now was history. When in after years an old woman, on seeing him in the street, called out "Wilkes and Liberty!" he called

[5] Fox's great "vice," however, was gambling, where Wilkes's was women. But they both at a certain period were hated, as no others were, by George III.

[6] Marat, it so happens, while living in England many years earlier, was a professed Wilkite.

back: "Be quiet, you old fool, that was all over long ago"; and when in 1794 a mob, either by mistake or from disapproving of his stance, broke the windows of his house—he had moved by then to Grosvenor Square—he refused to prosecute, remarking with a smile: "They're just some of my own pupils, who've now set up for themselves."

His own life, when the French Revolution had brought all sorts of repression and mental terror to a frightened England, was as peaceful and genial as it could elsewhere be tense and alarming. If the symbolic Wilkes had long ago ceased to signify danger, he had in no sense failed of fame; and for just that reason he was something more, socially, than just a lively, witty, gentlemanly diner-out whose "tongue seemed to have outlived his other organs"; he had, indeed, a historic past. The notable Mrs. Montagu, Queen of the Bluestockings, famous for her superior if stuffy *conversazioni*, her distinguished guests, her teas for a hundred, her breakfasts for seven hundred, now took up Mr. Wilkes, whom once she would have thrown up her hands at; now he was invited to the very first reception at Montagu House, and Polly became Mrs. Montagu's "respected friend." The rather prissy Hannah More confessed that Wilkes was "very entertaining"; Warren Hastings and his wife were good friends and hosts; another good friend was the famous admiral and victor at Cape St. Vincent in 1780, Lord Rodney. Indeed, Wilkes might be come upon in half of fashionable London. (Already in 1763, when he was spied on, he was, in one way or another, with the Honorable Mr. Townshend, Lord Harry Paulet, Lord Cornwallis, Lord Allen, Lord Petre, Lord Verney, and the French ambassador.) He had still in unfashionable bourgeois London his own title of chamberlain[7] and as such he performed his

[7] The banker-poet Samuel Rogers remembered Wilkes "walking through the crowded streets of the City as chamberlain . . . in a scarlet coat, military boots and a bag wig, the hackney coachman in vain calling out to him, 'A coach, your Honour?'"

And Leigh Hunt, when young, saw Wilkes "in an old-fashioned flap-waist-

rather pleasurable and only remaining public obligations very well. He performed the most public of them—his speech when conferring the freedom of the City on someone of consequence —less than a month before he died. Bowed and cadaverous, Wilkes addressed a one-armed hero of the day, who would become a far greater one—Horatio Nelson—in salute to his splendid victory at Cape St. Vincent in 1797. During all these years of relative retirement Wilkes had had the closest sort of relationship with Polly. Her own life, though an unmarried one, seems to have been extremely satisfying: she had many good and well-placed friends, in Paris as well as London; she was often asked out with the father she adored; she was his impeccable hostess at home, and became during the four years that she survived him, a distinguished hostess on her own part.

Her father's death—on December 26, 1797—resulted from catching a chill, which soon became too severe for him to leave his bed and enough to make plain that there was small if any chance of his survival. He had grown physically senile; and being mentally alert he knew and cheerfully resigned himself to what lay ahead. In facing death he remained what he had professed to be—religious enough to ask in his will for Christian burial;[8] honest enough to profess no deathbed penitence; Wilk-

---

coated suit of scarlet and gold" and tells of his father meeting Wilkes at someone's house without knowing who he was, talking to him, and saying something "in Wilkes's disparagement," whereupon Wilkes burst out laughing in his face.

[8] "I desire to be buried in the parish where I die, in great privacy and carried to the grave by six of the poorest men of the said parish, to each of whom I give a suit of coarse brown cloth and one guinea. I wish that a plain marble slab may be erected . . . with this inscription: *'The remains of John Wilkes, a Friend of Liberty.'* " Wilkes lies in a vault in Grosvenor Chapel, near where he last lived —a place where are also buried Lady Mary Wortley Montagu and the parents of the Duke of Wellington. He had thought and told his daughters shortly before his death that they would find a good deal of money at his bankers; actually, he died insolvent. Polly, however, paid Harriet the £2,000 Wilkes left to her, to be paid at age twenty-one, in his will; and paid Mrs. Arnold the £1,000 that she was left. (At her death, moreover, Polly left £3,400 to Harriet and £2,500 to Mrs. Arnold.) Harriet inherited the villakin and her mother the Kensington Gore house, with in each case all the contents as well; and Polly left to her "cousin Charles Wilkes, of New York in America . . . all the lands

ish enough to crack unseemly jokes with his doctor; clear-minded enough to read or be read to; and contented enough, since he was in no pain and always had Polly nearby. Were one to speculate on his thoughts and memories as he lay in bed, they must have traveled back through a great many years and have seldom resembled Queen Victoria's, as hers have very famously been charted. Hers were far more royal and decidedly more respectable; Wilkes's would be, for some peculiar reason, a very alliterative gallimaufry: Lord Mayor and Lord Mansfield; Samuel Martin and the Mansion House; his marriage and His Majesty; Medmenham and Middlesex; mistresses and mobs.

---

and houses" which had belonged to her parents in Cambridgeshire, Norfolk, Buckinghamshire, and Bedfordshire.

4

AN ASSESSMENT of Wilkes is not particularly difficult: what *is* difficult is to make the assessment cohere. The whole is made up of such different and ill-mated parts; the man, as an individual, is such a compilation of pluses and minuses as not to be characterized briefly; furthermore, to characterize the *man* is to leave out what is most important about him—the symbol he became and the power that the symbol exerted. Again, Wilkes sufficiently "grew" to assail great injustices and advocate great reforms; yet, if he later fell short of repudiating what he stood for, he clearly reverted to the kind of life he by temperament was attuned to. William Purdy Treloar perhaps goes a little too far, but in quite the right direction, in saying that Wilkes's "object in life *appeared* to be to live well, to do no work, to get as much amusement out of life as possible." Personally Wilkes shapes up as a worldly, picturesque, cultivated scamp, in a good many ways an eighteenth-century English type; he also, quite dissociated from this, stands out as a major force. The two are not easily reconciled; indeed, one might suppose that the public figure and the private man would fail to recognize each other.

Socially the witty, rakish, spendthrift Wilkes appears to have been desirable in any worldly setting; the same Wilkes, politically, was exposed to constant denigration, and he bared his back, morally, to constant chastisement. The Victorians regarded him as having far more of the Devil than his leer, and far more of the scoundrel than his lies. The Victorian Birkbeck Hill, who edited the standard edition of Boswell's *Life of Johnson*—it has since been revised—said of Wilkes: "What entered his ear as purity itself might issue from his mouth as the grossest obscenity . . . no principle restrained him." A Liberal Prime Minister, Lord John Russell, could tag Wilkes as "a profligate spendthrift without opinions or principles, religious or political, whose impudence far exceeds his talents, and who always meant licence when he cried liberty." On such terms, both the private man and the public figure were disposed of in the same sentence, just as the author of the *No. 45* and the publisher of the *Essay on Woman* were disposed of on the same day. A more distinguished and moralistic Liberal Prime Minister spoke differently: "The name of Wilkes, whether we choose it or not," said Gladstone, "must be enrolled among the greatest champions of English freedom." *This* Wilkes, the Wilkes who has a place in history, may be all that a certain kind of serious reader will be interested in: what he will envisage as an often unseemly and lickerish life story, as a biography that might be called *Sex and Middlesex,* he may feel he can dispense with.

But the other Wilkes, the extremely vulnerable Wilkes whom Byron called "a merry, cockeyed, curious-looking sprite," is not simply a type; he is a gifted individual at odds with his historical role. Never, perhaps, did so blatant a cynic become so embattled a reformer. Never did a man called by so many bad names stand for so much that had very great meaning. And never, certainly, was anyone else compared—indeed, frequently compared—to both Hampden and Casanova.

Such a man, of so mixed—or unmixable—ingredients, must forever stand trial in a biography. His faults were many, and some of them very serious; but we must distinguish, I think, between the real faults and the so-called—or call them the shocking—ones. Much in Wilkes's private life undoubtedly stained and damaged his public career. There is no scandal so succulent as sex scandal; and a man who confesses to what he calls a "warm imagination," and prints up an *Essay on Woman*, and flagrantly takes to bed all manner of womankind—a man who mingles profligacy with obscenity—is bound to be denounced by all prigs and puritans, most hypocrites, and vast numbers of scandalized, proper, and well-behaved people. In his own far from puritanical age this might not have mattered; indeed, had this been all, it might even have enhanced his position in society. But an ostentatious rake, with a Hell-Fire past and a filthy vocabulary, who also wrote *No. 45* and thrived off mobs, would be pelted from all sides. Actually, his profuse sexual life has remained the thing that many of his defenders have most been his apologists for. And since his life *seriously* hurt no one but himself—his wife, however badly misused, was totally mismated and in no way made miserable; and he nowhere seems to have mistreated or ill-paid his mistresses—this handiest of charges against him seems far from the most damaging of his faults.

The bad faults are faults of character, not of self-indulgence. Wilkes was often indefensibly irresponsible, whether in promises he made and broke or in doing nothing about money he borrowed; the irresponsibility, moreover, begot a belief that he fully deserved to be financed. He came to feel that the world, or at any rate the Whigs, owed him a living; and it was the people who didn't constantly help him—it was never himself—that he thought ungrateful. All the more because he shrugged at his debts, money matters contrived to make friends quarrel with him or end the relationship, which in turn could prevent him from ever forgiving those he had quarreled with. (His being always in debt was nothing unusual; so were Chatham, Pitt, Burke, and Fox.)

Wilkes's other serious faults were insincerity and untruthfulness. The insincerity was not just of a drawing-room sort—

praising out of politeness or agreeing with people to avoid arguments; it could be quite needless and even rather treacherous. Thus, for a small example, he would gratuitously tell the Speaker of the House that he was going to deliver a petition from "a set of the greatest scoundrels on earth" and on rising to present the petition, would inform the Speaker: "Sir, I hold in my hand a petition from a most intelligent, independent, and enlightened body of men." In a sense—because of his scorn for most members of the Commons—such insincerity was nine parts insolence. As a politician he might, to suit his ends, say things he didn't mean; as a demagogue, he might get so wound up as to make many exaggerated and groundless statements; and in much the same way, he used truth as a mere commodity. To re-quote him: "Give me a grain of truth and I will mix it up with a great mass of falsehood, so that no chemist shall ever be able to separate them." In making such statements, he may have thought that to confess a fault would excuse it.

As for his selfishness and self-seeking, they clearly existed and are not to be condoned; but they are in some degree understandable. During much of his life he was in trouble, or thwarted of his deserts, or denied backing that he had counted on, or—however culpably—flat broke and in debt. Such difficulties could hardly not turn an able and ambitious man into a self-promoting one. After all, he had constantly to rely on himself; and his disappointments and frustrations could make him extremely engrossed with himself. But Wilkes's was the genuine, and generic, selfishness of someone who wanted very much to enjoy life and at the same time achieve status and prestige. On just such terms of enjoyment and eminence he became a very good Lord Mayor and a well-functioning chamberlain. Horace Bleackley speaks of his "sublime egotism" in issuing, with one of his satellites, "a proclamation beginning 'We the people of England' and concluding 'By order of the meetings.'" Just what the two of them were proclaiming is not specified, but surely, coming from Wilkes, this seems in large part a joke (a sense of fun cohabits with much of his impudence). Wilkes's selfishness had little about it of the egomaniac; nor, as compared to his desire for place and prestige, any *innate* desire for power.

If to his serious faults we add a sometimes obnoxious impudence, a tendency to insult people—this the bastard child of his wit—and that he was a climber of sorts, the verdict comes off slightly worse. But aside from a few of his insults, Wilkes had no mean or cruel or bullying traits: a scamp and even a rascal he pretty clearly was, but he was something less than a scoundrel. He has again and again been called a demagogue and, if he could have, would no doubt have exploited such a role; but he lacked hortatory eloquence. "Wilkes and Liberty!" was a much more successful trumpet call than was Wilkes himself; and his objective was to rouse people but not to incite them, demagogically, to actual rebellion. He was delighted to have crowds at his back; but he most wanted useful supporters and followers; and wanted most of all what many of his supporters could not tender him: votes.

There is no reason to try to whitewash Wilkes, if only because his faults were glaring; but also because they were colorful and human enough to make him, simply as John Wilkes, a subject of interest. To be sure, his faults are of even greater interest for how far he rose above John Wilkes; but even as John at the lower level, perhaps no one else ever called forth so many and multitudinous mobs while also displaying such winning and polished manners. Wilkes's charm kept ladies and gentlemen sitting up very late with him—and could also squire many ladies to bed. His good nature was genuine and his hospitality delightful. And he has never lost his place as one of England's most celebrated wits. (Moreover, the famous French radical Louis Blanc said that a number of Wilkes's witticisms were long quoted and admired in France.) He had his off days at scintillating and his uncharitable lapses, but much that could only have been impromptu has survived. "Isn't it strange," said a fatuous young man trying to attract attention, "that I was born on the first of January?" "Not strange at all," said Wilkes. "You could only have been conceived on the first of April." Possibly his most brilliant impromptu came when a very smug Catholic asked him "Where was your religion before the Reformation?" "Where," answered Wilkes, "was your face before you washed it this morning?"

Wilkes's real significance and achievement obviously have about them an element of paradox. He never set out to be a participant, let alone a protagonist, in many of the large issues associated with him; and indeed it was not Wilkes but George III who made most of the issues large. The *No. 45* attacked the King through his ministers, and the King through his ministers retaliated: there may have been grounds for this, but the King's stance proved extremely unwise. Illegally arrested, his house illegally invaded, himself ill-advisedly imprisoned, Wilkes no sooner had a valid case than he had all the makings of a wildly contagious cause. For fifteen years it made Wilkes, if no Wilkite, very much of a warrior, and a warrior fighting on a number of fronts—enough for it to leave its mark on law, on constitutionality, and on human rights; enough for it to impede George III's ambitions to rule far more than to reign; and enough to become England's greatest *cause célèbre* of the century.

Obviously, much of Wilkes's career was shaped by politics and Parliament, with all the shifts, tergiversations, coalitions, contrivings, countercontrivings, and under-the-counter contrivings of a very important period in England's history. But such an atmosphere might do more to obscure than to illuminate the events in Wilkes's own history. For though party politics and ministerial and parliamentary actions often made for complexity and confusion, the issues that Wilkes fought for or fought against are almost always clear cut. Each is a concrete thing in itself and concrete enough to be readily understood. The earliest issue was the illegality of general warrants, first for arresting a man and then for entering his house and seizing his private papers; another was, by way of Colonel Luttrell, the sanctity of the *electors* choosing their representatives in Parliament;[1] yet another was the freedom of the press, as it was violated by forbidding the publication of parliamentary speeches; another still was Wilkes's efforts to extend the franchise to far more people than it had and to give seats in Parliament to many populous, even city-sized places that lacked them; and finally there were Wilkes's efforts to rid Parliament of the King's bought placemen and pensioners and to do away with rotten boroughs. A warrior often well ahead of his times, he set limits and gained victories of signal importance.

Wilkes's most splendid quality, and an indispensable one for what he faced and fought, was his courage. It stands forth as much in his political duel with George III as in his physical duel with Samuel Martin, in his denunciation of men in power as in his defense of men without any. Lacking such courage he would not have been capable of great audacity—an audacity that, among other things, endowed him with remarkable showmanship. Whether deified or damned, he was always in the public eye; he was always news. Even his squint became an

---

[1] A century after the Middlesex elections, Charles Bradlaugh in 1880 was refused a seat as M.P. for being an atheist; he was three more times chosen and "forcibly ejected"; no Luttrell appeared, but not until 1886 was Bradlaugh seated.

Earlier, Lionel Rothschild had been five times elected by the City, but for refusing as a Jew to take the oath "on the true faith of a Christian" had been debarred from his seat in the Commons by the House of Lords "with their serried ranks of bishops." He was finally seated in 1858 when each House could adopt its own form of oath, and Rothschild could omit the obstructive phrase. His fellow Jew David Salomans when elected in 1851 refused the oath but took his seat and delivered a "maiden speech," only, in spite of cheers, to be removed from the House by the serjeant at arms. Some years later, when the Parliament buildings were razed, Salomans bought the seat and had it placed in his billiard room.

object of showmanship, achieving all the cachet of a monocle.

Though I have just enumerated Wilkes's most dynamic roles, there were others—not least his services as a City man, when he curbed press-gang operations and brought about more humane treatment of prisoners and the poor. And though he could never himself put through parliamentary reform, his setting up of public meetings and of organizations for protest and petitions made him the father of reformists, the incubator of the "radicalism" that became militantly vocal by the end of the century. And much earlier, we are told, such "profound thinkers" as Diderot and d'Alembert welcomed Wilkes "almost as a brother in arms." If it is virtually impossible to integrate all sides of Wilkes, the very inability is perhaps not without value and certainly not without interest. The decided changes in tone, the shifts in levels, the extremes in behavior, the gains and losses in status may defeat a harmonious whole but are in themselves fascinating and humanizing segments. The cynic in Wilkes, the spendthrift, the rake constantly enter and exit but are never quite the center of the stage; they mingle something dissolute like Restoration comedy with high and turbulent drama; and there is nothing trumped up about the happy ending.

BOOKS CONSULTED

ALMON, John, *Correspondence of the Late John Wilkes with his Friends*, 5 vols., London, 1805.

ANGELO, Henry, *Reminiscences*, London, 1904.

BAYNE-POWELL, Rosamond, *Eighteenth Century London Life*, New York, 1938.

BERMANT, Chaim, *The Cousinhood*, New York, 1972.

BLEACKLEY, Horace, *Life of John Wilkes*, London, 1917.

BLUNT, Reginald, *Mrs. Montagu, Queen of the Blues*, 2 vols., Boston, (n.d.).

BOSWELL, James, *Life of Samuel Johnson*, 6 vols., Oxford, 1934.

BOULTON, James T., *Language of Politics in the Age of Wilkes and Burke*, London, 1963.

BRADSHAW, K., and PRING, D., *Parliament and Congress*, London, 1972.

BROOKE, John, *King George III*, London, 1972.

CHENEVIX TRENCH, C. P., *Portrait of a Patriot*, London, 1962.

CHRISTIE, I. R., *Wilkes, Wyvill and Reform*, London, 1962.

CONE, Carl B., *The English Jacobins*, New York, 1968.

DALY, J. Bowles, *The Dawn of Radicalism*, London, 1892.

DILKE, Charles W., *Papers of a Critic*, London, 1875.

DOBRÉE, Bonamy (ed.), *Letters of George III*, London, 1935.

——, *From Anne to Victoria*, London, 1937.

EVERETT, C. W. (ed.), *The Letters of Junius*, London, 1927.

FEILING, Sir Keith, *The Second Tory Party (1714–1832)*, London, 1938.

GEORGE, M. Dorothy, *London Life in the Eighteenth Century*, London, 1925.

HIBBERT, Christopher, *London: The Biography of a City*, New York, 1970.

HOLDSWORTH, Sir William, *Some Makers of English Law*, Cambridge, Eng., 1938.

HUDSON, Derek, *Sir Joshua Reynolds*, London, 1958.

HUTCHINSON, S. C., *History of the Royal Academy, 1768–1968*, New York, 1968.

KENT, C. B. Roylance, *The English Radicals*, London, 1899.

KRONENBERGER, Louis, *Kings and Desperate Men*, New York, 1942.

LA ROCHEFOUCAULD, F. de, *A Frenchman in England, 1784*, ed. by J. Marchand, Cambridge, Eng., 1933.

LEWIS, D. B. Wyndham, *The Hooded Hawk, or the Case of Mr. Boswell*, London, 1946.

LEWIS, W. S., *Three Tours Through London in the Years 1748, 1776, 1797*, New Haven, 1941.

LINDSAY, Jack, *1764*, London, 1959.

LONG, J. C., *George III: The Story of a Complex Man*, Boston, 1961.

MACDONOUGH, Michael, *The English King*, New York, 1929.

MARSHALL, Dorothy, *The English Poor in the Eighteenth Century*, London, 1926.

MUMBY, Frank A., *George III and the American Revolution*, London, 1924.

NICHOLS, John, *Literary Anecdotes of the Eighteenth Century*, ed. by Colin Clare, Carbondale, Ill., 1967.

NICHOLSON, Dorothy, *The Londoner*, London, 1946.

NOBBE, George, *The North Briton*, New York, 1939.

PARES, Richard, *King George III and the Politicians*, Oxford, 1933.

PLUMB, J. H., *England and the Eighteenth Century*, London, 1950.

——, *Men and Places*, London, 1963.

POSTGATE, R. W., *That Devil Wilkes*, New York, 1929.

POTTLE, Frederick A., *James Boswell: The Earlier Years 1740–1769*, New York, 1966.

PRIOR, Sir James, *Life of Edmund Malone*, London, 1860.

QUENNELL, Peter, *The Profane Virtues*, New York, 1945.

ROSE, J. Holland, *A Short Life of William Pitt*, London, 1925.

RUDÉ, George, *Wilkes and Liberty: A Social Study of 1763 to 1774*, Oxford, 1962.

SHERRARD, O. A., *A Life of John Wilkes*, London, 1930.

SMITH, William James, *The Grenville Papers*, 4 vols., London, 1852.

TINKER, Chauncey B., *Young Boswell*, Boston, 1922.

TRELOAR, William Purdy, *Wilkes and the City*, London, 1917.

TREVELYAN, Sir George Otto, *The Early Life of Charles James Fox*, London, 1881.

Books Consulted 255

TURBERVILLE, A. S., *The House of Lords in the Eighteenth Century,* Oxford, 1927.
——, (ed.), *Johnson's England,* 2 vols., Oxford, 1933.
VALENTINE, Alan, *Lord George Germain,* Oxford, 1962.
VENN, Olga, in *The English Wits,* ed. by Leonard Russell, London, 1941.
WALPOLE, Horace, *Letters,* ed. by Mrs. Paget Toynbee, 16 vols., Oxford, 1940.
WATSON, Steven, *The Reign of George III,* Oxford, 1960.
WEATHERLY, E. H. (ed.), *Correspondence of John Wilkes and Charles Churchill,* New York, 1954.
WHITE, R. J., *The Age of George III,* New York, 1969.
WRAXALL, Sir Nathaniel, *Memoirs,* 5 vols., London, 1884.
WRIGHT, C., and FAYLE, C. E., *A History of Lloyd's,* London, 1928.
WRIGHT, Thomas, *Caricature History of the Georges,* London, 1868.

Index

INDEX

IIA

Gentlemen   (Copy!)   King's Bench ?
                                                         March 30. ?

      I should sooner have acknowledged the ?
great honour of the letter Captain Bruce delivered to me, but from a real tend?
for you, and the other friends of liberty in America, still more than from ?
own important concerns. I did hope, that the spirit of persecution, which he?
forth against you, would have abated, and that I should have had it in my ?
to congratulate you on the recovery of your rights. If I had been permitted to ?
my seat in the House of Commons, I should have been eager to move the repeal ?
late Act, which lays the new duties on paper, paint, and other articles.)
      I would have done this from the full sense
not only of its being highly impolitic and inexpedient, but likewise absolutely ?
and unconstitutional, a direct violation of the great fundamental principles of
liberty. The present Session has been in many instances most unfavourable ?
public liberty, but I hope that the next, and a more upright Administration, ?
restore all the subjects of the British Empire to the possession of their rights, and ?
wish to enjoy the satisfaction of contributing to so noble a work.

      I have read with ?
and indignation the proceedings of the Ministry with regard to the Troops ?
to Boston, as if it were the capital of a province belonging to our enem?
in the possession of rebels. Asiatic despotism does not present a picture mor?
in the eye of humanity than the sanctuary of justice and law turned ?
main-guard. I admire exceedingly your prudence and temper on ?
intricate an occasion, maintaining at the same time your own digni?
and the true spirit of liberty. By this wise and excellent conduct ?
have disappointed your enemies, and convinced your friends that ?
entire reliance is to be had on the supporters of freedom at Boston in e?
occurrence, however delicate or dangerous. Your moderation prevented ?